The Jats

Their Role and Contribution to the Socio-economic Life and Polity of North and North-West India

Vol. 5

The Jats

Their Role and Contribution to the Socio-economic Life and Polity of North and North-West India

Vol. 5

Edited by
Dr. Rajendra Kumar

Originals
Delhi

First Published 2015

ISBN 13: 978-81-8454-148-9
ISBN 10: 81-8454-148-1

Published By

Originals

A-6, 2nd Floor, Nimri Commercial Centre,
Ashok Vihar Phase 4, Delhi 110 052 (INDIA)
tel.: +91-11-27302453 fax.: +91-11-47061936
website: www.LPPindia.com
e-mail: info@LPPindia.com

Printed At
IIP Printers
Delhi

PRINTED IN INDIA

Contents

Foreword

It is a matter of immense pleasure for me to write a few words about this significant publication of the proceedings of the Seminar, 'Contemporary Socio-economic Problems of the Peasant Community of North and North-West India and Remedial Measures', organized by Maharaja Surajmal Centre for Research and Publication, Surajmal Memorial Education Society in the series of The Jats : Their Role and Contribution to the Socio-economic Life and Polity of North and North-west India on 31st August 2013. The Seminar drew response from scholars, sociologists, economists, historians and representatives of several voluntary organisations. In all 27 papers were presented and discussed. Selected research papers presented are included in this collection which discuss the various economic and social problems of more than two-third population of India, directly dependent on agriculture.

The Indian economy is the fourth largest in the world, but the growth pattern is not uniform. Statistics show that the rate of growth for manufacturing, service and communication sectors has substantially improved but in vital sectors such as agriculture, infrastructure development, community and social services, and in rural development as a whole, our programme is not appreciable. Unfortunately, statisticians, economists, sociologists, social workers and government agencies have hitherto, overwhelmingly focused their attention on the study of the phenomena and problems of the urban society, though by far the greater portion of the Indian people lives in rural areas amidst conditions of immense hardship. Even the literature dealing with the factual data about the life of the agriculture community is very meagre. It is true that there has grown a literature, though insufficient, devoted to the study of different kinds of soil, manure, seeds, techniques of agriculture, land holdings, land tenures, process of marketing of crops and other matters pertaining to agrarian economy. There are even some fragmentary studies delineating the life of some castes and tribes and indicative studies of some villages. However, up till now, neither the problems of the peasant society have been adequately formulated in all their complexity and variety, nor have scientific diagnosis and solutions to these problems been offered satisfactorily.

Fact is that in the absence of the development in rural society, India can hardly claim to be developed. In recent years agricultural growth has fallen and so have investment and profitability in agriculture, net sown areas under crops, and the area under irrigation. According to the Economic Survey 2010-2011, low yield per unit area across almost all crops has become a regular feature. A multi-dimensional crisis of the rural economy in the post-green revolution phase of the agricultural development is going on. I must quote here Dr. M. S. Swaminathan, the distinguished agricultural economist, who said, "The agrarian crisis has its roots in the collapse of the rural economy........ Unemployment leading to out-migration of asset-less is growing. The minimum support price mechanism is not operating for most commodities. At every level of the livelihood security system, there is a tendency to make profit out of poverty. Something is terribly wrong in the countryside....."

A combination of economic factors, such as economic hardships of pauperized cultivator households, repeated crop failure due to unpredictable climatic variations, deliberately fixed low prices of agricultural commodities, reducing size of cultivated land holdings, lack of agricultural labour due to industrialization and urbanization, inability to meet the rising cost of cultivation and squeezing of profits, lack of procurement facilities, unemployment and increasing burden of debts are among the factors leading to frustration, pushing the victims even to end their lives. And this is happening in wake of decline of community spirit, and support mechanism as a result breaking social norms of this well knit, ages old rural society.

Village studies of the states of North-West India highlight features of peasant society that are often overlooked and overshadowed by macro-studies of the economy. A careful reading shows extraordinary rich, intensively disturbing data on agrarian relations, livelihoods, economic distress, discrimination and disadvantage faced by rural people. These studies leave one with a deep sense of fear and shock. That so many rural families continue to experience sever forms of injustice in India's more prosperous states is a matter of serious concern. By and large, the rural community is lagging behind in overall development, i.e., irrigation, power supply, road connectivity, markets, storage, medical and educational facilities, safety and security arrangements, training facilities to impart skills needed for competing with modern economic activities. And the result is more alarming among the young people, who are leading aimless, desperate, despaired life, inclined towards addiction, evils and crimes.

It is however, urgently necessary to make a systematic economic foundation and social and cultural superstructure, of its institutions. There is also a need to address the problems arising from the rapid process of disintegration which is undergoing and which even threatens its breakdown. Though some sporadic studies have been made earlier on various aspects of socio-economic problems of the rural society, no organized attempt was made to have a realistic approach to the issues involved and to find effective solutions for the problems faced by these people. The present Seminar had a much wider scope to look into problems pertaining to rural communities. I hope experts and policy makers ought to take note on the findings of the Seminar as they think of positive responses to reverse the plight of poor peasants across the country.

Since its inception Surajmal Memorial Education Society has strived to explore and encourage research on different aspects of rural community. Inspired by the ideals of Maharaja Surajmal, the 18th century ruler of the Bharatpur State, the Society was established in 1972, to provide educational facilities to weaker sections of the Society, especially those belonging to the rural areas. To fulfill its objectives, the Society established three professional institutes in its campus at C-4, Janakpuri, New Delhi, two public schools, one each in U.P. and Rajasthan. It is in process of establishing a new school in Haryana also. The Society also established Maharaja Surajmal Centre for Research and Publication, which has been undertaking the collection, preservation and publication of material on rural heritage, especially relating to the life and role of peasant community in our national endeavours. The Centre has published a variety of books, including research work of scholars, translation of prominent works into Hindi, reprinting of important works on peasants of North-West India and the proceedings of National Seminars organized from time to time.

Maharaja Surajmal Centre for Research and Publication has attained the status of a premier research institution. It is a matter of great satisfaction that Indian Council of Historical Research, New Delhi has approved our Centre in 2006 as a recognized Centre for their research projects in history. The Society is equipped with a rich library and collection of manuscripts and also provides boarding and lodging facilities to research scholars. The scholars can utilize the services of the Research Centre as an institution of affiliation for their research projects submitted to the ICHR. The Society also provides financial assistance to scholars in different universities who wish to pursue research on any aspect of the Jat community.

The Society has always striven for excellence and in that attempt, organizes seminars on various occasions. As a matter of fact, these seminars have become a regular feature of the activities of the Centre which are attended by eminent scholars from all over India to present their research findings.

I hope the readers would find the discussions and findings presented in these papers informative and useful. Collection of these papers is a result of sustained efforts put in by our Honorary Director Dr. Rajendra Kumar, who compiled, edited and brought out this volume in the present form.

S. P. Singh
President
Surajmal Memorial Education Society

Introduction

The present publication, fifth in the series of 'The Jats : Their Role and Contribution to the Socio-economic Life and Polity of North and North-West India,' represents selected papers presented in the National Seminar on the topic 'Contemporary Socio-economic Problems of the Peasant Community of North and North-West India and Remedial Measures' organized by Maharaja Surajmal Centre for Research and Publication, on 31st August 2013. The topic itself is very significant. Question arose, why seminar on 'Socio-economic Problems' by the Centre whose field is historical research on rural heritage, especially relating to the life and role of the Jats in national endeavour? And the question itself has its answer. As all know, last century saw the emergence of a new trend in history other than political history, that is, social history which with a great deal of labour distinguished itself from Political history, and by its emergence the political history was pushed behind. Social history came up freeing itself from the bondage of political incidence, marked by too much emphasis on it. The ideology of Karl Marx brought new categories for determining the course of materialistic history. Through his dialectical materialism, Marx tucked history to the past, not to the present, no to the future. Though incidents are there, but they are not important or emphasized because they have not deterministic role to play. Marx's formulations put forth transforming social formations based on the changing face of political economy, ultimately to a classless society. He did not formulate the pace of history as it will go about in future or as it is today. He only dispensed that economic conditions of people, in history, is a guide to the present or to the future and only provided a theoretical understanding of it as it happened in the past. Thus it can be assumed that Marx proclaimed the end of political history. That seems his presupposition, and that presupposition did not come about as true. However, it gave birth to the economic history—study of economic conditions of people of certain place and period, and its impact on the social, political and cultural life of people. And social and economic conditions of the people of particular area in particular time determine its role in history. Regarding the terms Jat, and Peasant, if we go with Ghurye, Jat and Peasant are same thing and who would believe that a person is a Jat and has no land holding? Or does not belong to the rural society? So, many times when we use the term Jat we mean to say a peasant. Hence the topic of the seminar is 'Contemporary Socio-economic Problems of the Peasant Community of North and North-West India and Remedial Measures'.

The Indian peasantry, the largest body of surviving small farmers in the world is facing a deep economic as well as social crisis of extinction. Being a classic land of agriculture, India's long past history, her complex social organization, varied cultural pattern can hence be understood only if a proper study is made of the rise, growth, crystallization and break up of the self-sufficient village community, the principal pivot of the Indian society only till recently. This unique agrarian socio-economic structure of the peasantry, especially of North-West India, experienced a decisive transformation as a result of the impact of the British conquest and rule. On the eve of the British conquest of this area in the beginning of nineteenth century, rural society was composed of a multitude of villages. Each village lived almost an independent, atomistic, self sufficient, social and economic existence. The village had from very early times perfected as an organization for harmonious adjustment of the interests of the individual and the interests of the community. Individual ownership of land or other means of production was recognized, but economic and social organization of village, khap and gotras was so strong and perfect that it prevented economic conflicts between individuals or co-sharers. The abode of these people was the home of the village republics, celebrated by C. T. Metcalfe in a memorable passage which caught Karl Marx's imagination that it formed the basis of the theory of the unchanging basis of Indian agrarian society. He writes, 'The village communities are little Republics, having nearly everything they want within themselves, and almost independent of any foreign relations. They seem to last where nothing else lasts. Dynasty after dynasty tumbles down, revolution succeeds revolution; Hindu, Pathan, Mughal, Maharattas, Sikh, English are masters in turn; but the village communities remain the same.'

Nothing more true or apt can be written of village communities than was penned by Lord Lawrence, then Collector of Delhi, in 1844, 'In no part of the North-Western Provinces are the tenures so complete and well-recognized as here; no districts in which the ancient village communities are in such excellent preservation, or where the practice of our civil courts has done so little harm. They are admirably adopted to resist the evil effects of bad seasons, epidemics and other evils incidental to this country. Bound together by the ties of blood connection and above all, common interest, like the bundle of sticks.....they are difficult to break. Drought may wither their crops, famine and disease may depopulate their houses, their fields may be deserted for a time, but when the storm blows over, if any survive, they are certain to return.....The most perfect ties are found in the oldest and largest Jat and Rajput villages.'[1] Sir George Campbell, speaks thus of the Jat Communities in his Essay on the 'Land Tenures of India' in the Cobden series, 'They are tributary republics rather than subjects or tenants of their conquerors. Those in possession of the village area were left in possession, and were allowed to manage their own affairs, subject only to the State right to receive its dues.'[2] The village represented a closed society based on economic autarchy and social life governed by caste and community rules, the rules of elders of the society.

William Crooke, under whom the Ethnographical Survey of the North-West Provinces of India was carried out, writes, 'In a village, the first great group.....the higher class of yeomen, such as the Jats and Rajputs........ They are followed by whose traditional business is the management of cattle... Next come people traditionally devoted to a religious life and the service of the gods, or who act as writers, genealogists, singers, rather a miscellaneous culture, Brahmans. The third group is that of the trading classes. Nearly all of them are Baniyas. Next we have the great mass of artisans and handicraftsmen, the Mallah, Kahar, Julahas, much of whose business has been ruined by competitions with Manchester and they have been forced to adopt other forms of labour. The Telis, or oil manufactures have, again, suffered by the increasing importation of kerosene oil...

---

1. Quoted in *Gazetteer of the Rohtak District, 1883-84*, compiled and Published under the Authority of the Punjab Government, Lahore, 1885, p. 70.
2. *Ibid.*

'The regular village menials constitute almost a distinct class of the community. The constitution of the old village body provided for a regular staff of these workmen–the barber, who performed the ceremonial shaving at the initiation of youths, shaved the corpse and acted an important part in marriage; the carpenter-smith, the two functions being often combined, who makes and repairs implements, and assists in building the hut; the potter, who prepares the earthen vessels so essential to village house wifery; the goldsmith, who makes jewellery; the washer-man, who cleans the foul raiment; the dhunia, who cards their cotton; the Julaha, who weaves cloth. These functionaries have each their body of constituents whose families they serve, and they are remunerated, not by a daily wage, more usually by a donation of grain at each harvest per family, or on cane-press (kolhu) which the peasant owns.'[3]

However during the British period the village experienced a steady transformation. The village economic self-sufficiency was dissolved. It slowly began to produce for the Indian and foreign market, and, not as before, for meeting out the needs of the village population. The village economy became increasingly an integral part of the national and even world economy. The influx of cheap foreign and, subsequently, of indigenous industrial goods into the village, progressively wrecked the rural artisan industries. The old self-sufficient economy based on the equilibrium between the agriculture and the village artisan's traditional industry was thus disrupted.

In the same way as all other Colonial and Semi-Colonial countries were kept, India was also kept underdeveloped

---

3. William Crooke : *The North-Western Provinces of India : History, Ethnology & Administration*, pp. 207-208.

by British Imperialism. It was kept predominantly as an agrarian, raw material producing appendage of British Imperialism. Her industrial development was strongly regulated to suit the needs of British Capitalism. Such type of practice led to lop-sided, asymmetrical, dependent and weak development of the country. The British rulers thus weakened the old technique and the old organization of production but did not replace them by new ones to any extensive degree.

Thus distorting and retarding the free harmonious development of the Indian rural economy, the British also made peculiar dent into the social organization, social institutions, and social outlook of the Indian people. The traditional self-sufficiency, which operated through the village panchayat, caste and joint family institution and was governed by customs and which subscribed to other-worldly, fatalistic, stationary outlooks, was almost fatally undermined. The rule of custom was gradually replaced by the reign of laws made by the centralized British State in India and administered by its own revenue, executive and judicial officials posted in the village.

After independence, the Indian government has done little to understand the problem, though top priority was given to the development of agriculture, land reforms and market reforms with the aim of achieving self-reliance. But soon this priority lost the attention as our leaders were over enthusiastic and over-ambitious on account of having the ready and well proved tools sought from the western world for combating the problem of development. Therefore, leaving the indigenous path of rural growth, we, being enticed and allured by the surprisingly fascinating fruits of industrialization, started our efforts in a haste. Thus we lost sequence in our development path. We ignored agriculture that was the spine of our economy. Thereby our agricultural development lagged behind the level required for feeding our industrialization up to the mark. Agriculture based small and cottage industries became shattered and the village got ruined.

This raised a huge bulk of unemployed people in the rural sector. The unemployed persons started migrating to the urban areas in search of employment. The urban development and industrialization there had no sufficient level to absorb the whole migrating mass and to provide them proper life facilities. As a result a mushroom growth of slums came about fast in cities within no longer period. This hampered urban growth and urban life. On the other hand in rural areas there emerged an acute crisis of labourer whereby agricultural development and rural life remained slang lower. Therefore, the state of affairs of rural India still remains almost the same as it was fifty years ago.

In the mid sixties of the last century, the rural areas of Punjab, Haryana and Western U. P. experienced a general spurt in their income after the green revolution. The potentials of green revolution technology began to be exhausted in the 1980s generating pressure of economic stress among the lower strata of peasants. The impact of economic distress and decline of traditional social support system based on community support made the poor people helpless and unable to fend for themselves as individual families and persons. The non-existence of formal and informal social support mechanism caused many poor peasants and agricultural labourers to break under economic and social stress leading to suicides.

Moreover, farming is de-linked from the earth, the soil, the biodiversity, the climate and linked to global corporations and global markets, and the generosity of earth is replaced by the greed of multinational corporations, the viability of peasants and small farms is destroyed. Farmers' suicides are the most tragic and dramatic symptom of crisis of survival faced by Indian peasantry. Rapid increase in indebtedness is mostly the cause of farmers taking their lives. Debt is always a reflection of a negative economy, a losing economy. Two factors have transformed the positive economy of agriculture into negative economy for cultivators—the rising cost of production and the falling prices of farm-commodities. Both these factors are rooted in the policies of trade liberalization and corporate globalization.

In 1998, the World Bank's structural adjustment policies forced India to open its seed sector to global corporations like Cargill, Monsanto, Syngenta. These corporations changed the input economy overnight. Farm saved seeds were replaced by corporate seeds, which needed fertilizers and pesticides in bulk and could not be saved, as prevented by patents as well as by the engineering of seeds with non-renewable traits, seeds have to be bought for every planting season by poor peasants. A free resource available to cultivator becomes a commodity which cultivators are forced to buy every year. This increases cost of cultivation and leads to indebtedness. As debts increase and become unpayable, peasants are compelled to sell their each and everything or even to commit suicide.

One alarming point of concern of investment pattern in agriculture is public investment. The public investment has been continuously decreasing and directly affecting agriculture negatively with less creation of infrastructure facilities. The public investment was 37 per cent in the tenth plan, recording a reduction of 50 per cent in 53 years.

A shift from diversity and multi-functionality of agriculture to mono-culture and standardization, chemical and capital intensification of production, and deregulation of the input sector, has led to rising costs of production. Deregulation of markets and withdrawal of state from effective price-regulation, has led to collapse in price of farm commodities.

Due to historical reasons, the existing rural society has become a veritable mosaic of various types of rural societies and hence reveals a diversified cultural pattern. The culture of food gathering tribes; the culture of hoe-agriculturists, further, all the varied cultures of people engaged in agrarian production with the plough and bullock, as also the modern culture of rural people influenced by a new technical and economic force—all these cultures are juxtaposed in the contemporary rural India. Further, the Indian rural community is also being influenced by the ideological currents of the modern era. Consequently we find in the Indian rural world today, the persistence of primitive cults of polytheism, pantheism of ancient India, monotheism and other idealistic philosophic world outlooks inherited from the ancient medieval periods as also a minor current of modern rationalist world view.

In social arena, as the rule of custom enforced by the joint family, the caste, village and khap panchayats was replaced by the reign of laws made by the British. After independence our government adopted the rule of law in the same way. This considerably undermined the powers of the joint family, the caste, community and village panchayats. The introduction of the modern means of transport and communication accelerated the process of disintegration of the rural society. Every aspect of the village life—economic, social, political and cultural, experienced a steady transformation. The old pattern of village life, the old structure of society appreciably changed, resulting a lot of social problems such as gender inequality, gender gap due to female foeticide and infanticide, dowry system, violence and crimes against women, alcoholism, crimes by juveniles, lack of access to education facilities, unemployment, urbanization, property disputes between family members, dowry, divorce, avoidable litigations, etc.

Rural women are at a particular disadvantage due to gender based violence and limited access to resources. Gender inequality in village society is a multifaceted issue that concerns men and women alike. Some argues that some gender equality measures place men at a disadvantage. However, when rural population is examined as a whole, women are at a disadvantage in several important ways. Causes of gender inequality lie with prevailing cultural beliefs and gender norms that promote the devaluation of women and social domination of men. Amartya Sen, the famous economist, highlighted the need to understand the socio-cultural forces that promote gender inequalities and result in poorer health outcomes for women in India.[4] In North-Western India such cultural forces result in immense pressure to produce sons. Social structures are in place that favours sons for reasons related to kinship, inheritance, marriage, status and economic security. These cultural factors cut across class and caste lines and result in discrimination of girls and women. The power of cultural inequalities is evident in the extreme case of honour killings where families kill daughters or daughters in laws who fail to conform to gender expectations about marriage and sexuality. When a woman does not conform to be expected gender norms, she is shamed and humiliated because it impacts both her and her family's so called honour.

4. Amartya Sen : Many Faces of Gender Inequality, *Frontline*, 18 (22), pp. 1-17.

It is said that the study of rural society, which varies from state to state, from even district to district, due to their extreme geographical, economic, historical, ethnic and other peculiarities hither to made, has been spasmodic, insufficient and often superficial. Such a study cannot give an authentic and composite picture of the variegated landscape of rural life, nor can it serve as a guide for evolving a scientific programme of reconstruction of the rural society so essential for the renovation of the entire society.

There is, however, an urgent need to make a scientific and systematic study of the rural society, of its economic foundation and social and cultural super structure, of its institutions and functions, of the problems arising from the rapid process of disintegration which ever threatens its breakdown.

The collection of papers contributed substantially to mitigate socio-economic problems of the rural masses, gives consideration to all the above ideas. In all twenty seven papers were presented and discussed at the sessions of the seminar, but it has not been possible to publish all the papers. This volume carries selected papers along with the valuable contributions in shape of the Inaugural Address by Dr. Ishrat Alam, Member Secretary, ICHR, New Delhi and Keynote Address by Shri Sompal, Former Minister of Agriculture and Member of Planning Commission, Government of India. It is hoped that the contents of this collection and recommendations in shape of remedial measures suggested by the experts are of relevance to the peasant society and governments and planning authorities as well as peasant community.

Shri Sompal, in his thought provoking key-note address, presents a brief, but deep account of the problems of the agrarian community and reasons behind them. Beginning from the short lived euphoria of Green Revolution of the 1970s, he describes its deleterious effects which became conspicuously visible within a decade. Its legacy continuous mono-cropping systems coupled with higher doses of irrigation and a host of agro-chemicals created numerous imbalances in soils, adversely affecting its fertility, polluted air and water and generated mass toxicity in the whole food chain. It increased the cost of cultivation faster than the prices realized by the peasants, and as a repercussion of the prosperity of 1970s, their cost of living too have risen faster than the incomes. Through the subtlety of discriminatory price mechanism and market distortions mass diversion of rural resources being affected. Lack of credit facilities, detrimental Mandi system, harmful land-acquisition policy, lacking of road connectivity, power and water supply, markets and storage facilities etc. are the grave economic problems, as well as threats of dowry, divorce, fratricide, matricide, foeticide and intoxication etc. are the social problems of rural society. The speaker suggested the remedial measures of all these problems point wise.

Kaptan Singh attempts to highlight the intensity of problems of the peasant-community increased after economic liberalization. The continuous reducing size of cultivated land holdings is the main reason behind the economic disparity in rural areas. Providing statistical data, he pleads for a dispassionate and deeper study of the issue. Absence of basic infrastructure and training facility to impart skills render the rural people unemployed. He suggests various remedial measures to remove these problems.

S.S. Rana presents some reflections on socio-economic life of the rural people, and through it highlights their day-to-day problems. Peasants are under economic depression which affects social life in several ways, even their capital, which they invest on education and professional training of their children, mostly fails to yield any returns as they along with the now trained and earning population, get sucked into the seamless monolith of the cities, lock stock and barrel. He raises various issues adversely affecting the peasant community. Zakir Husain and N.S. Alam make a thorough study of the economic problems of the peasant community from 600 AD and remedial measures in historical perspective and visualize the contemporary context. Parwez Nazir explores the problems faced by the peasants due to impact of urbanization on agriculture and shows ground realities and inside story of the village economy and concludes that by careful planning we can leave a strong legacy for the next generation to live peacefully in hunger free world.

Ramesh Kumar discusses authenticity of institutions of informal and formal self-governance and of synchronizing various practices of self-governance involving conflicting norms of peaceful and collective life at village level. The first section of his paper concerned with issues and experiences, describing controversies surrounding traditions in rural Haryana with reference to traditional practices of self-governance. In the second section he focuses on the puzzle of peasants where an attempt is made to identify the challenges of self-governance.

Nasreen Naqvi and Shirin Akhter present a brief survey of services and persisting poverty in India. Statistical data of the various economy survey reports show that the share of agriculture in GDP declined from 55.9% in 1950-51 to 14.6% in 2009-10, while those of services increased from 29.8% to 57.3% during the same period.

The authors attempt to over view the patterns of sectoral change in the Indian economy and to explain the persistence of poverty despite the magnificent growth exhibited in services sector. Ram Pande gives a brief account of the conditions and traditions of the peasant community of Rajasthan and drawbacks of White and Green Revolutions and Land Ceiling Act, etc., while Shirin Akhter presents an estimation of multi-dimensional poverty index for a resettlement colony of Delhi, based on data from Demographic and Health surveys, the Planning Commission and District Rural Development Authority and through survey of 55 households comprising 316 members of the Bhalswa resettlement colony. The paper proves that poverty in India is largely concentrated in the rural sector, with little or no provisioning of resources. The dummy response variables for access record a substantially higher value of deprivation in rural sector as well as for India as a whole, while given the quality of the resources available in the resettlement colonies, the respondents covered are hardly better off compared to the non-access average Indian poor.

K.S. Saxena discusses the problems due to traditionalism and conservatism of society and studies about the status of women in India, who suffer discrimination right from birth, not only in poorer families, but also in so-called rich and high class families increasing crimes and atrocities against them. He advocates to enact a uniform civil code to amend several laws and to implement them properly. S. Chandini Bi gives a brief account of the social problems that deter farmers from their jobs. Looking back to the pages of ancient history, particularly from Tamil land, she quotes the fame of farming as a profession, and saving the nature and girl child. She gives a brief account of the pitiable conditions of the farmers who feel the girl child as a burden, as one has to lose his land for the dowry of the girl. However, a village of Bihar has solved these twin problems of safeguarding the female child and also save agriculture land.

Mohammed Idris and Haroon Nayam Khan trace facts of the most serious struggle between the peasants and biswedars in Punjab in the first decade of the independent India, its reasons, the oppression and the three fold exploitation of the peasants by biswedars, officials of the Princely government and finally the princes and their relatives and conclude the achievements of the peasants movement that some laws were passed by the government in favour of the peasant which definitely improved their lot.

Manju Panghal discusses the development of agriculture in Haryana after green revolution and its impact on social and economy of rural community. Sumesta critically analyses the role of Caste-Panchayats and Caste Reforming Societies in having performed the remarriage of widows in western Rajputana, and its impact on social life of peasantry. Joga Ram Saran describes the socio-economic conditions of the peasant community of Marwar region of Rajasthan. Monika gives us useful information about the problems of the peasants of Marwar and the achievements of various economic and social movements which influenced the life of the peasants of Marwar. Malika Bohra presents a brief account of the Farmer Movement (1918-41), which was started from the village Bijolia of Bhilwara region of Marwar, in Rajasthan, by the Jats of Dhakar gotra against the atrocities of the Jagirdar imposing half part of produce as revenue and a large number of other taxes by the state, and taking of forced labour from peasants. The brutal suppression of the movement made the headlines and converted it into a wide-spread movement in other Princely

States too. Dharam Chand Vidyalankar pays attention on the role of cooperative movement in present context.

The publication of this volume is the result of the labour of the authors who promptly sent to me the written and revised copies of their papers. I tender my sincere thanks to them.

I express my sincere gratitude to Shri S.P. Singh, the President of Surajmal Memorial Education Society, for his constant and active inspiration, support and guidance extended to me in bringing out this volume.

I am thankful to Shri Kaptan Singh, Vice President of the Society and Shri Ajit Singh Chaudhary, Secretary, SMES for their help and support. Dr. S.S. Rana has stood by me as ever in giving this volume the final shape. I convey my heartfelt thanks to him. I may also make a special mention of Dr. Rajesh Kumar, Assistant Director, ICHR, New Delhi, who helped me in preparing some of the scripts. I am thankful to him.

I would not forget to acknowledge the hard work of my Research Associate, Mrs. Monika in publication of this work. I am also thankful to Shri Pradeep Mittal for publishing this volume in a short time with excellent get-up and printing.

Dr. Rajendra Kumar
Director
Maharaja Surajmal Centre for
Research & Publication
New Delhi

Inaugural Address

Agrarian Changes : Problems and Prospects

Ishrat Alam

I feel extremely privileged and grateful to the organizing committee of the Surajmal Memorial Education Society for giving me the opportunity to share some of my impressions on the theme chosen for the present seminar.

The theme opted for the seminar is particularly for its contemporaneity. The post-independence India's agrarian reforms transformed the agrarian relations beyond imagination. The majority of the people of Haryana, Punjab and Rajasthan are still rural and depend on rural economies with their shadow on relations of production.

First and foremost we are expected to concern ourselves with the nature, extent and degree of the development of capitalistic relations in the countryside. Secondly, agrarian relations are clearly marked by regional and sub-regional diversity and likewise asymmetrical unevenness in development.

In some regions sway of capital is clearly evident and it is particularly marked by extension of cash nexus, commercial agriculture and the residual part of feudal landlordism. Tenancy, varieties of labour service, many forms of servitude and bondage continue to coexist and above all the caste system continues to set the template for the development in the countryside across India.

The present seminar would possibly concentrate also on the question of contribution of agrarian policies adopted in post-independence India and in what manner, they have influenced the village population. Don't we find any change in the character of landlordism, forms of differentiation of the peasantry, nature and institution of money lending and the transformation in the role of merchant capitalists operating in the countryside (and getting their own modern houses built in the neighbouring cities) and the depressed rural labour force.

Related to the above two questions is the third part of the query i.e. in what manner a progressive transformation of production relations in agriculture and socio-economic conditions could be introduced?

Ever since India obtained its freedom from the colonial yoke, many steps were adopted by the subsequent governments introducing drastic changes in the agrarian sector. Post-independence till to date, agrarian policies witnessed (and continues to do so) various shades of socialist/capitalist (including globalization and liberalization) influences and as a result some of the following major tendencies could be identified.

1. The land reforms so envisaged during the independence movement and in the first few decades after independence, have been largely abandoned. The introduction of S.E. Zone in various parts of the country has actually rendered the earlier land ceiling acts meaningless and has consequently raised the land ceilings favouring non agrarian corporate world. Such policies are reducing the extent of land for redistribution, undermining the objectives of land ceilings, and accelerated the loss of land by peasants and worsened the inequalities in the distribution of land. Apart from corporate world, the new 'the real estate developers' are

eating up the most fertile tracts of land surrounding both big cities and *qasba* towns. In other words, market based reforms are alienating sizable section of rural population from their lands and consolidating the same in the hands of rich which has no root in countryside which it is busy uprooting.[1]

It has been rightly pointed out that government expenditure on agriculture and rural infrastructure (especially irrigation and roads) has been reduced considerably in recent years and as a result, the engines of growth in the countryside are withdrawn.[2]

The volume of rural credit has declined and the distribution of credit has switched in favour of large landholders and corporate world. The village level data show that the exploitation of the poor in the informal credit market – by moneylenders – has intensified as a result of financial liberalization.[3]

The new trade regime has been coercing the peasants to produce for distant (national as well as international) markets. Under the excruciating impact of globalization the tendency to produce commodities for predetermined destinations has led to mono-production on an ever increasing scale. This problem is further aggravated by sharp fall in the prices of primary commodities internationally. The new trade regime has extended the archaic putting out system under which the poor peasants receives money in advance for cultivating crops determined by the corporate world and in the process loose sight of

1. See V.K. Ramachandran and Madhura Swaminathan, eds.: *Agrarian Studies, Essays on Agrarian Relations in less Developed Countries*, New Delhi, 2002, pp. XIV-XV.
2. *Ibid.*
3. *Ibid.*

their own demand for certain staple commodities which are essential for their own survival. These factors are altering the methods of land use, cropping patterns and consequently hampering all efforts hitherto taken to help them attain self-sufficiency.

Related to the above is the fact of fiscal contraction. There is a growing international demand for reduction of food subsidies and 'exclusion of a large majority of nutritionally deprived and vulnerable people from access to systems of public food provision.

The current trade and patent regime is particularly unkind to government sponsored agricultural research. Instead agricultural research would be the responsibility of multinational corporations. As such there would be a paradigm shift in research policy orientation. Their priorities will be determined by market forces in place of any humanitarian consideration. This would prevent farmer's choice and collaborative international agricultural research.

In the states of Punjab and Haryana green revolution technology was introduced during the 1960s and 1970s with significant impact. The impact was rapidly felt at the countryside especially among the landowning ruling elite leading to consolidation and empowerment of dominant caste groups.

Some notable researches were conducted on the emerging scenario. According to a study of two villages of Haryana between 1988-89 to 2008-09, which may serve as an index to complexities involved, twenty years earlier, the two villages still had a predominantly agrarian character. It was providing employment to a majority of the working population and gave them the primary identity. Poor dalits and other landless villagers were supported by big farmers through twin mechanism of employment and credit. But this has witnessed changes in two decades. Less than 30% of all households identified agriculture as their primary occupation. There was an enormous rise in the category of labourers and they were not necessarily agricultural labourers. In fact it has been pointed out that most of them were 'working outside the agricultural sector and only occasionally worked on land'.[4]

Another significant aspect was the alienation of peasants from their lands. Nearly 95 per cent of the dalits and BCs were rendered landless.

Farmers have stopped the practice of giving their land on lease to tenants on long term basis. Earlier the demand for labour was provided by casual and contractual labour on fixed wages system. But in the last twenty years, a drastic decline in demand for labour was witnessed owing to the second phase of mechanization. Dalits were no longer working as labourers with local farmers.[5] Their vulnerabilities have increased manifold in the process.

In contrast to gradual land reforms in Kerala and Bengal, land reforms in Punjab, Haryana and Rajasthan have been quite asymmetrical with wide ranging differentiation and deprivation of the larger majority of rural population in these provinces. The agrarian changes obtaining in these provinces in the phase of Liberalization and globalization deserve a serious discussion, which I am sure scholars will attempt and enlighten us. I wish the seminar organizers a grand success!

---

4. See Surinder S. Jodhka: 'Emergent Ruralites, Revisiting Village life and Agrarian Change in Haryana', *Economic and Political Weekly*, Supplement, June 28, 2014, Vol. XLIX, Nos. 26 & 27, pp. 5-17.
5. *Ibid*, p. 13.

Key-Note Address

Contemporary Socio-Economic Problems of the Peasant Community of North & North-West India and Remedial Measures

— **Sompal**

I welcome you all and commend the initiative of convening this seminar, which I suppose has been long overdue. Significance of discussing the problems of more than 70 per cent people of India is easy to appreciate, demographically, democratically and economically. Having glanced through the backgrounder prepared by the Centre, I feel quite satisfied as it tries to capture the whole gamut of the multitudinous and complex problems being encountered by the peasantry of the north and north western regions of our country. It also rightly calls for setting an agenda to devise the remedies. In his just delivered inaugural address Dr. Ishrat Alam, the learned Member Secretary of Indian Council of Historical Research, has put the subject in right perspective. May I on behalf of the Institute, the participants and the peasant community congratulate and thank him for taking out his valuable time to enlighten us.

On my part friends, I must confess that I am no expert. So, what I propose to do is to share some of my observations, experience, perceptions and comments from the stand point of a farmer to that of a policy maker.

Historically, Indian peasantry, which broadly includes almost all the rural people directly or indirectly dependent on agriculture and allied activities, has been at the receiving end all through the Medieval, Moghul and British periods. Independence gave rise to a great hope, as the leaders of the freedom struggle, especially Mahatma Gandhi, very strongly championed the cause of rural India. The first government of independent India too did begin in right earnest. Recognizing the fact that agriculture is the mainstay of whole peasantry, top priority was accorded to development of agriculture, irrigation, land reforms and market reforms with the aim of achieving self reliance and freeing the farmers of distress and exploitation, which continued up to the Third Five Year Plan.

The Fourth Five Year Plan, however, started with an aberration, as emphasis shifted away from agriculture. A simultaneous blow came through the calling off of PL-480 assistance by the United States in 1966. At that point of time, our country neither had enough food nor adequate foreign exchange to buy it in the international market. The dreaded droughts of the following two years – 1967 and 1968 – further added to the woe. It was in this perspective that a new strategy and technology of dwarf cultivators of wheat and rice, supplemented with high doses of irrigation and fertilizers, was conceived and implemented successfully. Government policy of announcing and ensuring minimum support prices (MSPs) and making inputs available to farmers at reasonable prices paid rich dividends in making agriculture economically viable. All this met with great success, helped India attain self-reliance in food production, and is universally applauded as the Green Revolution of India. We were gung-ho to have belied the western prophesies of sliding back into the era of famines. For a while, it seemed as if all the problems of agrarian community had either been solved or would be tackled in due course. The euphoria, however, turned out to be quite short lived. The initial advantages of Green

Revolution started petering out within a span of about one and a half decade; and its deleterious effects became conspicuously visible towards the end of 1980s. A brief account of these should not be deemed out of place and irrelevant by those who are interested in understanding the problem(s) in a wholesome manner.

Continuous mono-cropping systems coupled with progressively higher doses of irrigation and a host of agro-chemicals–fertilizers, insecticides, pesticides, weedicides and fungicides–created numerous imbalances in soils, adversely affecting its fertility, polluted the air and water, depleted ground water sources, generated mass toxicity in the whole food chain, and posed disastrous environmental and health hazards. Newer and more dreaded chronic diseases started afflicting the rural masses raising their medical expenses. All these taken together have had very distinct twin impacts. Firstly, costs of cultivation have risen faster than the prices realized by the farmers resulting in squeezing of profits. Secondly, the costs of living too have risen faster than the incomes. Moreover, continuously reducing size of cultivated land holdings, approximately 80 per cent being in the category of small and marginal, have rendered the majority of farm units economically unviable. Several credible studies on terms of trade indicate that agricultural prices have always been laggard. Unfortunately, the British policy of keeping prices of agricultural commodities deliberately low to placate the vocal urban population and organized industrial labour, and help the capitalists with cheap raw material, has been kept in vogue even after independence but in a different garb. Through the subtlety of discriminatory price mechanism and market distortions mass diversion of rural resources is being effected, and farming sector indirectly taxed, which the poor ignorant rural people can hardly discern.

In spite of tall claims by the government(s) and economists, the financial system too, instead of helping, continues to fleece the rural sector. Without going into too many details, I cite only one index that would suffice to prove the point. For more than three decades, credit to deposit (C:D) ratio of all the rural branches of all the nationalized banks has been hovering around 30 per cent. It implies that only 30 per cent of the deposits put by the rural people in these branches are lent back to them, and 70 per cent, utilized to finance other sectors. Thus, the banks instead of bringing capital into the rural area are siphoning it off. There are several other related issues, which cannot be detailed here.

The *mandi* system created through the enactment of APMC Acts was brought in to end the exploitation by the unscrupulous hoarders and profiteer traders. Now, it has become an instrument of exploiting not only farmers but also the consumers. All recent efforts and exhortations to reform the system have been foiled by the vested interests in league with bureaucrats and politicians. Our import/ export policies too have always been detrimental to the interests of the farmers. The WTO regime that was touted to benefit the Indian farmers has failed to do so. Details can be shared if needed.

Land acquisition and diversion policies of the government are known to have caused immense harm to the peasantry, the main culprits being the concepts of "eminent domain" and "public purpose" enshrined by the alien rulers in the Land Acquisition Act of 1864, which after protracted agonies heaped on peasants are supposed to be ended through the latest legislation being enacted by the Parliament. If one goes by the past stances and intentions of the government(s) in such matters, fingers have yet to be kept crossed as to what the fine print of the draft says, and how the various provisions, after the subordinate legislation is in place, are implemented. Land revenue administration and records continue to be in mess and remain a major cause of large scale avoidable rural litigation and strife often culminating into violence and law and order situations. For obvious reasons of subjecting people to wily corruption, reforms and modernization of land revenue administration are doggedly being held at bay.

The fate of tribal people living in the hills and forests is yet more agonizing. These aborigines still do not have rights to the lands they are living on since ages, while the industrialists and other settlers enjoy these to the hilt, which is a new form of colonialism. The conditions of this hapless lot have been made more pitiable by the new environmental and forest laws, through which the unscrupulous officialdom exploits them mercilessly. Pastoral communities are equal or maybe greater sufferers.

A recent NSSO survey has shown that more than 40 per cent farmers want to quit farming. But where are the alternative opportunities ? The reason is not difficult to find. Even in the matter of infrastructural development the rural areas have been getting a raw deal. Road connectivity, power supply, housing, water supply, irrigation, medical and educational facilities, safety and security arrangements, markets, storage etc. are highly lacking; and whatever exists is of very poor quality. Absence of this basic infrastructure, and training facilities to impart skills that are required by the emerging modern economic activities, render the rural people unemployable. Consequently, the incidence of unemployment in rural areas is much higher than that in the urban areas. Hence, many of them are compelled to live in utter insecurity and desperation, which is more alarming among the youth. The desperate, dejected and directionless youth are turning to be desperadoes and druggies. Large scale unabated migration to the large urban centres is an obvious consequence thereof. Living in ghettos and shanties there, these migrants live under miserable and frightening physical and social conditions. Another related or unrelated phenomenon is the brain drain from villages. All educated, wise and enterprising persons and families are leaving their traditional abodes for good, rendering the rural areas yet poorer in every respect.

There are several other dimensions and details of the economic rot affecting the peasantry, but those have to be left for some other occasion. Now, I switch over to the socio-political arena.

On the societal plane, it seems the problems are even more complex and difficult to solve. Traditionally, the Indian village society has since times immemorial been more settled and well knit. In spite of the ages old proverbial illiteracy, ignorance, superstition and poverty, the Indian villages were cultured in their own way, harmonious, self sustaining and peaceful. Even the oft denounced caste and communal divisions, although rightly so, seldom disturbed the peace and harmony. These were accepted as norms and mutually respected according to certain codes evolved over hundreds or may be thousands of years. Life was simple, as needs were minimal; and to a large extent the economy was based on barter system of exchanging and sharing almost everything, be it manpower, inputs, goods and domestic use items on all occasions such as of sowing, harvesting, festivals and marriages. All communities would come together to build and maintain community services and places like the wells, ponds, irrigation channels, places of worship and also celebrate festivals, fairs and hold games. The most outstanding feature of the rural life was its self rule through the ancient time tested Panchayat system, which had a well established hierarchy and code of conduct and rules.

Yet more outstanding was an informal need based activation system of justice administration, where the disputes of all types were heard and resolved in an open assembly. No doubt, the system had certain weaknesses and sometimes injustice was done, but such instances were exceptions and aberrations only. Many of us have seen these happening during our childhood. Prof. M.C. Pradhan's book entitled 'The Political System of The Jats of Northern India' published by Oxford University Press in 1966, and reprinted by this Institute, provides a good peep into this novel system. We find mention of such self rule and a list of 35 republics, the Lichhivi Ganatantra being one of them, in the great epic *Mahabharata*.

In this context, I am tempted to quote a story from epic. The legend says that Bhishma Pitamah, the great grand patriarch of the Kaurav-Pandava clan, having been shot by his illustrious grandson Arjuna, was lying on the bed of arrows awaiting death. As customary, daily at sunset the battle would cease and the senior warriors of both sides would come by his side to seek his blessings and discuss various issues. On one such occasion, Yudhisthira, the eldest of Pandavas, sought to know the history of their dynasty's rule. Having got the details, he wanted to know, who the rulers were before that of their dynasty? He also wanted to know if there were none, how the system used to run? Bhishma Pitamah's answer is found in for of the following *shloka* enshrined in the Shanti Parva:

Na raajya eva na cha raajaaseen, na cha dando na daandikah,
Sarve prajaah dharmenaiva rakshanti sma parasparam.

It means that before the beginning of their rule, there were no rulers and no system of administering justice, and no judicial officers. All the communities, however, would come together to protect and order themselves mutually. The inference is that the society and its members were so matured and enlightened that they did not need an outsider to rule them. It is perhaps this state of affairs that prompted Karl Marx to observe that India's rural society and its village units have been the best laboratories of human civilization. This is precisely the concept that Mahatma Gandhiji had in mind for bringing in the real *gram swaraj*.

If we examine the present *Panchayati Raj* brought about through the 73rd Amendment of the Constitution, it stands nowhere near the spirit of the ancient system. Rather, we find that perhaps it is doing more harm than good to the rural social and moral fabric. Through the so called decentralization and empowerment, it is extending the claws of corrupt power system to the remotest of villages and tribal habitats, and training these hitherto innocent people in the crafts of corruption, deceit and manipulation. The wily players of the game at the village level are systematically colluded in, aided, abetted and promoted by the equally or maybe more wily officials and politicians to achieve their petty untoward ends – political as well as monetary. The unholy nexus perpetrates all sorts of crime in an unabashed manner. The fact is that the whole system has been designed by the people who have no inkling whatsoever of the propensities and needs of the rural people. In addition to frittering away the valuable natural and financial resources, it is damaging the very weave of rural community and morality beyond repair.

At the familial level too things are tending to get more and more dismal day by day. Not only the joint family system now belongs to the past, even the very basic building block of our society - the nuclear family is experiencing great stress. Menaces of dowry, divorce, fratricide, matricide and foeticide are becoming common day by day. Acute materialism and individualism are taking a heavy toll of the long cherished family values. All the bonds are being sacrificed at the altar of myopic short term aggrandizement. Relationships that used to sustain for several generations are tending to rupture in no time. Law and order has totally broken down. Avoidable litigation, murders, loot, rape and mass violence have become so common. All these have totally engulfed and consumed the rural order, harmony and peace. Legislation to curb the malpractices like caste discrimination and dowry etc. are more misused than used to address the genuine problem. Most of the time, energy and resources of rural people are wasted on such negativities. In the whole melee, the government is becoming too intrusive, which obviously it relishes.

The conclusion is that even living at a very low standard economically, the rural society of yore perhaps was happier than that of today. All available evidence suggests that in spite of the material progress and prosperity, which is visible all around, the rural people are tending to becoming more and more restive and insecure.

Coming to the remedial measures, my first suggestion is that all these phenomena need to be systematically and scientifically studied. The governmental claims of addressing these problems through legislation and resource allocation also have to be objectively evaluated. The cases of the so highly hyped Panchayati Raj and priority accorded to the development of agriculture and rural areas are conspicuous examples of governments' double speak. Going by the actual resource allocation and implementation of various measures and schemes, which I have seen from within the system, one finds that these sectors have received mere lip service rather than real help. This needs to be brought out through research and publicized in order to make the rural masses see through the trick played on them; and also to enable them to articulate their concerns and aspirations rightly.

The second and related important issue is the development of basic infrastructure and facilities – irrigation, roads, power supply, education, healthcare, rural markets, storage, housing, transport and security system etc. – at par with the urban areas, without which the alternate opportunities of employment in rural areas cannot be expected to come up.

The third requirement is a complete overhaul and modernization of revenue and justice administration making the arrangement adequate, transparent and time bound.

The fourth very important need is to enhance the employability of rural people, especially the youth, by offering facilities for imparting technical and other skills warranted by the emerging modern economic activities. In this regard, we have to glean a lesson from China, where such training is given in more than 6,000 trades, while India's tally is hardly 600. This is the only way to shift the unsustainable burden of people from land to other professions, which has become more imminent than ever before. The measure would help us achieve two objectives – provide gainful and productive employment to people, and enhance the size of land holdings making them economically viable.

Fifthly, we should mobilize and articulate the public opinion rightly for exerting a mass democratic pressure on government to increase investment in agriculture and allied activities, which since the Fifth Plan has remained stuck at 1.3 per cent of GDP that includes private investment. Government allocation during this period has been a mere 1 per cent of the budget, 0.3 percent of GDP and less than 3 per cent of Plan outlays. Is it at all adequate for a sector that sustains 62 per cent of country's population and provides employment to 56 per cent of its work force, contributes 14 per cent to GDP and 12 per cent to exports, produces all the food and nutrition and important raw materials for industry?

Sixthly, the Government has to be convinced to allot waste lands to the unemployed youth, small, marginal, landless farmers and rural entrepreneurs in economically viable sizes backed up with appropriate technological and financial packages.

At the seventh place comes the urgency of drastically reforming and redesigning the rural and agricultural marketing and financial systems, modalities of which are available and can be discussed.

Eighth, all food storage and processing facilities including cold stores have to be strictly reserved for and located in the rural side, where the advantages of cheaper land and labour are likely to make them more viable and convenient, and can offer additional employment.

Ninth, the MSP regime and the financial system have so far been favouring a few food grain crops only. Prices and finances for other on-farm activities and products such as those of dairy, horticulture, animal husbandry and breeding etc. need greater focus to restore balance and promote diversification, and reduce risks.

Tenth, the use of agro-chemicals has to be minimized and ultimately phased out. The alternate health and environment friendly strategies are available. It is essential for sustaining the production systems as well as health and environment. Organically produced items have great potential in the national and international markets.

On the social side, the work has to be undertaken by the voluntary social workers and organisations, especially the well off people. The onus squarely lies on the civil society. I must remind that it is not at all a new concept. In past, we have seen such reform, awareness and enlightenment campaigns succeeding. Raja Rammohan Rai, Mahatma Gandhi, Swami Dayanand Saraswati etc. pioneered great social reforms, which were carried on with utmost commitment later too by institutions founded by them. The mass voluntary and proactive movements for abolition of caste system and untouchability, establishing educational institutions in rural areas with the meagre resources of the community, shunning dowry and extravagant expenditure in marriages and death feasts, abjuring drinking and other malpractices were launched by the leaders of our previous generation with a missionary zeal and these scored great successes, of which almost all of us sitting here have been direct witnesses and beneficiaries. This Institute itself is a living testimony to a similar endeavour of our immediate ancestors. One of them was Shri Ramniwas Mirdha, in whose memory a lecture is slated for today just after this seminar.

Some important things in this regard, however, need to be kept in mind. There has to be a continuous informed debate on these and related issues to generate right kind of public opinion. That, in my view, is the most potent device to sensitize the government(s). Here I must also remind that mere criticizing the system, or adopting an agitational approach, does not help. Working out an agenda of social reforms and suggesting alternate policies that are financially feasible, administratively doable and democratically acceptable, are equally important. Secondly, all actions cannot be left to the government. We have already seen the fallacy and futility of several legislative and administrative measures. I once again emphasize that the initiative has to be taken by the better off like us. We cannot abdicate this responsibility. We must not abandon our moorings. Thirdly, we have to begin by practicing certain things at our own end first and pose as the active role models. I am pleased to report that several decades ago leading families of our community, my own included, have courageously and successfully taken lead in such matters. Only then we will have a solid and sound moral ground and confidence to convince others. A Bhagwat Gita *shloka* seems quite apt to quote in this context. And I quote:

Yad yadaacharati shreshthastad tadevetaro janah,
Sa yatpramaanam kurute lokastadanuvartate.

The way the leading men of society act is followed by the other people, whatever is testified by him is emulated by the society. With these observations and a few humble suggestions, I conclude, and thank the conveners for the opportunity to present my views and listen to the enlightening speech of Dr. Alam. Thank you all for your patience, and kind attention.

1

उत्तर व उत्तर-पश्चिमी भारत के किसानों की समकालीन सामाजिक-आर्थिक समस्याएँ एवं निदान

कप्तान सिंह

उत्तर व उत्तर-पश्चिमी भारत में हिमाचल, उत्तराखण्ड, हरियाणा, दिल्ली, उत्तर प्रदेश, राजस्थान व मध्य प्रदेश राज्यों का क्षेत्र आता है। यह वह क्षेत्र है जिसके किसानों ने भारत में खाद्यान्न आत्मनिर्भरता का लक्ष्य प्राप्त करने में महत्त्वपूर्ण भूमिका निभाई। ज्ञातव्य हो कि पिछली सदी में 70 के दशक तक हम खाद्यान्न की आवश्यकता की पूर्ति अन्य देशों से प्राप्त सहायता व आयात से करते थे। 70 के दशक में योजनाबद्ध तरीके से हरित क्रान्ति का श्रीगणेश हुआ जिसकी सफलता में हरियाणा, पंजाब व पश्चिमी उत्तर प्रदेश के किसानों द्वारा खाद्यान्न उत्पादकता में वृद्धि कर उल्लेखनीय योगदान दिया गया। परन्तु आर्थिक उदारीकरण के बाद के वर्षों में कृषि क्षेत्र की उपेक्षा के कारण इन अग्रणी राज्यों की उत्पादकता में ठहराव आया तथा अन्य राज्यों में उत्पादकता में वृद्धि नहीं हुई। कृषि क्षेत्र व गैर कृषि क्षेत्र में आर्थिक असमानताएँ बढ़ी। कृषि आय में कमी आयी और बेरोजगारी बढ़ी। फलस्वरूप कृषि एक अलाभकारी व्यवसाय बनता जा रहा है। आज भी देश की 70 प्रतिशत आबादी गावों में रहती है और किसी न किसी रूप में कृषि पर निर्भर है। अतः इस बहुसंख्यक जनजीवन की सामाजिक-आर्थिक समस्याओं पर गम्भीरता से विचार कर ऐसी कार्यनीति बनाने की आवश्यकता है जिससे इन समस्याओं का देशहित में समाधान हो सके।

समस्याएँ

1. कृषि जोतों का विखण्डन

आबादी बढ़ने के साथ जोतों की संख्या बढ़ रही है और जोत का आकार घट रहा है। वर्ष 1960-61 से 2010-11 की अवधि में देश में जहाँ कृषि क्षेत्र 133.48 मिलियन हैक्टेयर से बढ़कर 159.20 मिलियन हैक्टेयर हुआ वहाँ जोतों की संख्या 50.77 मिलियन से बढ़कर 137.80 मिलियन हो गई। परिणाम स्वरूप इस अवधि में जोत का औसत आकार 2.63 हैक्टेयर से घटकर 1.16 हैक्टेयर रह गया। उल्लेखनीय तथ्य यह है कि वर्ष 2000-2001 के बाद कृषि क्षेत्र में वृद्धि नहीं हुई परन्तु जोतों की संख्या निरन्तर बढ़ी। निम्न तालिका से यह स्थिति स्पष्ट हो जायेगी।

तालिका 1

विषय	1960-61	2000-2001	2005-2006	2010-2011
क्रियात्मक जोतों की संख्या (मिलियन)	50.77	119.93	129.221	37.80
कृषि क्षेत्र (मिलियन है०)	133.48	159.43	158.323	159.2
जोतों का औसत आकार (है०)	2.63	1.33	1.23	1.16

इस अवधि में लघु व सीमान्त कृषकों का प्रतिशत बढ़ा है तथा मध्यम व बड़े कृषकों का प्रतिशत कम हुआ है। स्पष्ट है कि वृहत जोत मध्यम में, मध्यम अर्द्धमध्यम में, अर्द्धमध्यम लघु में और लघु जोत सीमान्त में परिवर्तित हो रही हैं। यह प्रक्रिया भविष्य में अबाध गति से चलती रहेगी। यह स्थिति तालिका 2 से स्पष्ट हो जायेगी।

तालिका 2

आकार के अनुसार जोतों का प्रतिशत

श्रेणी (हैक्टेयर)	1960-61	2000-01	2005-06	2010-11
सीमान्त (<1.0)	39.1	62.3	64.8	67.04
लघु (1.0-2.00)	22.6	19.0	18.5	17.93
अर्द्धमध्यम (2.0-4.0)	19.8	11.8	10.9	10.05
मध्यम (4.0-10.0)	14.0	5.5	4.5	4.25
वृहत (>10.0)	4.5	1.0	0.8	0.73

प्रश्नगत राज्यों में हरियाणा, पंजाब व राजस्थान अन्य राज्यों की तुलना में बेहतर स्थिति में हैं। वर्ष 2005-2006 के आंकड़ों के अनुसार इन राज्यों में क्रियाशील जोतों के आकार समूह के अनुसार जोतों की संख्या का विवरण तालिका 3 में दिया जा रहा है।

तालिका 3

क्रियाशील जोतों के आकार समूह के अनुसार संख्या (2005-2006)

राज्य	सीमान्त (0-1.00 है॰)	लघु (1.00-2.00 है॰)	अर्द्ध मध्यम (2.00-4.00 है॰)	मध्यम (4.00 -10.00 है॰)	वृहत (>10.00 है॰)	कुल
हरियाणा	7,64,278	3,11,397	2,82,849	1,96,029	48714	16,03,267
	(47.67%)	(19.42%)	(17.64%)	(12.24 %)	(3.03%)	(100.00%)
हिमाचल	6,36,619	1,75,651	88,447	29,136	3,530	9,33,383
	(68.21)	(18.82)	(9.47)	(3.21)	(0.38)	(100.00)
मध्यप्रदेश	31,98,918	21,47,723	15,66,422	8,68,149	1,26,785	79,07,997
	(40.45)	(27.16)	(19.80)	(10.98)	(1.61)	(100.00)
पंजाब	1,34,762	1,83,062	3,19,933	2,95,749	70,960	10,04,466
	(13.43)	(18.23)	(31.86)	(29.46)	(7.02)	(100.00)
राजस्थान	20,73,099	13,21,126	12,60,369	11,03,263	4,28,625	61,86,482
	(33.52)	(21.35)	(20.37)	(17.83)	(6.93)	(100.00)
उत्तराखंड	6,58,214	1,62,881	77,785	21,370	1304	9,21,554
	(71.42)	(17.67)	(8.45)	(2.32)	(0.14)	(100.00)
उत्तरप्रदेश	1,75,07,112	31,03,166	13,91,564	4,27,879	27,873	2,24,57,594
	(77.96)	(13.82)	(6.20)	(1.90)	(0.12)	(100.00)
दिल्ली	14047	5691	3446	1931	196	25311
	(55.50)	(22.49)	(13.61)	(7.63)	(0.77)	(100.02)
सम्पूर्ण भारत	8,36,94,372	2,39,29,627	1,41,27,120	63,75,340	10,95,778	12,92,22,237
	(64.77)	(18.52)	(10.93)	(4.93)	(0.85)	(100.00)

पंजाब में 31.66 प्रतिशत किसान सीमान्त व लघु श्रेणी के हैं, हरियाणा में यह आंकड़ा 67.09 प्रतिशत, हिमाचल में 87.03 प्रतिशत, मध्यप्रदेश में 67.61 प्रतिशत, राजस्थान में 54.6 प्रतिशत, उत्तराखण्ड में 89.09 प्रतिशत, उत्तर प्रदेश में 91.78 प्रतिशत है। इन राज्यों में विभिन्न श्रेणी की जोतों के औसत आकार में अधिक अन्तर नहीं है। केवल पंजाब, मध्यप्रदेश और हरियाणा में कुल औसत अन्य राज्यों से बेहतर है। यह विवरण तालिका 4 से स्पष्ट हो जाएगा।

तालिका 4

आकार समूह के अनुसार जोतों का औसत क्षेत्र (2005-2006) हैक्टेयर में

राज्य	सीमान्त	लघु	अर्द्ध मध्यम	मध्यम	वृहत	समस्त जोत
हरियाणा	0.45	1.44	2.83	6.05	16.47	2.23
हिमाचल	0.41	1.39	2.72	5.66	17.00	1.04
मध्यप्रदेश	0.50	1.43	2.75	5.86	15.29	2.02
पंजाब	0.62	1.41	2.67	5.75	15.03	3.95
राजस्थान	0.49	1.43	2.83	6.16	17.88	3.38
उत्तराखण्ड	0.40	1.39	2.70	5.48	25.13	0.94
उत्तरप्रदेश	0.40	1.40	2.73	5.55	15.20	0.80
दिल्ली	0.43	1.38	2.85	5.83	14.60	1.49
सम्पूर्ण भारत	0.23	1.38	2.36	4.38	12.99	1.23

समय के साथ वृहत व मध्यम किसान भी लघु व सीमान्त श्रेणी में आ जायेंगे। शनैः शनैः सीमान्त श्रेणी के किसान भूमिविहीन या नगण्य भूमि के स्वामी रह जायेंगे। वर्तमान में भी भूमिविहीन किसानों की संख्या कम नहीं है। भूमिविहीन किसानों की संख्या का कुल किसानों की संख्या से प्रतिशत निम्नानुसार है-

हिमाचल	21.87 प्रतिशत	राजस्थान	12.73 प्रतिशत
हरियाणा	25.95 प्रतिशत	उत्तराखण्ड	21.15 प्रतिशत
पंजाब	29.50 प्रतिशत	उत्तरप्रदेश	16.31 प्रतिशत
मध्यप्रदेश	22.75 प्रतिशत	सम्पूर्ण भारत	31.12 प्रतिशत

2. तुलनात्मक रूप से कम होती कृषि आय और बढ़ती बेरोज़गारी

आबादी बढ़ने व जोतों के घटते आकार के कारण अधिकांश किसानों के लिए कृषि अलाभकारी व्यवसाय बनता जा रहा है। तालिका 5 से पता चलता है कि मध्यम या वृहत श्रेणी के किसान ही अपनी आय से अपने उपभोग व्यय की पूर्ति कर पाते हैं। इस प्रकार देश के 4.95 प्रतिशत किसान ही अपने परिवार का व्यय अपनी आय से निकाल पाते हैं शेष 95.05 प्रतिशत किसान अभाव में जीवन व्यतीत करने को विवश हैं।

तालिका-5

जोत के आकार के अनुसार पारिवारिक मासिक आय व उपभोग व्यय (रू०)

श्रेणी	आकार (है०)	आय (रू०)	उपभोग व्यय (रू०)	अन्तर
लगभग भूमि विहीन	0–01	1380.00	2297.00	–917
सीमान्त	0.01–0.04	1663.00	2390.00	–727
लघु-सीमांत	0.04–1.00	1809.00	2672.00	–863
लघु	1.00–2.00	2493.00	3148.00	–655
अर्द्धमध्यम	2.00–4.00	3589.00	3685.00	–96
मध्यम	4.00–10.00	5681.00	4626.00	+1055
वृहत	>10.00	9667.00	<418.00	+3219
सभी आकार	1.16	2115.00	2770.00	–655

प्रश्नगत राज्य, जिनमें से अधिकांश कृषि उत्पादकता में अग्रणी हैं, भी अच्छी स्थिति में नहीं हैं यह स्थिति तालिका 6 से स्पष्ट हो जाती है।

तालिका-6

किसान परिवार की आय व व्यय (जुलाई 2002-जून 2007) (रु०)

राज्य	वार्षिक कृषि आय	वार्षिक कुल आय	वार्षिक कृषि व्यय	वार्षिक कुल व्यय	अन्तर 3-5	अन्तर 4-6
हरियाणा	17928	34584	18270	52963	-342	-18384
मध्यप्रदेश	11952	17160	8886	28068	3066	-10908
पंजाब	33864	59520	25945	58080	791	+1440
राजस्थान	4308	17976	7668	39456	-3360	-21480
उत्तरप्रदेश	10,032	19596	9151	34788	881	-15192
भारत	11628	25380	8791	33240	2837	-7860

स्पष्ट है कि पंजाब प्रदेश को छोड़कर किसी भी प्रदेश का किसान अपने पारिवारिक व्यय की पूर्ति अपनी आय से करने की स्थिति में नहीं है। यह आंकड़े 2002-2003 के हैं। वर्तमान में स्थिति में सुधार के बजाय गिरावट आने की ही सम्भावना है। इस स्थिति का निवारण आवश्यकता पड़ने पर किसान कर्ज़ लेकर या जमीन बेचकर करते हैं।

यह भी देखने की बात है कि कृषि क्षेत्र व गैर कृषि क्षेत्र में काम करने वाले श्रमिक की आय में भारी अन्तर है।

तालिका-7

क्षेत्रवार प्रति श्रमिक आय (2004-2005) रु० में

राज्य	कृषि	गैर कृषि	अनुपात
हरियाणा	26192	85128	3.25
हिमाचल	9796	69818	7.13
मध्यप्रदेश	6606	44980	6.81
पंजाब	35087	70138	2.00
राजस्थान	10609	56830	5.36
उत्तर प्रदेश	10367	42683	4.12
भारत	12371	61432	4.97

इस अन्तर के कारण श्रमिक कृषि क्षेत्र में काम करने के बजाय गैर-कृषि क्षेत्र में काम करने को वरीयता देते हैं। इससे भी लघु व सीमान्त कृषकों को मुश्किलों का सामना करना पड़ता है क्योंकि उनके कृषि उत्पादन कार्य मूलतः श्रम आधारित होते हैं।

कृषि उत्पादन की दृष्टि से इन अग्रणी राज्यों में भी ग्रामीण व शहरी क्षेत्र में प्रति व्यक्ति मासिक उपभोग व्यय में भारी अन्तर है। इससे शहरी व ग्रामीण जीवन की गुणवत्ता की असमानता साफ दिखाई देती है।

तालिका 8

औसत प्रति व्यक्ति मासिक उपभोग व्यय (2009-2010) रु॰ में

राज्य	ग्रामीण	शहरी	अनुपात
हरियाणा	1510.00	2321.00	1.53
हिमाचल	1536.00	2654.00	1.72
मध्यप्रदेश	903.00	2437.00	1.84
पंजाब	1649.00	2109.00	1.27
राजस्थान	1179.00	1663.00	1.41
उत्तर प्रदेश	899.00	1574.00	1.68
भारत	1054.00	1984.00	1.88

आकलन से यह तथ्य भी सामने आता है कि हरियाणा, हिमाचल व पंजाब के लगभग 70 प्रतिशत किसानों का प्रति व्यक्ति मासिक व्यय 600.00 रुपये से अधिक है जबकि मध्यप्रदेश, राजस्थान व उत्तर प्रदेश के 60 से 70 प्रतिशत किसानों का प्रति व्यक्ति मासिक व्यय 600.00 रुपये से कम है। स्पष्ट है कि मध्यप्रदेश, राजस्थान व उत्तरप्रदेश के किसानों की स्थिति अपेक्षाकृत अच्छी नहीं है।

अपनी आर्थिक आवश्यकताओं की पूर्ति हेतु किसान ऋण लेने को विवश है। राज्यवार विवरण तालिका 9 में दिया जा रहा है।

तालिका 9

किसानों पर ऋण की स्थिति (जनवरी-दिसम्बर 2003)

राज्य	अनुमानित कृषक परिवार सँख्या लाख में	अनुमानित ऋणग्रस्त परिवार लाख में	ऋणग्रस्त परिवार	प्रति परिवार औसत ऋण रु०
हरियाणा	19.445	10.33	53.1	26007
हिमाचल	9.061	3.03	33.4	9618
मध्यप्रदेश	63.206	32.11	50.8	14218
पंजाब	18.442	12.069	65.4	41576
राजस्थान	53.080	27.828	52.4	18372
उत्तराखण्ड	8.962	60.644	7.2	
उत्तर प्रदेश	171.575	69.199	40.3	7425
सम्पूर्ण भारत	8395.04	4342.42	48.6	12858

यह आंकड़े पुराने हैं और भारत सरकार के व राज्य सरकारों के द्वारा ऋण किसी सीमा तक माफ भी किया गया है। जब भी किसानों के ऋण माफ किए जाते हैं तब विभिन्न क्षेत्रों से आलोचनाएं की जाती हैं। उद्योग के क्षेत्र में 40,000 करोड़ से अधिक ऋण की वसूली नहीं हो सकी है परन्तु इस बारे में ध्यान नहीं दिया जाता जबकि किसानों से ऋण वसूली जबरदस्ती की जाती है।

स्थिति यह बन गयी है कि आय की कमी व ऋणग्रस्तता के कारण आज किसान जगह-जगह पर आत्महत्या कर रहे हैं। एक अध्ययन के अनुसार वर्ष 1997 से 2006 की अवधि में 1,66,304 किसान आत्महत्या कर चुके थे। इनका वर्षवार विवरण तालिका 10 में दिया हुआ है।

तालिका-10

किसान आत्महत्या की संख्या

वर्ष	किसानों की संख्या	कुल आत्महत्याएं	किसानों का प्रतिशत
1997	13622	95829	14.2
1998	16015	104713	15.3
1999	16082	1,10,587	14.5
2000	16603	1,08593	15.3
2001	16415	1,08,506	15.1
2002	17971	1,10,417	16.3
2003	17164	1,10,851	15.5
2004	18241	1,13,697	16.0
2005	17131	1,13914	15.0
2006	17060	1,18,112	14.4
कुल	1,66,304	10,95,219	15.2

कृषि जोतों के निरन्तर विखण्डन, गैरकृषि रोजगार के अभाव, रोजगारपरक शिक्षा के न होने और ग्रामीण क्षेत्र में कृषि आधारित लघु उद्योगों के अभाव के कारण गांवों में बेरोजगारी तेजी से बढ़ रही है। 15-59 वर्ष की आयु के व्यक्ति बड़ी संख्या में बेरोजगार हैं। इसका आकलन तालिका 11 में दिया हुआ है।

तालिका-11

विषय	हरियाणा	पंजाब	हिमाचल	उत्तरप्रदेश	राजस्थान	मध्यप्रदेश	भारत
जनसंख्या, लाख	253.53	277.04	68.57	1995.81	686.21	725.97	12101.93
मुख्य वर्कर्स का कुल जनसंख्या से प्रतिशत	29.5	32.2	32.3	23.7	30.9	31.7	30.4
कृषि वर्कर्स का प्रतिशत	51.3	39.0	68.5	65.9	65.9	71.5	58.2
बेरोजगारी का प्रतिशत	8.6	10.5	5.9	8.0	17.5	7.9	8.2
कृषि क्षेत्र में बेरोजगार (लाख)	3.3	3.65	0.89	24.93	24.45	12.99	175.57

इसमें वे किसान शामिल नहीं है जिन्हें पूरे वर्ष रोजगार नहीं मिलता। ग्रामीण बेरोजगारी को दूर करने के लिए भारत सरकार के द्वारा समय-समय पर कई योजनाएं प्रारम्भ की गई परन्तु उनके द्वारा न तो स्थाई परिसम्पत्तियों का सृजन हो सका और न रोजगार के स्थायी अवसर सृजित हो सके। ये योजनाएं अपने उद्‌देश्यों में सफल नहीं रही।

वस्तुत: बेरोजगारी एक अभिशाप है। यह समाज में अनेक बुराइयों को जन्म दे रही है। सामाजिक अपराध बढ़ रहे हैं और कानून व व्यवस्था चरमरा रही है। नक्सलवाद में भी कहीं न कहीं बेरोजगारी का योगदान है। सामाजिक मूल्यों का ह्रास हो रहा है। नि:सन्देह यदि हमने बेरोजगारी का नाश नहीं किया तो बेरोजगारी हमारा नाश कर देगी।

3. कृषि क्षेत्र में गतिरोध

स्वतंत्रता के पश्चात कृषि क्षेत्र पर ध्यान दिया गया। सिंचाई सुविधाओं, प्रसार सेवाओं का विस्तार हुआ, फलस्वरूप फसलों की उत्पादकता व उत्पादन में वृद्धि हुई। "हरित क्रान्ति" के बाद तो उत्पादकता

में उल्लेखनीय वृद्धि हुई। वर्ष 1951 में खाद्यान्न की उत्पादकता केवल 522 कि. ग्राम प्रति हैक्टेयर थी जो अब बढ़कर 1876 कि. ग्राम प्रति हैक्टेयर हो गई। परन्तु गतवर्षों में प्रगति में ठहराव आ गया है। यह स्थिति तालिका 12 से स्पष्ट हो जाएगी।

तालिका-12

खाद्यान्न उत्पादकता (किलो ग्राम/हैक्टेयर)

राज्य	1990-2000 से 2001-02	2002-03 से 2004-05	2005-06 से 2007-08	2008-09 से 2010-11
हरियाणा	3078	3087	3286	3390
हिमाचल	1691	1679	1787	1663
मध्यप्रदेश	1100	1107	1122	1204
पंजाब	4033	3932	4086	4185
राजस्थान	986	1056	1038	1146
उत्तराखण्ड	1727	1626	1797	1778
उत्तरप्रदेश	2152	2049	2221	2329
दिल्ली	1944	2922	2653	3651
सम्पूर्ण भारत	1688	1638	1918	1876

पंजाब व हरियाणा में खाद्यान्न उत्पादकता अन्य राज्यों की तुलना में बेहतर है परन्तु यहां भी वर्ष 1990-2000 की तुलना में नगण्य वृद्धि हुई है। अन्य राज्य अभी पीछे हैं। निःसंदेह अच्छी प्रसार सेवाओं, सिचाई सुविधा, अच्छे बीज, खाद्य व अन्य तकनीक के उपयोग से उत्पादकता में कई गुना वृद्धि की जा सकती है। यह उल्लेखनीय है कि विभिन्न फसलों की उत्पादकता में भारत अभी अनेक देशों से पीछे है। यह स्थिति तालिका 13 से स्पष्ट हो जाएगी।

तालिका-13

उत्पादकता (सन् 2010)

फसल	भारत में औसत उत्पादकता टन/ हैक्टेयर	विश्व में सर्वाधिक उत्पादकता टन/ हैक्टेयर	सम्बन्धित देश
धन	2.24	10.8	आस्ट्रेलिया
गेहूँ	2.95	8.9	नीदरलैण्ड
गन्ना	68.9	125	पेरू
कपास	0.51	4.6	इजरायल
आलू	19.90	44.3	यू.एस.ए.
टमाटर	19.30	524.9	बैल्जियम
सोयाबीन	1.1	3.7	तुर्की
सब्जियां	13.4	76.8	यू.एस.ए.
प्याज	16.6	67.3	आयरलैण्ड
दालें	1.1	5.5	इण्डोनेशिया

सकल घरेलू उत्पाद में कृषि क्षेत्र का योगदान निरन्तर घट रहा है। यह स्थिति निम्न तालिका से स्पष्ट हो जाएगी।

तालिका-14

कृषि क्षेत्र का 2004-2005 के मूल्यों पर सकल घरेलू उत्पाद में योगदान

राज्य	2004-05	2006-07	2008-09	2010-11	2011-12
हरियाणा	23.10	21.32	19.49	16.74	16.27
हिमाचल	25.47	22.71	21.03	19.17	15.84
मध्यप्रदेश	27.66	26.35	23.99	22.79	23.76
पंजाब	32.64	29.05	26.66	24.18	22.77
राजस्थान	18.59	16.65	14.40	8.22	7.94
उत्तरप्रदेश	29.74	27.08	25.34	23.01	22.53
उत्तराखण्ड	22.27	17.37	12.84	11.27	10.99
भारत	19.03	17.37	15.77	14.45	14.10

विकास की यह स्वाभाविक प्रक्रिया है कि उद्योग तथा अन्य क्षेत्रों में प्रगति के साथ सकल घरेलू उत्पाद में उद्योग व सेवा क्षेत्रों का प्रतिशत योगदान बढ़ा है। परिणामस्वरूप कृषि क्षेत्र का योगदान घटा है। परन्तु यह तभी स्वागत योग्य है जबकि कृषि क्षेत्र पर कार्यरत जनसंख्या का भार भी तुलनात्मक रूप से कम हो। वर्ष 1950-51 में लगभग 70 प्रतिशत जनजीवन कृषि कार्य में लगा था तथा सकल घरेलू उत्पाद में कृषि का योगदान 55.4 प्रतिशत था। वर्ष 2011-2012 में लगभग 50 प्रतिशत जनजीवन कृषि कार्य में लगा है परन्तु सकल घरेलू उत्पाद में उसका योगदान 14.10 प्रतिशत रह गया है। इसे सन्तुलित विकास नहीं कहा जा सकता।

यह भी तथ्य है कि योजना परिव्यय में कृषि क्षेत्र का भाग घट रहा है। प्रथम पंचवर्षीय योजना से लेकर वर्ष 1979-80 तक यह भाग औसतन 10 से 17 प्रतिशत तक रहा परन्तु उसके बाद घटकर औसतन 4 से 5 प्रतिशत ही रह गया।

4. आधारभूत सामाजिक सुविधाओं का अभाव

आज ग्रामीण क्षेत्र में शिक्षा, ऊर्जा, परिवहन, स्वास्थ्य आदि सामाजिक सुविधाओं का नितान्त अभाव है, कानून व्यवस्था में भी गिरावट आ रही है। फलस्वरूप कुछ लोग तो रोजगार के लिए गाँव छोड़ रहे हैं और कुछ लोग सामाजिक सुविधाओं के लिए गाँव छोड़ रहे है। जनजीवन के पलायन से शहरों पर आबादी का दबाव बढ़ रहा है और गाँव अभाव के केन्द्र बन रहे हैं। आकलन से यह बात सामने आती है कि शहरी आबादी में वृद्धि का लगभग 50 प्रतिशत भाग जनजीवन के ग्रामीण क्षेत्र से पलायन से आया है।

समस्याओं के निराकरण की कार्यनीति व उपाय

विकास का माडल

विकास का वर्त्तमान माडल कृषि क्षेत्र की समस्याओं का निराकरण करने में असमर्थ है। इसका मूल कारण है कृषि अर्थतन्त्र का आबादी बढ़ने के साथ संकुचित होना जबकि गैरकृषि क्षेत्र का अर्थतन्त्र आबादी बढ़ने के साथ विस्तार पाता है। आबादी बढ़ने के साथ जोतों का विखण्डन अपरिहार्य है। इसलिए खेती की आय पर किसानों की निर्भरता को कम करने के उपाय खोजने होंगे। यह उल्लेखनीय है कि चीन में औसत जोत का आकार भारत से कम है। परन्तु वहाँ कृषि उत्पादकता व विकास भारत से कहीं अधिक है। चीन में कृषि आबादी के बड़े भाग को अन्य व्यवसायों में प्रशिक्षित कर

रोजगार के स्थायी अवसर उपलब्ध कराते हुए कृषि पर आबादी भार को कम करके उसे लाभकारी बनाया गया है। फलस्वरूप चीन ने गरीबी के स्तर को 80 प्रतिशत (1980) से घटाकर 15 प्रतिशत (2005) करने में सफलता प्राप्त की है। भारत में भी विकास के वर्त्तमान माडल पर पुन: विचार कर इसमें वांछनीय परिवर्तन करने होंगे।

इस कार्य नीति के निम्न अवयव होंगे-

1. उत्पादकता में वृद्धि
2. कृषि उत्पादों के भण्डारण व विक्रय की सुव्यवस्था
3. उचित एवं सन्तुलित कृषि उत्पाद समर्थन मूल्य
4. ग्रामीण क्षेत्र में सेवा क्षेत्रों का विस्तार
5. ग्रामीण क्षेत्र में कृषि आधरित लघु व कुटीर उद्योगों की स्थापना व विस्तार
6. शिक्षा का विस्तार व उसे व्यावसायिक बनाना
7. ग्रामीण क्षेत्र में सामाजिक सुविधाओं का विस्तार

1. उत्पादकता में वृद्धि

(1) यह निर्विवाद है कि प्रभावी कृषि प्रबन्धन के द्वारा भारत में उत्पादकता में कई गुना वृद्धि की सम्भावना है। परन्तु इसके लिए आवश्यक है कि किसान को आवश्यक कृषि निवेश, यथा, 1. अच्छा बीज, 2. खाद व कीटनाशक दवाएँ, 3. सिंचाई, 4. ऋण, 5. सबसिडी व तकनीकी जानकारी उपयुक्त मात्रा व समय पर मिले। वर्तमान में प्रसार सेवाओं की अदक्षता के कारण ये निवेश समय पर नहीं मिल पाते अत: उत्पादकता प्रभावित होती है।

(2) पंजाब, हरियाणा व पश्चिमी उत्तर प्रदेश में खाद के अत्यधिक प्रयोग, जल ठहराव व भूमि उपचार न करने के कारण उत्पादकता प्रभावित हुई है। अत: इस बारे में अनुसन्धान कर उपयुक्त कार्यवाही की आवश्यकता है।

(3) यह आवश्यक है कि प्रत्येक किसान को अच्छी से अच्छी तकनीक की जानकारी उपलब्ध करायी जाए। वस्तुत: वर्तमान कृषि पद्धतियों में सुधार की आवश्यकता है क्योंकि न तो ये किफायती हैं और न पर्यावरणीय दृष्टि से धारणीय। कई फसलों की उत्पादकता कम है, जिसके

लिए अदक्ष सिंचाई व्यवस्था व प्रसार सेवाओं की कमी जिम्मेदार है। इस बारे में कृषि अनुसन्धान संस्थाओं व कृषि विश्वविद्यालयों को किसानों के साथ मिलकर कार्यवाही करनी होगी। दुर्भाग्यवश कृषि से सम्बन्धित कई तकनीकों का विकास तो हुआ है परन्तु वे किसानों तक नहीं पहुँची हैं। प्रसार सेवाओं का लाभ भी किसानों को नहीं मिला है। वस्तुतः हरित क्रान्ति के बाद कृषि अनुसंधान व प्रसार के क्षेत्र में उल्लेखनीय कार्य नहीं हुए हैं। यह तो सही है कि अनुसंधान संस्थाओं के प्रायोगिक फार्म्स में कृषि उत्पादकता विश्व स्तर की है परन्तु किसानों के खेतों में यह आधी रह जाती है। स्पष्टतः किसानों के पास वे सुविधाएँ नहीं हैं जो अनुसंधान संस्थाओं के पास उपलब्ध हैं। आवश्यकता इस बात की है कि किसान की परिस्थितियों को ध्यान में रखते हुए व्यावहारिक तकनीक विकसित की जाए।

(4) विभिन्न गतिविधियों के सम्पादन हेतु कृषकों को कई तरह के ऋण उपलब्ध कराने की व्यवस्था है। परन्तु प्रणाली की जटिलता, जानकारी के अभाव, कर्मचारियों के नकारात्मक दृष्टिकोण व निहित स्वार्थ के कारण प्रायः लघु व सीमान्त कृषक सरकारी ऋण सुविधा से वंचित रह जाते हैं और निजी संस्थाओं/व्यक्तियों से उच्च ब्याज दर पर ऋण लेने को विवश हो जाते हैं। ये लोग किसानों का शोषण करते हैं। सरकारी व संस्थागत बैंकों से कार के लिए ऋण प्राप्त करना आसान है परन्तु ट्रैक्टर के लिए ऋण प्राप्त करना कठिन है। वस्तुतः वर्तमान व्यवस्था में सुधार करने की आवश्यकता है ताकि एक आम किसान को बिना किसी बाहरी सहायता के उचित मात्रा में समय पर ऋण मिल सके। ऋण प्राप्त करने की प्रक्रिया सरल हो और ब्याज दर 4.00 प्रतिशत हो जैसा कि नेशनल कमीशन फॉर फारमर्स के द्वारा संस्तुति की गई है।

(5) इस समय किसानों को विभिन्न मदों में सबसिडी दिए जाने का प्रावधान है। सबसिडी एक विशद योजना का अंग होना चाहिये जिसका लक्ष्य लघु व सीमान्त कृषकों को सहायता पहुँचाना हो ताकि वे खेती में ऊर्जा सहित विभिन्न निवेशों पर आ रहे अतिरिक्त व्यय को वहन कर सके।

2. कृषि उत्पादों के भण्डारण व विक्रय की सुव्यवस्था

(1) इस समय भण्डारण की आधुनिक सुविधाओं का अभाव है फलस्वरूप फसल उठाने के बाद काफी हानि उठानी पड़ती है। एक

आकलन के अनुसार हानि की मात्रा 30 प्रतिशत तक आँकी गई है। इसमें सुधार करने की आवश्यकता है।

(2) कृषि उत्पादों के विक्रय की वर्तमान व्यवस्था भी बिचौलियों व व्यापारियों के हक में कार्य करती है। सरकारी एजेन्सी भी प्रायः किसानों के बजाय इन बिचौलियों का साथ देती है। जब किसान अपना उत्पाद लेकर सरकारी केन्द्रों पर जाता है तो वे कई बार अनावश्यक आपत्तियाँ लगाकर उत्पाद लेने से मना कर देती है फलस्वरूप किसान समर्थन मूल्य से कम दर पर अपना उत्पाद बिचौलियों को बेचने को विवश हो जाता है। लघु व सीमान्त कृषकों की आर्थिक स्थिति ऐसी नहीं होती कि वे अपने उत्पाद का भण्डारण कर सकें क्योंकि उन्हें साहूकारों का ऋण चुकाना होता है।

(3) ये बिचौलिए कृषि उत्पाद को उच्चतर मूल्य पर उपभोक्ताओं को बेचते हैं। इस प्रकार एक तरफ उपभोक्ताओं का शोषण होता है और दूसरी तरफ किसानों का। एक अध्ययन के अनुसार उपभोक्ता कृषि उत्पाद का जो मूल्य चुकाता है उसका मात्र 10 से 23 प्रतिशत ही किसान को प्राप्त होता है। अधिकांश भाग हानि, अदक्षता व बिचौलियों की भेंट चढ़ जाता है। विकासशील देशों में भण्डारण व विक्रय की अच्छी व्यवस्था होने के कारण किसान को 64 से 80 प्रतिशत मूल्य मिल जाता है। यह विडम्बना है कि कुछ वर्षों में ही व्यापारी तो कृषि उत्पाद का विक्रय कर धनवान हो जाता है परन्तु उसका उत्पादन करने वाला किसान गरीबी और अभाव से जूझता रहता है। वस्तुतः कई कारणों से किसान बिचौलियों को अपना उत्पाद बेचने को विवश है। ये हैं बाजार से गाँव की दूरी, परिवहन पर व्यय, ऋण व इन्श्योरेन्स उपलब्धता की कमी, भण्डारण का अभाव, उत्पाद को रोकने की अक्षमता, निजी क्षेत्रों के ऋण लौटाने का दबाव आदि। किसान व उपभोक्ता के हित में इन कारकों को दूर करना आवश्यक है।

(4) आवश्यकता इस बात की है कि विक्रय की ऐसी व्यवस्था की जाए जिसमें कृषि उत्पाद के विक्रय का लाभ किसान, उपभोक्ता व व्यापारी को न्यायोचित व अनुपातिक आधार पर मिले। इसके लिए या तो किसानों को अपना उत्पाद सीधे विक्रय करने के लिए आवश्यक सुविधाएँ उपलब्ध करायी जाएँ या किसानों और उपभोक्ताओं की सहकारी समितियाँ बनायी जाएँ। यह भी उपयुक्त होगा कि सम्पूर्ण भारत को एक बाजार के रूप में मानते हुए किसानों को अपना उत्पाद किसी भी स्थान पर विक्रय करने की स्वतंत्रता हो।

3. उचित एवं संतुलित कृषि उत्पाद समर्थन मूल्य

(1) समर्थन मूल्य निर्धारित करने की वर्तमान अवधरणा भी किसानों के हित मे नहीं है। यह आदर्श मूल्य के बजाय प्रारम्भिक (Threshold) मूल्य है। आदर्श समर्थन मूल्य का अर्थ है कृषि तथा गैर कृषि उत्पाद के मूल्यों में सन्तुलन। कृषि उत्पाद की इकाई की तुलनात्मक अर्थात क्रय क्षमता में गिरावट को रोका जा सके। आज किसान एक क्विन्टल खाद्यान्न से उतना गैर कृषि सामान नहीं खरीद सकता जितना पहले खरीद सकता था। इस प्रकार वह इस बात से अनजान है कि वह निरन्तर गरीबी की ओर बढ़ रहा है। स्पष्टत: कृषि उत्पाद का समर्थन मूल्य समानता के आधार पर निर्धारित होना चाहिए।

(2) इस बारे में राष्ट्रीय किसान आयोग (National Commission on Farmers) की सस्तुंतियाँ विचारणीय हैं। इनके अनुसार किसी भी कृषि उत्पाद का समर्थन मूल्य आ रहे इकाई व्यय का 150 प्रतिशत होना चाहिए (कृषि व्यय+50 प्रतिशत) उपयुक्त होगा कि ये संस्तुति तत्काल लागू की जाएँ।

4. गाँव में सेवा क्षेत्रों का विस्तार

(1) ग्रामीण क्षेत्र में आवश्यक सेवाओं का विस्तार नहीं हो पाया है। विपरीत इसके गाँव के कारीगर रोजगार व बेहतर कमाई की आशा में शहर की ओर पलायन कर रहे हैं। यदि पूर्व की भाँति गाँव की रोजमर्रा की आवश्यकताओं की पूर्ति की व्यवस्था गाँव के पास ही की जाए तो इससे उन्हें लाभ तो होगा ही गाँव के नवयुवकों को रोजगार भी मिलेगा।

(2) गाँव के नवयुवकों को प्रशिक्षित कर तथा उनके प्रभावी ग्रुप बनाकर निम्न सेवा क्षेत्रों में लगाया जा सकता है-

1. कृषि उत्पाद के लिए वांछित विभिन्न निवेशों की ट्रेडिंग
2. नर्सरी का कार्य
3. बायो गैस यन्त्रों की स्थापना व अनुरक्षण
4. सामाजिक वानिकी योजनाओं का प्रबन्ध
5. फूड प्रोसेसिंग कार्य
6. हैण्डपम्प, पम्पसेट्स, ट्रेक्टर आदि तथा उनके पुर्जो की ट्रेडिंग व मरम्मत के कार्य

7. कृषि उपकरणों की ट्रेडिंग व मरम्मत के कार्य
8. भवन निर्माण सामग्री की ट्रेडिंग
9. कम्पाउंडर एवं नर्सो के प्रशिक्षण केन्द्र

5. ग्रामीण क्षेत्रों में कृषि आधारित लघु व कुटीर उद्योगों की स्थापना व विस्तार

(1) गाँव की बेरोजगारी दूर करने तथा गैर कृषि आय में वृद्धि करने के लिए यह आवश्यक है कि वहाँ कृषि आधारित लघु व कुटीर उद्योगों का जाल फैलाया जाए। आधुनिक उद्योग प्रायः रोजगार रहित विकास को प्रोत्साहित करते हैं। कृषि ही ऐसा क्षेत्र है जो रोजगार आधारित विकास की सुविधा प्रदान कर सकता है।

(2) गाँव के लोग आर्थिक दृष्टि से इतने सम्पन्न नहीं है कि उद्योगों का जाल फैला सकें। वहाँ पूंजी की कमी है। उद्योगों के लिए आवश्यक इन्फ्रास्ट्रक्चर, परिवहन, संचार व बिजली की कमी है। हमारी वर्तमान तकनीक एवं औद्योगिकी ग्रामीण क्षेत्र के लिए बहुत उपयोगी नहीं है। आज हमें गाँव की आवश्यकताओं की पूर्ति के लिए ऐसी औद्योगिकी की जरूरत है जिसमें स्थानीय प्रतिभा, स्थानीय कृषि उत्पाद व स्थानीय संसाधनों का अधिकतम उपयोग हो सके, प्रति इकाई पूंजी से वांछित उत्पादन हो सके तथा अधिकतम रोजगार की व्यवस्था हो सके।

(3) किसानों के हित में यह एक महत्वपूर्ण कार्य है। इसके लिए सरकार को आवश्यक पूंजी, इन्फ्रास्ट्रक्चर व तकनीकी उपलब्ध करानी होगी। साथ ही साथ किसानों तथा ग्रामीण नवयुवकों के आवश्यक प्रशिक्षण की व्यवस्था करनी होगी।

6. शिक्षा का विस्तार व व्यावसायीकरण

(1) ग्रामीण क्षेत्र में शिक्षा का विस्तार व व्यावसायीकरण रोजगार सृजन का सशक्त माध्यम बन सकता है। इसके लिए वर्तमान शैक्षिक प्रशासन, शिक्षा व्यवस्था, अध्यापक प्रशिक्षण, पाठ्यक्रम आदि में सुधार करने की आवश्यकता है। इसके लिए एक उच्चस्तरीय समिति या आयोग के गठन की आवश्यकता है जिसमें ग्रामीण पृष्ठभूमि के विद्वान भी सदस्य हों।

(2) शिक्षा को रोजगार से जोड़ने के लिए प्राइमरी स्तर से लेकर डिग्री स्तर की शिक्षण संस्थाओं में पढ़ाई के साथ-साथ क्राफ्ट, कुटीर धन्धे के

प्रशिक्षण की व्यवस्था होनी चाहिए।

(3) ग्रामीण क्षेत्रों में ग्रामीण तकनीकी इन्स्टीट्यूट खोले जायें जिनमे कृषि प्रसार, कृषि उद्योग, ग्रामीण अभियन्त्रण, ग्रामीण प्रबन्धन, मार्केटिंग आदि के डिग्री स्तर के पाठ्यक्रम हों। इनसे जुड़े ग्रामीण पोलीटेकनीक खोले जाएँ। इनको क्षेत्र में स्थापित उद्योगों से जोड़ा जाए ताकि समय-समय पर विद्यार्थियों को उन उद्योगों में प्रशिक्षण दिया जा सके।

7. सामाजिक सुविधाओं का विस्तार

गाँव को रहने योग्य बनाने के लिए यह आवश्यक है कि वहाँ सामाजिक सुविधाओं का विस्तार किया जाए। आज अधिकांश गाँवों में बिजली की कमी है, शिक्षण संस्थाओं की कमी है, अच्छे अस्पताल नहीं हैं, सड़कों की दशा अच्छी नहीं है, कम आमदनी तथा बेरोजगारी तो है ही सामाजिक सुविधाओं का भी अभाव है।

आज विभिन्न राज्यों में 20 से 50 प्रतिशत ऐसे कृषक हैं जो कृषि का धन्धा छोड़ना चाहते हैं। परन्तु वैकल्पिक धन्धा न मिलने के कारण छोड़ नहीं पा रहे हैं। कोई भी साधन सम्पन्न व्यक्ति गाँव में रहने को वरीयता नहीं देता। विश्व के विकासशील देशों में गाँव तथा शहर की सामाजिक सुविधाओं में लगभग समानताएँ हैं। यदि भारत में इस स्थिति का निराकरण नहीं किया गया तो एक दिन शहर और गाँव के बीच संघर्ष होगा।

सन्दर्भ

1. Statistical outline of India 2012-2013, Tata Services Ltd.
2. Economic Survey, 2012-2013, Government of India.
3. N. S. S. Surveys.
4. Agricultural Statistics at a Glance 2011, Government of India.
5. Survey of Indian Agricultural 2012, *The Hindu*.
6. Article by Sri Vikas Rawal on Ownership Holdings of Land in Rural India. Putting the Record straight.
7. Agriculture in India from Wikipedia, the free encyclopedia.
8. कप्तान सिंह : *ग्रामीण क्षेत्रों में शिक्षा के विस्तार, नियोजन व प्रबन्धन में सुधार।*
9. कप्तान सिंह : *ग्रामीण क्षेत्रों में लघु व कुटीर उद्योगों का विस्तार।*
10. Article by Sri K. Nagraj.

2

Some Reflections on Socio Economic Life of the Peasant Community of North India Today

Dr. S.S. Rana

India has, since the Vedic times, been primarily an agricultural country[1]. Vast majority of its population lives in villages and depends on agriculture for subsistence. Not withstanding the green revolution, happening first in north-west, and gradually but inevitably extending to the eastern parts of the country, and conjointly the white revolution taking place in several parts, agriculture and its natural ally, cattle rearing and dairy farming have not received the amount of attention required in terms of micro planning and fund allocations. The scenario today continues to be the same as aptly diagnosed by Michael Lipton 'where the countryside may get the priority but the city will get the resources'[2]. As the country marches forward, we find among the beneficiaries, mostly those who are either already firmly settled in the big cities or those among the landless who having little stake in their villages, manage to flee and settle on the fringe of a city or town in semi-urban conglomerations. This phenomenon is more notable in the north, especially in

1. *Akshairma diyah, krishimit krishasva-Rigveda*-10.34.13
2. Michael Lipton : *Why Poor People Stay Poor: Urban Bias in World Development*, p. 18.

the country's capital. Their new habitats, though generally substandard, receive fancy names, mostly ending in 'Vihar' or garden, with patronage of the vote hungry political class. The residual population of villages finding itself tied with their meagre land holdings has hardly any alternative but to stick on, slogging in the hope of an elusive turn around. This phenomenon pervades among the peasant communities of the North and North-West India, though observed in varying degrees from region to region. The capital, which the rural people invest on education and professional training of their younger generation, mostly fails to yield any returns as the same, along with the now trained and earning population, gets sucked into the seamless monolith of the cities, lock stock and barrel. The system of rewards and opportunities is so designed that the city appears to draw to it, as if magnetically, the young and youthful men and women from their chronically stagnant habitat. The usual emerging scenario in the villages is one of dearth of capital. Compounded by dearth of talent (which too has drained out), the result is an eternal famine of enlightened leadership. The situation leaves the arena free for the unscrupulous elements to have a field day. In many cases the Panchayats get manipulated at the hands of the wily in the government agencies, who manage to milch the funds meant for development for their personal benefit, leaving only crumbs for the gullible among the Panchayats. With negligible infrastructure in place, initiatives for growth on the part of private persons get frustrated.

Economic depression affects social life in several ways. Kinship and family relationships start getting fragmented. Increasing alcoholism, fostered by contraband activities on the part of anti-social elements adds to the prevailing hopelessness of the situation and also to the sense of helplessness among the people. The local politician finds himself on the horns of a dilemma. Generally, he (occasionally she) is least academically oriented and is as such clueless of the impact of the piling legislation concerning the life of peasant communities, who themselves have hardly any clout with the media in shaping its stance regarding issues touching their lives viz. gender issues, time honoured social customs (evolved in a homogeneous kinship based settlement pattern), land rights, pricing of their products and their marketing etc. Squatting remains the birth right of equally the rich and the poor of the cities alone, but the same is considered infra dig for a peasant to resort to such methods to dispose of his produce. He is perpetually under pressure (as if a prisoner) to sell off his produce to avoid diminishing returns (for the obvious reasons of inadequacy of safe and secure storage). It is a different world where the buyer virtually decides the price of the product.[3]

Social conditions: A basic and prevalent social structure in the area is not only threatened to be degraded but is also sought to be replaced by a monolithic and so called model of modernity through road rolling legislation. Those involved in this process, from the bureaucracy to the levels of legislatures and courts, at both the state and central levels are either arrogantly oblivious of the prevailing social milieu in the rural and semi urban settlements in the region or are revengefully contemptuous of the same being unworthy of even a serious examination. For historical reasons the feebleness (or one may say, the total absence) of intellectual protest has been partly responsible for turn of circumstances adversely affecting the peasant community through legislation in independent India. Further, the neutralization through voluntary choices of community

3. *Manushyanam vritirarthah, manushavatibhumirityarthah* – *Kautilya's Arthashastra* 15.1.1

members (both individuals and the community at large), of adverse impact of such unimaginative measures–be it the land succession laws or the laws governing matrimony, as can be seen, has perhaps been responsible for the slumber and indifference of the populace, amply unmindful of what awaits their future progeny. For the present, 'de-facto' the customary laws prevail (leaving out rare cases). But such *manipulation* of law, however well intentioned, is no solution. The thaw should be translated into new initiatives whereby the problems of the traditional laws are addressed squarely and comprehensively, leaving no quarter for any injustice anywhere.

Take, for example, the land succession laws. The traditional law, for certain esoteric reasons, had no place for the girl child in the chain of successors in the land of a deceased person. This omission was explained by the argument of land being an immovable entity can not be parceled out to accompany the girl when she is married off *(which as per custom should be at a considerable distance-duhita doore hita)* and settles away in her 'in-laws' home. Secondly, the element of *'quid pro quo'* present in almost all cases renders the question of a girl having share in her late father's land redundant. But let it be admitted that a small, but serious problem remained to be tackled. One shuddered to think of the plight of a girl child having no male sibling. The customary law is silent on its' solution. It should be possible to have a legal and statutory arrangement by which such a girl is given the right to enjoy her late father's land income all her life and in case of her early demise her children take her place till they attain adulthood. Thereafter the land might revert to co-laterals. Any mutual arrangement, duly documented, between the girl and the co-laterals at any stage should prevail. Now that a wife is *ipso facto* equal owner in the ancestral property of her husband, the question of giving a girl child the right in her late father's land begs for a serious review. All along, the basic principle of 'the land belongs to the village as a whole' ultimately; should be kept in mind. It is another matter that the initially 'de facto' occupants became 'dejure' owners in due course of time. Even the domestic animals had their share in the common land left as meadows *(a good animal lawyer has a brief ready!)*. Let us learn from Kautilya that all wealth is created on the earth[3]. Let us not fragment it on a sly and attempt to parcel it out to our outgoing daughters awaiting to be compensated through the package of our incoming daughters-in-law. If the process goes on for a few decades one can hardly imagine the devastation that could be inflicted on land holdings by a complicated fragmentation–the very reverse of our avowed policy of consolidation of land holdings for economic viability. Surely, the issue merits a serious thought and the existing law, perhaps, a review.

Peasant communities in North and North-West, as else where in India have never before since independence, come under strains in their social life as they have come now with a series of legislation either in the name of freedom of choice or of expression. Whether it was the times of the imperial rulers like the Mauryas, the Guptas, the Pushyabhutis (especially under Harsha) or the Delhi Sultanate rulers, the Mughals and the British, peasant communities enjoyed autonomy of some degree in regulating and managing their social life.[4] Even in war times enemy armies observed the norm of letting the agriculturists do their work unhindered[5] – plausibly for the reason that they were engaged in creating wealth to be had at appropriate time or perhaps for the

4. For example the Mughals issued sanads to the *Khap Panchayats* to this effect, vide M.C. Pradhan: *The Political System of the Jats of Northern India*.
5. *Chachnamah*, edited and translated by Kalichbeg.

reason that if distracted they might direct their plough as a weapon against the enemy. We have in our mythology the story of Balarama *(elder brother of Shri Krishna)* raising his plough as a weapon of war against the enemies for good effect.[6] Agriculture, not being a mere vocation has been a way of life and the two are inseparable like fibre and fabric. No wonder then, that all along the stream of Indian history we find the rulers uninterfering as far as the social life and ways of the people were concerned.

Matrimony is the core fibre which goes on to construct the web of social life among members of a community. Social relationships are determined and governed primarily by blood and matrimony supplemented by the brotherhood of geography. The pattern of settlements in our rural areas simply bears it out. The well thought out and well adhered to institutions of endogamy and exogamy, the by-products of the pattern of settlements and way of life, have served our society well for millenniums. But with the onset of modernity, aided by new scientific technologies and abetted by the primacy of individualistic approach to life, guaranteed by our constitution, the social fabric of peasant communities is encountering challenges, which do not appear to be easily met with.

Matrimony is one aspect which, at the present juncture, has thrown up issues requiring serious in depth examination and pragmatic solutions. The prevailing laws relating to matters of matrimony and land succession incorporating the so called progressive measures, especially those taken in the name of women empowerment need to be re-looked closely and afresh in light of the experience gained so far at different places and among different communities *(if unity is to be achieved diversity must be respected and honoured).* If

---

6. Balaram is called Langali (having plough as his weapon).

our constitution itself can be amended umpteen times, its byproducts i.e. the related Acts could easily be amended both at the central and state level. It is a pity that the Central government sneered at perhaps a solitary realistic land succession law enacted by the Haryana government decades ago which needed the former's nod.

Lack of appreciation of the ground realities on the part of the law makers has resulted in enactment of laws which contribute to disintegration of the social fabric of the peasant communities settled in the rural areas. Under the circumstances they find their own solutions which at times are not only in serious violation of the prevailing law, but are in several cases blatantly savage. But the irony is that the otherwise well informed urban elite is reluctantly clueless about what lies behind the symptoms. Even an erudite scholar of peasant studies like Dr. Prem Chaudhary, in her brilliant case studies in 'Contentious Marriages and Eloping Couples'[7] appears reluctant to go beyond the obvious and examine the basics in the relevant context. Certainly poverty of philosophy is the ultimate culprit here. Any one sparing a thought for the issue will not fail to discover the dilemma of these communities when they are faced with situations which threaten their very existence as communities. It is a pity that no serious efforts have been made to discuss the issues involved on wider intellectual fora.

Conflict resolution is the function of the state. In a country of diversities unity can be brought about by creating common meeting ground between conflicting standpoints. It is here that the peasant communities need greater understanding of their view point tied as they are to their land. Dispersed in their respective fields and preoccupied in the noblest of

7. Prem Chaudhary: *Contentious Marriages and Eloping Couples*, Oxford University Press, Delhi, 2007.

vocations they inherently refrain from forming vocal groups to agitate sustainingly to snatch concessions from the state. Our constitution has freedom of choice and liberty among its corner stones. But at the same time the over all principle is the need for public order and social harmony. It is in this context that the laws regarding matrimony need to be made to achieve this ideal. Individuals must have freedom of choice but within the overall good of the community in which they live. Freedom does not come free. It entails certain obligations to fellow citizens and the community at large. In this context one can venture to suggest to add certain provisions in the Hindu Marriage Act and the Special Marriage Act. The degrees of prohibition already provided in the prevailing laws accommodate the customary law to a limited extent.[8] It prohibits marriage between persons who are *sapindas* (have common ancestry for a varying number of generations on either side).[9] This prohibition is relaxable if the local custom permits such marital liaisons. A similar provision could be added making *gotra* (being an extension of *sapindata,* to an unspecified number of generations) also as a degree of prohibition with a similar provision for relaxation if local custom takes no objection. Local custom here should be decided upon by the gramasabha (which has lately been duly recognized by the 73rd constitutional amendment Act 1992). Conflict resolution has been listed among the functions of the *gramasabha.*[10] Cases out side the ambit of the *gramasabha* could continue to be dealt with under the present provisions. Such an innocuous addition to the

---

8. Hindu Marriage Act, 1955 (25 of 1955) sub section (v) of section 5.
9. *Ibid,* sub section (F) (i) (ii) of section 3 (definitions).
10. The Seventy Third Constitution Amendment 1992 adds article 243-B giving *Panchayats* status of Constitutional Bodies.

prohibitions will only state what is already in practice. The legal provision will only prove to be a disincentive to those who have no regard for the local custom and community harmony. But if such couples still insist, they may exercise the option to go elsewhere to settle down for a home. Issues of different *gotras* in the same village are minor and can be settled with mutual understanding once the *gramasabha* is brought in as an arbiter. The recent reports of a khap panchayat in Haryana welcoming inter caste marriages as long as the other traditional degrees of prohibitions are observed is an example of how the rural communities are pragmatic and are capable of finding solutions with in the framework of tradition and custom. The outsiders have to have patience.

We may now point out here how the poverty alleviation schemes of the states and the central government are adversely affecting the economic activities of peasants. The peasant proprietors, many a times, do not get labour force to work on their fields when most needed as the former prefer to engage themselves in the schemes like MNREGA which seems to give more dignity or status - the ultimate master being the government. The peasant lands up paying either higher rates for labour or ends up suffering loss due to poor cropping. No cognizance is taken of such phenomena in determining the procurement price or support price of the agricultural products. Agriculture is perhaps the solitary production sector where production cost is arrived at without Taking into account major components of inputs such as manpower including also women and children of the family *(translated into hours)*, land value *(or its notional rental)* and last but not the least, the cost of animal power utilized in the process. A meticulous cost accounting is likely to throw up stunning results.

The sedentary life of the peasant communities is in itself a blessing but with the capital formation taking place in the urban centres the developmental cake also gets consumed before it can reach the village. They do not have easy access to good educational institutions or affordable health services. These are the times of mobility. The mobile become upwardly mobile and then do not mix up with the immobile peasants, no matter that the two once huddled together. The peasant appears rarely mobile - either when brought to some *maidan* or park in the cities on a free ride to the rallies of the canny politicians or some more foxy god-man promising to him the mythical rule of the still mythical king of distant times. In the later case he is most likely to shell out a good part of his hard earned money for contributing to a 'grand' mission which the impatient godman is hell bent to accomplish to save the nation from some perceived danger. Education, the most important factor next to religion in shaping human life, has yet to reach the desired levels in its different parameters viz. accessibility, availability, quality assurance etc. The increasing induction of private sector in the domain of education has not been in the best interest of the rural people, both for the reasons of high costs and generally poor quality of education made available.

In the end we may say the rural urban divide must end and the desired portion of the development cake must go to the rural sector if we want to save the urban sector from becoming a stinking place in the not so unforeseen future. The rat race for city ward immigration is sufficient signal for all to watch out.

3

Economic Problems of the Peasant Community of North and North-West India and Remedial Measures in Historical Perspective

Zakir Husain, N.S. Alam

The Socio-economic problems of peasant community of North comprising contemporary Delhi, Uttar Pradesh and Uttarakhand and North-West India constituting Jammu and Kashmir, Punjab, Himachal and Haryana and the remedial measures have their origin in history in Indian context. In India the agriculture revolution and the first urban revolution coincide in the Indus or Harappan revolution within 2600-1800 BC as the fabric of Indian agriculture, totally depended on plough cultivation. The domestication of cattle especially that of ox, that had already been converted into a draught animal for pulling the cart had become well established in respect of Indian people.[1] Interestingly enough the most remarkable of the Indus crops is cotton which ushered the industrial crops because the use of plough explains the really large extent of Indus agriculture, covering the north-western plains and extending into Gujarat.[2]

---

1. Marshall : *Mohenjodaro and Indus Civilization*, Vol I, pp. 31-32.
2. Irfan Habib : *Essays in Indian History-Towards a Marxist Interpretation*, Delhi, 1995, pp. 110-115.

Irfan Habib has argued in favour of the two crops annual cycle in Indus and Rig Vedic civilizations as well as of 'free' peasant who were the masters of their own field, which term however specifically appears in early 14th century medieval period as *hurr* or free men by birth in *Insha-i-Mahru* of Ainul Mulk Mahru Multani.[3]

A long transit took place in the Gangetic Basin where extensive tract were cleared by the Indian peasantry as the area of the heaviest concentration of rural population in India today was probably then densely forested down to 2000 B.C.

Till the beginning of early medieval period from 600 A.D., the peasant community suffered many travails and turbulence which had far reaching effect on socio-economic problems of the peasant community of north and north-west India for which remedial measures used to be applied simultaneously yet the picture become much more crystal clear since the very inception of the medieval period.

We are acquainted with the fact that when the Arabs confronted Dahar in battle in 712-713A.D., the ruler of Sindh was accompanied by 'sons of king' (*abnaul muluk*) numbering 5000 horsemen,[4] which is the literal translation of the rajputras (rautas, ancestors of the modern Rajputs) yet the treatment continued to be met with the Zutt [or Jats) remained unchanged as this peasant community in Sindh suffered the old taboos of discrimination imposed by the Brahmans upon them. The fate of the Meds or the modern Meo community became much better as they gradually began to embrace Islam from 712 A.D. onwards

3. *Insha-i-Mahru*, ed. Shaikh Abdur Rasheed, Lahore, 1965, p. 61.
4. *Chachnamah*, edited by Umar Daudpota, Delhi, 1939, p. 169.

till they became a complete Muslim community by the end of 16th century A.D. at their own choice.

Agriculture and the irrigation technology in the arid soil of Haryana and the torrid climate of Rajasthan (Rajputana) simultaneously attracted the attention of the rulers, who constructed the tanks and lakes for irrigation purposes and also provided relief to the caravans of travellers and businessmen. As a contemporary Persian epigraph records the construction of a *hauz* (lake) Palwal by Badruddin Sunqar, the officer-in-charge of the town, in 1211A.D. both for benefit of people and cattle.[5]

Similarly the first lake constructed in Delhi by Sultan Shamsuddin Iltutmish near the Idgah (for offering two Eid prayers) outside the Ghazni gate was used for irrigation as well.[6]

Such irrigation facilities were a real solution or the remedial measures for the peasant community in the early thirteenth century which practice was also opted by the nobles in Bari Khatu district Nagaur in Rajasthan, as recorded in an inscription of 1232 A.D. by Masood, son of Ahmad Khalji, which have provided relief both to cultivation and travellers in the torrid climate of the desert.[7]

Sultan Alauddin Khalji is known for taking much interest in developing the means of irrigations in the Delhi Sultanate for the promotion of agriculture as he constructed Hauz-i-Khas known as a Hauz-i-Alai.[8]

---

5. Cf. *Epigraphia Indo-Muslemica*, 1911-12, ed. J. Horovitz, pp. 1-3.
6. Ibn Battuta : *The Travels of Ibn Battuta*, English Translation by Sir Hamilton Gibb, Cambridge, 1971, Vol 3, p. 624.
7. Z.A. Desai : 'Inscriptions of the Mamluk Sultans of Delhi', *Epigraphia Indica : Arabic Persian Supplement.*
8. Ziauddin Barani : *Tarikh-I-Firoz Shahi*, ed. Syed Ahmad, Aligarh Ghazipur, 1862, p. 48.

Though Irfan Habib has argued about the introduction of Persian wheel in India sometime in the fifteenth century,[9] yet Thorkid Schioler has established its presence in Baghdad in 1100 A.D.[10] and the references to the *saqiya* and *charkh* set upon the wells that were owned both by the state and private cultivators in the early period of Sultan Muhammad bin Tughluq in and around Delhi to water their field and gardens[11] since irrigation facilities in the Delhi Sultanate were provided which have also been properly documented.[12] Muhammad bin Tughluq is credited for advancing loans to peasants for digging wells for the extension of cultivation,[13] as masonry and *cutcha* wells are mentioned in one of our medieval texts,[14] probably the latter was found in abundance. Interestingly in some localities water blocked up by constructing dams *(bandhs)* upon system provided another source of irrigation which was built by the local peoples and some by the government.[15]

---

9. Irfan Habib : Presidential Address, Medieval India Section *Proceedings of the Indian History Congress*, Varanasi, 1969, pp. 152-53.
10. Thorkid Schioler : *Roman and Islamic Water Lifting Wheels*, Odense (Denmark), 1973, pp. 168-73.
11. Shihabuddin-al-Umari : *Masalikul Absar fi Mamalik al Amsar*, Khursheed Ahmad Fariq, Delhi, 1961, p. 23.
12. Tatsuru Yamamoto, Mastu Ara and Tokifusa Tsu Kinowa : Delhi : Architectural Remains of the Delhi Sultanate period, *Water Works*, Vol. 3, Tokyo, 1970, p. 120.
13. Ibn-i-Battuta : Translation by Agha Mehdi Husain, pp. 88-89.
14. Amir Hasan Sijzi : *Fuwaidul Fu'ad* (Conversations of Shaikh Nizamuddin Auliya recorded in 1307-22A.D.), ed. Latif Malik, Lahore, 1966.
15. Anonymous : *Sirat-i-Firoz Shahi*, manuscript [1371 A.D.] photo print, K.B.O.P. Library Patna, pp. 36 (a), 38 (a), 106 (b), 107 (a).

Since fourteenth century we become acquainted with the canals which seem too have been inspired from Central Asia. Though Ghiyasuddin Tughluq (1320-24) was known for digging canals for promotion of agriculture yet it was under Firoz Shah Tughluq (1351-1388) the biggest network of canal came into existence in India until nineteenth century. He dug two canals, the Rajab-Wah and the Ulugh-Khani, from the Jammu River, carrying them to Hissar. He however cut again the Firoz-Shahi from the Sutlej and one from Ganga.[16] One canal ran from Hindan River in the Doab to join the Jamna near Delhi.[17] Ghiyasuddin Tughluq was deeply interested in developing water supply and providing irrigation facilities for the people while Muhammad bin Tughluq devised an elaborate agricultural policy, known as *asalib*, to promote agriculture which according to Barani could in the event of implementation would not have left any fallow land in the country but only Firoz Shah succeeded in this mission, as one of his dams is still functional in Wazirabad in Delhi supplying the water even after 650 years.

We are informed that Firoz Shah was the first ruler who seriously planned for restoring the rain water through the constructions of dams in the territory that faced the scarcity of water which is also confirmed by Farishta that the sultan built thirty huge reservoirs in territories that suffered from scarcity of water to serve for irrigation. Furthermore an anecdote *in Javamial-i-Kilem* about Shaikh Nizamuddin Auliya brings to light the fact the Persian wheel had gained general acceptance in Delhi, sometime in the thirteenth century as the Shaikh observed the Persian wheel set up on a well and the cultivator who was drawing the bullocks

16. Barani : (Manuscript), pp. 106 (b), 107 (a).
17. Sharfuddin Ali Yezdi : *Zafarnama*, ed. M. Allahdad, p. 86.

for lifting the water exhorted the animals, saying "*age barh, age barh*" (speed up, speed up) in a melodious tone.[18]

Surprisingly the construction of canals by Firoz Shah Tughluq resulted into the springing up of 1000 villages of the peasant community on these canals and cultivation. We may also take into consideration the fact that mangoes and grapes were possibly cultivated as Muhammad bin Tughluq also encouraged to raising grapes (and dates).[19] This device of Persian wheel seems to have spread in different territories in north India by the turn of 14th century thereby resolving irrigation problems of the peasant community.

Though Ghiyasuddin Tughluq sought to give relief to the peasant community as a whole by remitting additional cesses that used to be levied on all sown lands both such as yielded crops and as failed to do so, yet under Muhammad bin Tughluq [1324-51] followed the same rigorous system of taxation as prevalent in villages of Doab that was implemented in the entire empire with enhancement of agrarian taxation which caused an agrarian uprising of great intensity covering a vast area near Delhi and Doab in 1332-34 AD, which even continued around Kol (Aligarh) by the rural rebels as late as 1342 AD. Thus the contraction of cultivation in the Doab, the ruin of peasant community, the reduction in numbers of grain carriers, and the failure of grains to reach Delhi from the provinces of Hindustan, a serious famine began to spread in Delhi and the entire Doab which led to high rise in grain prices that was coupled with the scarcity of rains owing to which the famine became widespread for some years. The famine

---

18. *Javami' al Kilem* conversations of Saiyid Muhammad Husaini, Gesu Daraz, Kanpur, 1356 hijri, p. 150.
19. Barani, pp. 498-99.

that had begun in 1334 AD, lasted for about seven years till 1341-42 AD.

This failure of Muhammad bin Tughluq, which provoked an agrarian rebellion of unprecedented intensity by increasing taxation also became the first ruler to formulate a systematic policy of promoting agriculture. He advanced *sondhar*, or loan to peasants known as *taqavi* in Mughal administration, to enable them to extend cultivation and dig wells. The word taccavi from *taqavi* (literally, strength giving) for the pre-harvest loans in contemporary context was introduced by Muhammad bin Tughluq of the system throughout the Delhi Sultanate.[20]

But the Mughal administration not only rigorously followed the taxation system on peasant community but also extended grant of loans designated as *taqavi* to enable them to buy seed and undertake cultivation of waste land. But economic differentiation had progressed considerably among the peasant community as there were large cultivators using hired labour and raising crops for the market and there were small peasants who could barely produce food grains for their own sustenance. Though much has been said about the so called regressive taxation system of the Mughals yet the peasant community was side by side cooperating them and also rebelled against them.[21]

During the Mughal period no great famine or any other calamities took place in north and north-west India, otherwise the Mughal government as a rule had to remit

20. Shams Siraj Afif : *Tarikh-i-Firoz Shahi*, Calcutta, 1890, pp. 129-30.
21. Shaikh Farid Bhakkri : *Zakhiratul Khawanin*, Maulana Azad Library, Habib Ganj Collection, Manuscript no. 32/74, p. 108 (a).

the revenue, to the peasant community and would import food grains from surplus ones to open government shops and free kitchens for the afflicted people as these measures were occasionally emulated by *zamindar* and other local magnates too.

Interestingly enough the peasant community of north and north-west India had been facing problems as well as occasionally getting redresses of their grievances since the time immemorial. But since the British period this indigenous phenomenon did not last long as the 'land revenue' also drawn from peasant community as understood by the succeeding British administrators, the property of the ten-elevenths of the country. How the British government in India exploited the peasant community and the economy of the country has been a matter of much debate since 19th century especially from the middle of that century.[22] However Maulvi Muhammad Baqir of the *Delhi Urdu Akhbar* fame had specifically drawn the attention of the Indians about the drain of wealth policy through the exploitation of the Indian economy by the English East India Company in his weekly newspaper column.[23] The peasant community were converted by the British Government into mere farms, producing opium, cotton, indigo, hemp and raw materials in exchange of British stuff.[24]

---

22. Cf Irfan Habib : Marx's Perception of India : Process of Accumulation in Pre Colonial and Colonial India; Colonolization of Indian Economy 1757-1900 and Studying a Colonial Economy, without Perceiving Colonialism, in his *Essays in Indian History : Towards a Marxist Interpretation*, Delhi 1995, pp. 14-58, 259-366.
23. *Delhi Urdu Akhbar*, Volume 19, No. 25, 28 Shawwal 1273AH/21 June 1857, p. I Column I.
24. Karl Marx : *On Colonialism and Modernization*, ed. Scolomo Avinari, p. 498.

In United Provinces the merchants and moneylenders began extensively to buy land.[25] Similar position prevailed in Punjab where after the formation of Unionist Party by Sir Fazl-i-Husain and Sir Chhotu Ram after 1923 as the above two classes were deprived from acquiring the lands of the peasant community which became a bone of contention to them because it was the real solution to their problems which was so progressive a step in the interest of peasants in the pre-partition India as it continued to dominate Punjab till the elections of 1946 as it was the largest province in British India presently constituting Punjab, Haryana and Himachal Pradesh including Pakistani Punjab.

Taking cue from the above historical perspective we can easily visualize the contemporary context of the socio-economic problems of the peasant community of north and north-west India and their solutions. Though we know that irrigation, natural calamities, market control, advancing the *taqavi*, or agricultural loans and several other problems and their solutions have been applied from time to time, yet the replacement of pulley wheel for drawing water out of well the counterweighted scoop (*dhenkali* in Hindustan), being a lever and the use of the ox as a draught animal to pull up water in a leather bag out of well by tying to a rope thrown over a pulley and then the replacement of the Persian wheel by diesel and electric pumps have today made them a thing of the past. Introduction of the tubewells in 20th century, the use of electricity in Delhi since 1901, the continuance and expansion of canal system introduced by Firoz Shah Tugluq and re-excavated by Akbar and British Governments and its further extension to other areas of the region under study, the establishment

25. Cf. Eric Stokes in *Cambridge Economic History of India,* Vol II, pp. 46-47, 49, 52.

of Gramin Banks, the continuation of taccavi, the use of agrarian structure established by Alauddin Khalji and improved by Sher Shah which was further embellished by the recommendations of Raja Todar Mal in 1582, and the waving off of the agriculture loans to the peasant community and the introduction of Food Security Bill are the off shots of the old agrarian policies being brought afresh in contemporary context which are basically aimed at the improvement of the lot of the peasant community.

Under the contemporary circumstances the scheme of waving off loans to the peasant community aimed at bailing out them from the financial crisis and other remedial measures have to some extent brought relief to them. However, keeping in view the slow pace of relief there is still a great need of giving much agricultural facilities and concessions on the pattern of European countries and the USA and several other welfare measures need to be followed on humanitarian grounds in India especially in north and north-west India which are the largest corn producing areas of the country. As India has already come of the age of science and technology which has introduced not only the green revolution but also pioneered in field like dairy reforms, and other related agriculture improvements of far reaching consequences which has brought India on the map of progress and development in the competitive world.

4

Agriculturalist Community in India : Confronting Neo Socio-Economic Challenges

Dr. Parwez Nazir

From time immemorial or the beginning of Indus civilization,[1] the agriculturalist community confronted different kinds of problems, besides facing the wrath of nature. They developed their indigenous methods or mechanism for tackling the natural calamities and sustaining it. One problem they faced throughout the historical period was exploitative taxation system, arbitrarily assessed and high-handedly realized. But they were humanely treated at the time of failure of the crop due to natural calamities or any other reasons and they were extended every kind of help by the rulers, encouraging them to start agriculture afresh. During the British rule agriculture and agriculturalist community suffered most because of their exploitative

1. Indus valley civilization or popularly known as Harappa culture was highly urbanized. With the help of 'thriving agriculture economy the Harappa people built their rather unimaginative but comfortable civilization'. For detail see Sir R.E. Mortimer Wheeler, *The Indus Civilization*, Cambridge, 1953.

policies.[2] Consequently agrarian revolt against the British at different places started.[3] It was their participation which provided a mass base to the ongoing anti colonial struggle. Mahatma Gandhi is credited to bring them in the main stream by raising their grievances from the platform of the Indian National Congress.[4] After independence some of the problems solved by the government and their position ameliorated by the adoption of land reform[5] somehow they continued to face new challenges successfully.

In the 21st century mankind has made remarkable progress in every field of life. Agriculture is not an exception. With new inventions and discoveries, agriculture too has developed beyond imagination. Path breaking development in genetic engineering and by applying scientific method with better manure and chemical fertilizers, using high yielding seeds and by use of insecticides and pesticides the per acre agricultural production has tremendously increased and available in market for the consumption. But ever increasing population especially in the third world and African countries is posing serious threat to the policy makers and people are facing acute problems of shortage of food leading to hunger consequently death of millions of people every year.

India is also facing the problems of shortage of food grains because of the growing population and unprecedented

2. See Meghnad Desai, Susanne Rudolph and Ashok Rudra (eds) : *Agrarian power and Agriculture Productivity South Asia*, Barkley, 1984.
3. For detail see A.R. Desai (ed.) : *Peasant struggle in India*, 1982, London.
4. For instance Faizpur Session of the Indian National Congress in 1936 is known for talking up the agrarian issue.
5. See David Lehmann (ed.) : *Agriculture Reform and Reformism : Studies of Peru, Chile, China and India*, London, 1974.

urbanization. Both Government and media can play a decisive role and offer a better solution to tackle the problems confronted by the agriculturalist community in particular and people of the country in general. Since demand is very high but supply is not in that proportion, price is bound to be high some time beyond the purchasing capacity of the people leading to the crises. Thousands of farmers were committing suicide every year because of the failure of the crops either due to changing weather or failure of the monsoon. Environmental changes have created havoc and affected the agriculture community a lot. Some of the government policies are also responsible for the agrarian crises faced by the village community.

Traditional joint family system however, is rapidly disappearing leading to fragmentation of land where application of scientific methodology and extensive farming becomes difficult which naturally affects production. Agriculture these days needs heavy investment but because of poverty and other reasons people are not in position to invest heavily. Therefore agriculture is bound to suffer. During the British period, since the village community was over burdened and exploited, they generally abandoned agriculture. The British heavily invested in railways but deliberately neglected irrigation which was essential for agriculture development. After independence government of India initiated several measures to relieve the peasant community including land reform and establishing cooperative societies. Financial assistance was provided to them. Somehow their condition improved but soon they were confronted with new sets of problems which needs to be tackled carefully by the government to ensure agriculture progress by providing sound financial basis and infrastructural development.

Impact of Urbanization[6] on Agriculture

During the last decade of the 20th century the process of urbanization accelerated to a great extent. In the early decade of the 21st century it assumed an alarming proportion and attracted the attention of the people. Growing urbanization is identified with development having both positive as well as negative impacts on society. Urbanization leads to industrial growth which creates employment opportunities and standard of living improves with better facilities as compared to the rural areas. Simultaneously, since arable and fertile tract of land was urbanized, it was not available for agriculture production and entire segment of the rural population got affected by diminishing income and losing employment. Since the cultivated land is urbanized consequently, availability of land for cultivation is reduced. In India only 43% of geographical area is available for cultivation, out of this if any portion of land is urbanized it will cause the shortage of food problem in future.

Earlier the process of urbanization was confined to a few cities or to metropolitan cities only but after liberalization and globalization the process, however, expanded to almost all the cities with varied degree. Therefore, for production of food, small proportion of land is available around the cities which requires reorganization of agriculture sector based on scientific methods to increase the productivity per unit and traditional system of farming needs to be changed keeping the growing urban population in view. Urbanization is accompanied by industrial development and both small and large scale industries started coming

---

6. For detail see Smailes, A.E., 'The Definition and Measurement of Urabanization' in Jones, Ronald (ed.) : *Essays on World Urbanization*, London, 1975.

up. Therefore according to the industrial needs agriculture production is to be modified which leads to commercial use of agriculture in place of food crops therefore shortage in food grain is noticed.

The self sufficient agriculturalist community now depends on outside supply. For the urban industrial product the neighbouring rural area served as the market and rural industry lost its relevance causing displacement of the artisan class who ultimately migrate to cities in search of employment. Statistically speaking the migration from the rural to urban areas is on massive scale. Consequently there is a short fall in labour force earlier available for agricultural sector which has badly affected the production. In this way we can say that urbanization has further widened the gap between urban and rural population.

Urbanization is a parameter of development in any society. Therefore it should be promoted but not at the cost of agriculture. Urbanization in India is unplanned, unorganized and lop sided depending on the mood of real estate developers. It is strictly to be controlled by the district administration and state government at the first stage and finally by the central government. There is no regulatory body to regulate the unplanned and unorganized ongoing process of urbanization. Neither there is any commission to decide the level of urbanization and percentage area to be urbanized. The urbanization regulatory body if established should work in collaboration of agriculture land regulatory body to demarcate and identify the area to be urbanized. But corruption in the real estate is a great challenge along with bureaucratic delays in stopping it, which needs to be checked. The fertile tract of land should be saved for the production keeping in mind the year 2050, when India's population will touch 150 crores and there will be huge gap in the food production. To save the country from hunger likes situation agricultural land should be saved from reckless urbanization. Urbanization of rural areas can oust the farmers from their traditional profession and render them poor.

Agriculture is the main source of livelihood for more than 70 per cent population but the productivity is considerably low in agricultural sector. During the last fifty years population has increased by 50 per cent and from the trends a high growth rate can be predicted. Punjab has shown a direct correlation between urbanization and agricultural productivity. Urbanization in Punjab is accompanied by progress in agriculture along with agro-based industries which is a healthy sign of development.

Urbanization has resulted in deforestation and again it is a loss to the agriculturalist community. Due to rapid urbanization the level of water is now getting depleted around the big cities and therefore water in unavailable for agricultural or industrial activities. Cultivation on the available land according to the needs of growing population has necessitated the use of high yielding seeds and chemicals for specialized crop which is deteriorating the fertility of soil in due course of time resulting in low productivity. Due to urbanization there is increase in the price of land. Marginal and small land holders are opting to sale it out since agriculture has become unsustainable because of increasing prices. It results in farmers becoming landless labourers. Urbanization has resulted into the decline of natural vegetation and industrialization is causing great damage to climate and environment.

Ground Realities and Inside Story of the Village Economy

Urbanization has necessitated the reorganization of rural order and needs readjustment in accordance to the growing demand of the urban market and money economy by giving up the traditional system of production and previously isolated, self sufficient and subsistence production for the local market. The agriculturist community at present is grappling with new kind of challenge at different stages which is unfortunately not highlighted by the media and brought in to notice of the government.[7] To know the real problems faced by the village community visiting a village in necessary for better understanding of the problems and suggesting remedial measures. Unfortunately most of the surveys conducted and data collected are fictitious. NGOs and other government agencies working in the rural areas and exploring to find out the actual problems are appreciable but their report and suggestions are not taken seriously by the state or central government. Therefore problems continue to prolong affecting agriculture. To know the actual problems of a middle and lower level farmer, during summer vacation, I visited my native village and interviewed hundreds of the farmers not only of my village alone but also of the neighbouring villages. For better understanding of the problems I also talked to the landless labourers and tried to know the complexities of the rural life in wake of industrialization and globalization which the modern society has created.

The findings are astonishing to me since I also belong to that community itself. Knowing the actual problems confronted by a farmer which I never tried to understand

7. R. Dutt and K.P.M. Sundharam : Agriculture, Productivity Trends and Crop Pattern, *Indian Economy*, New Delhi.

became a great surprise to me. For instance one of my findings was that agriculture for the agriculturalist community is not remunerative. When I asked if agriculture is not at all remunerative then why you people still indulge with agriculture sector. The explanation given by them was purely in sociological perspective and it was devoid of any financial or economic implication. Their argument was that they are not associated with their holdings because of the economic gains but emotional attachment with the ancestral property has forced them to continue farming.

The agriculturist community having large or small holdings have different story to grind with. They informed me that agriculture has become so unprofitable that they have preferred to lease out their holdings on crop sharing, what is known as *batai* system and nearly 90 per cent land is under *batai* system in my village alone. The reason they explained was simple to understand. There was huge gap between the amount invested on agriculture and the return and that analysis was more or less based on the facts and figures of previous ten years. They calculated the loss and finally reached to the conclusion that it was not at all profitable and leasing it out was the only solution. On the other hand, *bataidar* has no intention or inclination to improve agriculture by heavily investing as he too was not sure of return; therefore in due course of time production started decreasing.

Secondly, the farmer is confronting the problem of uncertainty of monsoon or no monsoon. In that situation he depends on tube well. Because of the rise in the price of petroleum products irrigation has become a costly affair. Besides this, seeds and chemical fertilizers and other insecticides and pesticides used from time to time are very costly. Due to changing environment and global warming agriculture is also affected by various kinds of deceases to tackle which farmers need finances. But afterwards there is less return on agriculture.

Thirdly, due to urbanization the labour force started migrating towards industrial towns and cities in hope of getting better job opportunities. Somewhere agriculture sector too has made remarkable progress because of the adoption of the extensive farming, for instance in Punjab and Haryana or South Indian states. Migration from Bihar and Eastern Uttar Pradesh is prominently recorded. Therefore there is shortage of labour in the agriculture sector in these areas, demand is high and supply is short because of migration. Therefore cost is bound to be very high and it is very difficult to carry agriculture by farming community themselves.[8]

Fourthly, environmental changes are also of a great concern for the agriculturalist community since global warming and extreme weather is not conducive for the agricultural pursuits. Due to climate change the crops are affected by many diseases for which no cure is available and researches are going on. Recently there was news that the paddy crop is getting affected by a particular kind of disease creating an alarming situation. Excessive rain at some places has created flood like situation and some places known for growing paddy have received minimum rain causing distress for the farmers.[9]

Fifthly, another challenge of a very serious kind is being faced by the farmers of Bihar and eastern Uttar

---

8. K. Adiseshaiah : Urbanization in India a Lopsided development, *Asian Economic Review*, 1979.
9. A. Kundu, S. Gupta : Migration, Urbanization and Regional Inequality, *Economic and Political Weekly*, 13 (52) December 26, 1996.

Pradesh the area which I have studied is, the increasing population of *Neelgai*. Since *Neelgai* is considered to be endangered species whose population was reduced to an alarming level. Therefore government included it into the list of protected animals.[10] Killing and hunting is strictly prohibited and killing is a punishable crime. But the farmers are facing a problem which is not highlighted by local media neither it has become a subject of debate due to communal considerations. I was told by many farmers that they have stopped growing certain crops which are under attack by moving caravans of *Neelgai* whose population has increased largely. The crops got affected and farmers have stopped sowing the crops like oilseeds and cereals for example, *moong, til, massur, arhar,* maize etc. Due to this reason the production has drastically decreased. This needs immediate attention of the government to provide some relief to already over stressed farming community.[11]

Lastly we can say that the financial institutions meant for lending finances to the poor farmer are not functioning properly and there is lot of corruption. Various schemes started by the central or state governments facilitating the farmers are being appropriated by the government officials and if reaching to the people, the percentage is very low.[12] We should take a lesson from the medieval rulers who developed a better system of managing the agrarian crises and provided every kind of facility at the time of natural calamities. Because of inadequate marketing facilities the farmers could not get better return on their

10. Ashish, Bose : *India's Urbanization 1901-2001,* New Delhi, 1980.
11. Biplab Dasgupta : *Urbanization, Migration and Rural Changes*, 1988, New Delhi.
12. Davis, K : Urbanization in India : Past and Future in R. Turner (ed.) *India's Urban Future,* 1962, Barkley.

production. Real producer is not the major beneficiary but the intermediaries.

Conclusion

After independence of the country the economic progress was slow but after globalization when open market policy was adopted, the process of urbanization started but India cannot be categorized in the list of over urbanized countries. Urbanization in India is 'certainly expanding and not exploding' as described by some scholars. Urbanization has greatly contributed in the overall economic progress of the country and standard of living considerably improved. But after 2006 the urbanization is fast and at the cost of agriculture which needs attention of government. Both print and electronic media should highlight the problem with concern of availability of food for all by 2050. By careful planning we can leave a strong legacy for the next generation to live peacefully in a hunger free world for which Mahatma Gandhi dreamt all his life.

5

Modernity of Self-Governance and the Puzzle of Peasant Community in Haryana

Ramesh Kumar

Recently, turbulent experiences of peasant community with institutions of formal (statutory) and informal (traditional) self-governance in Haryana attracted attention of many newspapers, journals, magazines, television-talk-shows, and film industry. Although the prime phase of media trial of the controversies is over yet the puzzle remains unresolved. However, it is more important to address the question as to why this puzzle of peasant community has emerged in Haryana rather than to deal with the reasons for the failure of media trial in resolving the puzzle.

The puzzle, which is multidimensional and complex, involves questions concerning authenticity of institutions of informal and formal self-governance. One of the important questions posed by this puzzle is that of synchronizing various practices of self-governance involving conflicting norms of peaceful and harmonious collective life at village level. Such questions have emerged partly because of the widening gap between 'modern' principles of law and conventional wisdom of peasant community in the wake of global impact of human excellence demonstrated through unprecedented technological advancement.

To, what extent the phenomenon of globalization has influenced the nature of self-governance at village level in rural Haryana? This paper addresses this question with reference to issues concerning women's security-with-dignity, matrimonial relations, and ethics of collective life.

The paper consists of two sections. The first section is concerned with issues and experiences. It begins with a description of the controversies surrounding traditions in rural Haryana followed by a discussion on experiences of peasant community with reference to traditional practices of self-governance. Next, it highlights issues and challenges emerging from these experiences. The second section focuses on the puzzle of peasant community where an attempt is made to identify the challenges of self-governance.

I

The Controversies

For over six decades, peasant community in rural Haryana has been struggling with the problem of accommodating indigenous practices evolved through conventional wisdom and the principles of law imported from colonial rulers. Recently, this struggle has emerged as a matter of concern in the wake of growing discontentment among many members of peasant community over the processes through which institutions of formal and informal self-governance have tried to settle cases of conflicting claims concerning norms and practices of collective life at village level. The main issues involved in the controversies include women's security-with-dignity, matrimonial relations, ethics of collective life and self-governance at village level.

Women's Security-with-Dignity

In recent years, peasant community in rural Haryana has been criticized for not being sensitive to women's security-with-dignity.[1] Criticisms from various angles are substantiated by highlighting rapidly falling sex-ratio in Haryana.[2] It is alleged by radical advocates of women's rights that even while ensuring security for women within the family institution, their dignity (as equal partners in the making of the primary unit of human society) is generally ignored. The root cause of this sort of undignified security is often traced back to the act of voluntary sacrifice of a share in paternal properties by daughters. It is alleged that such sort of sacrifices made by daughters are not recognized by society.

As a result of non-recognition, radical critics allege, daughters' education at home and at public institutions is designed in discriminatory ways, which deny them basic rights such as freedom of choice in terms of livelihood and matrimonial socialization. This very process of educating daughters substantially affect their status as capable human beings thereby blocking the prospect of dignified space- after marriage- within the prospective family where they are sent for the rest of their life. Such a discriminatory treatment, results into unequal and problematic matrimonial relations.

Matrimonial Relations

In recent decades, there has been an increase in discontentment among advocates of women's rights on

---

1. Prem Chowdhary : *The Veiled Women: Shifting Gender Equations in Rural Haryana*, Oxford University Press, 1994; *Contentious Marriages, Eloping Couples; Gender, Caste and Patriarchy in Northern India*, Oxford University Press, 2007.
2. According to Census 2011, sex ratio (females per 1000 males) in Haryana is 877, which is the lowest among rest of the states of India, http://www.censusindia.gov.in, accessed on March 28, 2011.

the issues surrounding matrimonial alliances in the wake of controversies surrounding matrimonial relations in rural Haryana.[3] According to advocates of women's rights, matrimonial relations reflect the psychology behind daughters' status within family system. It is alleged that matrimonial relations in rural Haryana are decided on the basis of an assumption according to which daughter-givers' status is treated secondary to daughter-takers' status. Such a secondary treatment of daughter-givers negatively affects the nice ties of matrimonial relations. One of the negative impacts of such treatments often surfaces in the claims of gotra-superiority within a caste and the claims of caste-superiority within religious communities; both the claims directly contribute for daughters' status as inferior to that of son's status and thereby deny them right to equality among members of family system. This sort of treatment reduces their status down to the level of disclaimed daughters or someone else's wealth, radical critics allege. Such criticism is further extended to the domain of ethical concerns of collective co-existence.

Ethics of Collective Life

These ethics involve select norms and practices of collective life which are crucial in maintaining peaceful and harmonious coexistence of different groups at village level. For example, in rural areas of many districts of Haryana such as Bhiwani, Karnal and Rohtak, the ideas of honor and traditions are found to be the core of ethical codes of collective village life. Critics argue that honor and traditions need to be reinterpreted in the light of both modern principles of law and conventional wisdom

---

3. Personal interview with Jagmati Sangwan (Rohtak), June, 2011.

of peasant community because many of these norms and practices are dated now and therefore irrelevant to the changed socio-economic and political context in rural areas.

The need for reinterpretation has gained importance in the wake of an increase in media reports describing controversial cases of marriage alliances and the resultant troubles (loss of human life, unnecessary violence, unwarranted divorces, uncertain marriages etc.) experienced by the members of peasant community at local, state, national, and international level. The main controversy in this regard has been that of conflicting interpretations of honor and traditions concerning same-gotra marriage alliances. The controversy has posed serious questions before peasant community in Haryana regarding self-governance of matrimonial alliances.

Institutions of Self-Governance

The controversies surrounding social life of peasant community discussed in the preceding few paragraphs have been addressed from time to time by institutions of both formal and informal governance in post-colonial rural Haryana. To refresh, the Constitution of India provides for a formal institution of state controlled-and-regulated self-governance at village level, namely, Gram Panchayat. Gram Panchayat is composed of the village people, by the village people, and for the village people. It does not have the privilege of being at the highest level in the hierarchy of state institutions; therefore, it becomes one of the horizontally organized institutional mechanisms at village level.

A general review of local government at village level suggests that Gram Panchayat is the lowest hierarchical institution representing modern nation-state.[4] Apart from formal institution of Gram Panchayat, informal institutions such as customary village councils still find their existence relevant to most of the concerned people in India.[5] As far as institutions of informal self-governance in Haryana is concerned, their roots can be traced back to pre-colonial times when traditional panchayats used to deal with disputes at village level while functioning as justice delivery mechanism on ad hoc basis. One variant of such panchayats was the tradition of *Khap Panchayats*, which are

4. Under the constitutional scheme of local governance, in most states of India, there exists three-tier system of Panchayati raj institutions–a council at district, block and village level with varied names. Therefore village councils (here statutory panchayats) are at the lowest levels of institutions of local self-governance. (*The Constitution of India*, Part IX , Articles 243).
5. Customary village councils in Karnataka, for example, as Kripa Ananthpur & Mick Moore argue, enjoy "considerable local authority because the opportunities for them to abuse these powers for personal or small-group gain are limited" as their clients have options to exit the domain of this authority. Seen from this angle, instead of exercising control over access to land or other valuable assets, these informal institutions in India, face a competitive, pluralist, institutional environment in relation to their judicial functions in particular. Besides, they have "significant roles as gatekeepers between their populations and the higher-level electoral and bureaucratic institutions that offer access to growing volumes of public money" (Kripa Ananthpur & Mick Moore :Ambiguous Institutions: Traditional Governance and Local Democracy in Rural South India, *Journal of Development Studies*, 46: 4, 2010, pp. 605-606).

still considered to be useful in rural areas.[6] During colonial times, modern judiciary had little impact on the process of justice in rural areas;[7] therefore, institutions such as Khap Panchayat used to function independently.

During colonial times, according to oral tales, the central areas of Khap Panchayat activities ranged from

6. Importance of these institutions because of their long existence in the ideological domain of cultural and socio-economic aspects of rural Haryana makes them "old institutions", Prem Chowdhary argues, they should take "reformist agenda" [*'Khaps Have To Reform'*, Sheela Reddy Interviews Prem Chowdhary, Outlookindia.com, Retrieved on January 13, 2011]. For more on *Khap Panchayats* see K.S. Sangwan. According to a survey conducted by a sub-committee headed by K.S. Sangwan under the guidance of the Haryana Backward Class Commission, most people in Haryana prefer *khap panchayats* for various reasons (*Times of India*, December 16, 2012). Inspired by the ideals of preserving institutional arrangements evolved for the sake of good life of people, writers such as Sompal (2006) considers khap panchayats as institutions of community governance [Sompal : 'A Paradigm of Self-Reliant Village India: The Modern Context' in Y.P. Singh (Ed.) *Indian Villages 2020, Vision and Mission,* Vol. 1, Concept Publishing Company, New Delhi, 2006:94]. On the other hand, while acknowledging historical, 'Khap Panchayats in Haryana' in Kalpana Kannabiran and Ranbir Singh, ed., *Challenging the Rule(s) of Law: Colonialism, Criminology and Human Rights in India*, (Sage Publication India Pvt. Ltd. 2008), pp. 331-350.
7. It was partly because of the fact that the British model of administration of justice was non-participatory, extremely formal, and alien to Indians (114th Report of the Eleventh Law Commission of India, 1986, p. 7).

present Hisar to Bharatpur and Bijnor to Aligarh.[8] Khap Panchayat were named according to *numberdari* which was a system of numbers of a particular gotra/clan/caste in a village or khap area. Membership of Khap Panchayat was both territorial (khap area) and ascriptive (clan and caste). Representation in Khap Panchayat was hereditary and there was no direct participation of women. M.C. Pradhan (1966) has extensively dealt with Khap Panchayat organizational units which included the following: *khandans* (networks of nuclear and joint families belonging to common ancestor), *thoks* (a number of *khandans*), clan (consists of khandans, and thoks), village panchayat, *gawand* (informal political unit of the khap area), *thamba* (consists of neighbouring villages ranging from five to twenty), and khap (inhabitation area of people organized into different clans and castes in nearly placed villages).

One of the founding principles of Khap Panchayat was the idea of collective defense of peasants' interests against exploitative feudal and colonial rulers. Therefore, the primary objective of Khap Panchayat was to protect the khap areas (a geographical territory, comprising of some villages–ranging from twelve to 84) against cultural and territorial invasion during pre-colonial and colonial times. In order to fulfill the objective, Khap Panchayat used to practice military activities. Since KPs were helpful to peasants in terms of safeguarding their collective local interests against the atrocities of mughal and colonial rulers, they became popular among rural masses, and eventually traditions of *bhaichara* (brotherhood) was internalized in order to resolve intra-khap and inter-

8. Personal interviews with K.S. Sangwan (Rohtak), Hawa Singh Sangwan (Bhiwani), Bhaleram Beniwal (Dupedi, Karnal) and Col. Risal Singh Sangwan (Charkhi Dadri, Rohtak), April-June 2011.

khap disputes concerning land rights. However, with the demise of feudal and colonial rule, military functions of Khap Panchayats also became irrelevant.

Contemporary rural Haryana is experiencing a number of changes in its social, economic and political spheres in the wake of rapidly declining ajmani system and when the gap between various interpretations of law and self-governance is widening. In such turbulent times, especially when peasant community is getting exposed to the danger of being misunderstood and misinterpreted, one needs to look into the puzzle from a broad perspective.

II

The Puzzle

Since the last decade of 20th century, one of the biggest challenges of democratic decentralization in rural Haryana has been the problem of dealing with ambiguous areas of self-governance. The controversial issues discussed in the preceding section highlight the fact that rural Haryana is at the crossroads of developmental democracy in the wake of conflicting claims of self-governance at village level. Conflicting claims have given rise to the puzzle which can be expressed in very simple words: Which way of self-governance is to be preferred and why? However, answering this puzzle is a very difficult task. There has been an ongoing conflict between competing claims of self-governance the ethics of collective village life and honor codes related to village traditions, social structure, and social institutions.

Modernity of Self-Governance and its Limitations

In recent years, questions have been asked repeatedly whether the local state institutions such as *Gram Panchayats* and *Gram Sabhas* alone are capable enough to deal with these areas in the wake of controversies surrounding institutions of informal self-governance such as *Khap Panchayat*. Partly because of competing answers to such questions, probably for the first time in the history of post-colonial rural Haryana, the existential authenticity of traditional panchayats, i.e. *Khap Panchayat* has been viewed by some as in conflict with the spirit of *Gram Panchayats* and *Gram Sabhas*. The conflict, which has substantially influenced the nature of politics in rural Haryana, is mainly due to the nature and scope of *Khap Panchayats* which cover many aspects of *Gram Panchayats* and *Gram Sabhas* thereby transcending the legacy of colonial rulers.

The conflict is something new, for it is not only an evidence of increasing political participation of the people in rural areas of post-colonial north India, but most importantly, it points to the fact that the debate on development and democracy has started influencing politics at village level. This is a promising state of affairs as far as deliberative aspect of local democracy at village level is concerned. However, this developmental aspect of democracy is paradoxical; the debate represents conflicting claims regarding substantial and procedural aspects of self-governance at village level. As such, it has become a challenging task for the people of Haryana to deepen local democracy at village level.

To refresh, the preceding section has highlighted controversies surrounding issues of women's security-with-dignity, matrimonial relations, ethics of collective village life, self-governance etc. As stated earlier, such controversies direct our attention to internal contradictions of village life which are increasingly emerging in the form of conflicting claims of traditions and self-governance. Loaded with historical legacies, such claims have problematised the life of peasant community. As such, in the wake of rapidly changing social, political and economic aspects of human society in various parts of the globe, ethical dilemmas emerging from a complex socio-political scenario at village level have turned out to be the puzzle of peasant community. One of the core constituents of this puzzle is the growing discontentment of peasant community. The discontentment is an outcome of many factors, globalization is one among them.

Globalization and Changing Nature of Self-governance

While addressing the controversial issues in rural Haryana in the wake of globalization–which has contributed for faster interplay of technology and politics thereby substantially influencing the making of contemporary peasant community in rural Haryana, one has to drop the colonial notion of a village community.

In our times, the power of 'modern' technology has made it feasible for a peasant from rural areas in Haryana to build an online network and exchange ideas with peasants residing in other parts of the globe. What are the attributes of this technologically globalized peasant self and how it differs from the classical 'local' peasant self? This question deserves enough time and space which is beyond the scope of this paper. However, this question, as a guide to our attempt in understanding the growing discontentment, direct us to look into the factors which have influenced the making of peasant self in rural Haryana. Among many factors, the role of traditions and self-governance remains crucial.

While dealing with the issue of tradition and modernity of Indian society, Rajni Kothari suggests that any political system is likely to acquire stability if its procedures and symbols are transformed into carefully nurtured tradition. Doing so becomes necessary because, according to him, "No society lives without traditions and essential challenge of modernity is not the destruction of tradition but the traditionalisation of modernity itself".[9] Kothari's suggestion is important in that it points out the importance of syncronising dynamic and dialectical elements of a political system. Such a syncronisation involves participation of various stakeholders who need not necessarily agree on each and every set of norms and practices. This is where the scope for consensus decision making opens up which is nothing but a practice of consensus self-governance.

The process of self-governance through consensus decision making necessarily involves stakeholders from institutions of both formal and informal self-governance. Seen from this angle, civil society organizations such as khap associations can play constructive role in this process. It is so because, a broad meaning of governance is taken to be free from the restrictions of a binary relationship between state/society, formal/informal institutions; governance is generally understood in relation to the term government. In this sense, governance is seen as broader than government; government is understood here as the hierarchy of institutions representing modern nation-state, whereas governance is viewed as more than top down institutional arrangement–more about persuasion rather than coercion (Neera Chandhoke, 2003; Niraja Gopal Jayal, 1997).

Governance, as Niraja Gopal Jayal suggests, is now viewed as a broad process encompassing "state-society interactions and partnerships". The stakeholders involved in such a process of governance include a range of organizations, as well as the complex relationships

9. Rajni Kothari : *Politics in India,* Orient Longman Pvt. Ltd: Hyderabad, 1970, p. 23.

between them. The list of such stakeholders, according to Jayal, include institutions of local government (such as panchayats); civil society organizations (ranging from social movements to nongovernmental organizations and from co-operatives to civic associations); and private corporations as well as other market institutions are all relevant actors in the new lexicon of governance.

Governance is therefore viewed as not an exclusive domain of state institutions and hence not restricted to civil service reform, or with the application to public organizations of management strategies devised in the private sector. Now, emphasis is more on participation, decentralization, accountability, governmental responsiveness including social equality and justice.[10] If this is so, then peasant community emerges as the single largest stakeholders in the consensus decision making process regarding issues concerning traditions and ethical aspects of village life.

It becomes clear that any notion of self-governance remains incomplete if it does not include participation of peasant community in self-governance. If khap associations can succeed in uniting peasant community for such participation, then they have an enabling role for peasant community.[11] The history of khap associations suggests that these associations have been helpful in uniting peasant community against exploitative ruling classes. As such, with all limitations to be addressed, khap

10. Niraja Gopal Jayal : 'Locating Gender in the Governance Discourse', in *Essays on Gender and Governance*, pp. 97-99.
11. The significance of caste associations as a tool of political mobilization has also been highlighted long back by scholars such as Rudolph and Rudolph (See, *Modernity of Traditions: Political Development in India*, University of Chicago, Chicago, 1984).

associations can be considered as one among many civil society organizations. As a constituent of civil society, such associations can contribute, as a legitimate partner, to the process of democratic governance.

Democratic governance is more than democracy and governance taken separately; it is not even a mere sum of democracy and governance. Seen from this perspective, democratic governance can be viewed as a condition of realizing various material and spiritual promises of justice, liberty and equality in a democratic political framework—where security and satisfaction of people in terms of their identities, aspirations and needs are taken into account by a sensitive government.[12]

Governance at village level, as we understand here, is a horizontally institutionalized coordination mechanism within which actors negotiate, bargain, and decide public policies for public purpose. At village level, government, that is, Gram Panchayat becomes one among many actors in governance process. This complicates the fact that at village level, especially in north India, an individual actor often performs multiple roles, for instance, a village Sarpanch often works as a village caste council's headman, local elite such as party leader, landlord, businessperson etc.

At village level, one can hardly depend on sources of authenticity of life external to village culture for a long time. Therefore, any demarcation of life into 'formal' and 'informal' becomes immaterial when it comes to social life at village level. This blurring of boundaries is one aspect of the puzzle of peasant community in that it masks two facets of society, i.e. civil society and political society at

12. K.C. Suri : 'The State of Democratic Governance in India', paper presented in *An Asian Barometer Conference on the State of Democratic Governance in Asia,* 2008, pp. 1-2.

village level. The difficulties in identifying the 'civil' and the 'political' aspects of social life at village level often generates confusions regarding authenticity of judgments concerning an individual or a group activity. This brings us back to the issues (of women's security-with-dignity, matrimonial relations, and ethics of collective life) which have posed challenges before peasant community.

The most important challenge is to retain the niceties of institutions such as family and civic associations in an era of rapid social, economic and political transformations. In our times, when there has been an unprecedented increase in the compartmentalized knowledge, it becomes essential for us to understand the complexities involved in the life of a peasant community. A reinterpretation of social responsibility is crucial and relevant. Further, any interpretation of the term 'social responsibility' needs to take into account the implications of such interpretation on peasant community and the very nature of peasant self in rural Haryana.

Changing Context and the Sources of Peasant Self in Rural Haryana

In rural Haryana, an important source of peasant self can be found in the Vedic ideal of 'Arya', which has occupied central space in the epical stories and figures revolving around Kurukshetra region of Haryana and in our times in reform movements such as Arya Samaj Movement. For our understanding, the term 'Arya' can be interpreted as an ideal human being, not necessarily belonging to a particular breed of human race.

However, in our times, institutionalization of human being in the light of a particular interpretation of the ideal human being as an authentic source of reference point of collective life is disputed by many radical critics; the conflict emerges here. For example, many radical advocates of women's rights dispute the patriarchal system of collective existence; they hold this system responsible for the crisis of women's security-with-dignity and troubled matrimonial alliances. On the other hand, allegations of social irresponsibility are made on such advocates by those who treat themselves as the guardians of good society. There are some who want to take a central position while interpreting the crisis of falling number of women. The real issue lies somewhere else.

One needs to keep in view that human relationship in terms of the hierarchical nature of family system and civic associations in rural areas differs substantially from that of urban areas, at least in many parts of India. This brings us to the ideas of bhaichara and honor which need a fresh interpretation against the backdrop of peasant community's recent experiences. If one examines bhaichara and honour in the literature on peasant community in rural Haryana, one can easily notice that these ideas have gone through many changes as far as women's security, matrimonial relations, and ethics of collective village life is concerned. However, it is important to note that the presence of modern justice delivery institutions has not enabled the peasant community in avoiding the crisis.

Human Virtues and Limits of Technology

Peasant community in rural Haryana remains a skeptical observer of technology driven cultural norms as far as the issues of internalization or traditionalisation of the cultural contents of technological advancements are concerned. The reasons may be many : (1) Cultural contents of technological revolution are coextensive with the mode of technological advancement and therefore the life span of these contents is restricted to a temporary cultural trend emerging out of a particular mode of technology; (2) Technological advancement and human relations are not coextensive, therefore, mere technological advancement and material richness are no guarantee to sustaining human virtues; (3) Human virtues and cultural contents of a particular mode of technology are not identical in their intent and scope. The reluctance of peasant community regarding traditionalisation of cultural contents of technological advancement points once again to the communication gap between the law makers and policy makers who are born, brought up, and trained in urban areas to make laws for their counter parts in the rural areas.[13]

The reality of human relationship in village life is not identical to that of urban life. The ethical codes therefore are likely to differ as far as social relations are concerned. In village life, the meaning of freedom, honour, and responsibility practiced in a particular context is likely to differ from other villages due to different geographical settlements and local practices of peasant community. If we agree on this then we also agree that the task of ensuring women's security-with-dignity, harmonious matrimonial relations, and peaceful coexistence at village level is not as easy as suggested by the media trial of the controversies surrounding these issues.

The task of balancing radical elements of human efforts aimed at betterment of material and spiritual life involves building capability of peasant community in terms of legal awareness, rethinking the scope of cultural contents of a particular mode of technology, reorienting civic associations and so on. However, this task will remain a partial attempt

13. This gap and the resultant problems were highlighted by Dr. S.S. Rana, Dr. Vir Singh and Jaipal Vidyalankar during the author's group discussion with them at Maharaja Surajmal Centre for Research & Publication, New Delhi, June 2011.

if we ignore challenge of bridging the gap between a peasant community guided by the geographical limitations of rural areas and the law makers and implementers who are socialized and trained in urban areas.

Conclusion

This paper, which is only an elementary reflection on the puzzle of peasant community in rural Haryana regarding tradition and modernity of self-governance, discussed the controversies surrounding women's security-with-dignity, matrimonial relations, and ethics of village life. In doing so, various aspects of the life of peasant community have been analyzed. It is important to keep in view that a paper like this is a very small space to discuss the totality of the puzzle of peasant community even if it is of a particular part of India; therefore, any generalized statements on any aspect of the puzzle is tantamount to be a premature conclusion. However, it is possible to highlight central tendency of this puzzle, which may be understood as the growing discontentment of peasant community with the results of one dimensional development process. The impacts of such a process have been noticed more prominently on women's security, matrimonial relations, and ethics of collective co-existence at village level.

The unprecedented process of globalization and its influence on various virtues of human life has come to inform the limitations of human excellence in material advancement in an age of rapidly increasing gap between the rich and the poor. In such turbulent times, civic associations such as khap associations can play a constructive role in consensus decision making and self-governance. There is a need to contextualize khap associations through reformative steps; the reform process would be much easier if it emerges from within these associations.

6

Services Sector and Persisting Poverty in India: Analysis of Sectoral Trends

Nasreen Naqvi
Shirin Akhter

Economic development has traditionally being associated with transition of the economy from a traditional agrarian economy to a modern industrial economy. This transition involves a shift in the labour force from low productivity-low returns agricultural labour to high-productivity, high returns industrial labour. W. Arthur Lewis in his celebrated dual economy model describes this movement of labour. As the industrial sector begins to grow and the profits are reinvested, the economy begins to grow; this growth is augmented by technological advances that lead to still higher yields, there by pulling more workers from the traditional agricultural sector to the modern industrial sector.

Industrial sector keeps growing, pulling at first only surplus workers from the traditional sector but soon the modern sector begins to attract more workers and the traditional sector starts shrinking. However, increase in output of modern sector is larger than decrease in output of traditional sector and the economy keeps growing. Process continues till the traditional (agricultural) sector is transformed into a commercial sector with advanced technology and a few workers (with high marginal productivity) and a large output.

In case of India share of agriculture in GDP declined from 55.9% in 1950-51 to 14.6% in 2009-10 while those of industry and services increase from 13.3% and 29.8% to 28.1% and 57.3% respectively during the same time period. Economy survey (2011-12) reports the share of services at 55.1% (excluding construction) and 63.3% (including constructions). Considering the share of employment, agriculture continues to be the primary employment provider. The services sector (including construction) occupies the second place following the NSSO report on employment and unemployment situation in India 2009-10, on the basis of usually working persons in the principal and subsidiary status for every thousand people employed in rural and urban India 679 and 75 people are employed in the agriculture sector, 241 and 683 in services sector (including construction) and 80 and 242 in the industrial sector. In terms of percentage agriculture sector witnessed the fall in employment share from 74.7% in 1951 to 53.1% in 2009-10, while manufacturing and services witnessed an increase in employment share from 10.1% and 15.2% to 21.5% and 25.4% respectively in 2009-10 (NSSO).

This data clearly shows that sharp increase in the share of services sector in GDP has not been accompanied by a corresponding increase in share of the services in employment. Thereby, though services leap-frogged manufacturing in output, employment growth in services has been allegedly jobless. This paper is an attempt to overview the patterns of sectoral change in the Indian economy and to explain the persistence of poverty in India despite the magnificent growth exhibited by services sector. Further, this paper is an exercise in explaining the alleged jobless growth and the services sector.

Review of literature

In its simplest terms economic growth is the result of abstention from current consumption the Harrod Domar model firmly links the growth rate of the economy to two fundamental variables, the ability of economy to save and the capital output ratio. There by, making economic growth a function of "savings and technology".

Solow Model of economic growth is based on the law of "Diminishing returns to individual factors of production" It claims that in the absence of technical progress a country cannot sustain per capita income growth indefinitely. In other words unless the effective labour grows, growth dies out. Again economic growth is made contingent on technological advances.

In his famous dual sector model W.A. Lewis puts movement of labour from traditional to modern sector on the centre stage. Economic development here is viewed as progressive transformation of traditional sector into modern sector. The traditional sector is viewed as the supplier of unlimited labour. Starting with a situation where entire labour force is in agriculture and there exists surplus labour, beginning of industrial activity gives rise to a movement in surplus labour from agricultural sector towards the industrial sector. Following Lewis-Renis-Fei model (1961), the minimum wage require by each labourer in the industry must be such that each industrial worker is able to buy back his food packet. Since Lewis assumes an unlimited supply of labour* this movement of labour from agriculture to industry does not decrease agricultural output (at least in the phase of existence of surplus labour). As the phase of surplus labour and disguised unemployment in agriculture ends the industrial wages start rising (in response to increasing food prices). As industrial sector keeps expanding, agriculture sector shrinks and the wages in both industry and agriculture increase till agriculture becomes commercial in nature. Capital accumulation in the industrial sector acts as the engine of growth.

The classic theory of rural urban migration based on the Harris-Todaro (1970) Model views migration as a response to a significant rural-urban wage gap, a worker in the rural job market will wish to move to the urban sector to get a high paying job. This high paying formal job may not always be attainable; the probability of getting such a job will depend on the ratio of formal job seekers to available formal jobs. Those who remain unemployed may enter the urban informal sector where jobs are easy to find but relatively low paying.

Any attempt to decrease the size of informal sector will eventually lead to an increase in its size. This can be explained as under, if government views urban informal sector as an outgrowth of urban formal sector it may try to increase the number of jobs in the urban formal sector,

---

* Unlimited supply of labour refers to a situation where presence of labour is so large that the marginal productivity per unit of labourer is either negative or zero. That is to say that withdrawal of workers from labour force will not lead to a decline in total output produced. In extreme cases, however, the output may actually rise once the surplus labour has been withdrawn.

thereby initially decreasing the size of urban informal sector, However an increase in number of jobs in formal sector leads to a higher expectation of a job being attained by the rural worker in the urban formal sector. This increased expectation pulls more people to the urban formal sector thereby increasing the size of urban informal sector (forming a vicious circle).

The traditional growth models thus explain economic growth as a shift from agriculture to industry via capital accumulation and reinvestment. Following the traditional growth theories, economic development will lead to a sectoral transformation of the economy from an agrarian economy to a manufacturing based economy. These growth models were confirmed to by today's developed countries in their phases of development. Contemporary developing countries however do not show similar patterns of structural transformation. Services sector has leap-frogged manufacturing in share of contribution to GDP and employment in almost all developing economies. The shift of labour from agriculture has almost entirely been mopped up by the services sector. The contemporary literature reveals that the share of services increases more than that of manufacturing however almost everywhere services sector is the major employer in economy.

Empirical evidence shows that as an economy matures the share of services in output increases consistently. To begin with, the increase occurs along with an increase in the share of industry. Thereafter, the service share grows more rapidly, accompanied by a stagnant or declining share of the industrial sector. Cross-country experience suggests that the first stage occurs until the country reaches lower middle income status, while the second stage commences once it becomes an upper middle income country.

The importance of service sector in India is highlighted in a study by Eichengreen (2011) saying that while India is distinctive among developing countries for its fast-growing service sector; skeptics have raised doubts about the quality and sustainability of this service-sector growth and its implications for economic development. They show that while growth of the sector has been unusually rapid, the share of services has now converged to the international norm; this raises questions about whether it will continue growing rapidly. In particular, whether service-sector output and employment continue to grow in excess of international norms will depend on the continued expansion of modern services (business services, communication and banking) but, also, on the application of modern information technology to more traditional services (retail and wholesale trade, transport and storage, public administration and defence). They conclude that sustaining economic growth and rising living standards will require shifting labour into both manufacturing and services. They also conclude that employment in modern services can be a useful supplement to employment in manufacturing as a route out of rural poverty.

Gordon (2004) analyzes the factors behind the growth of the services sector in India. The paper shows that growth acceleration of the services in the 1990s was mostly due to fast growth in communication services, financial services, business services (IT) and community services. While factors such as a high income elasticity of demand for services, increased input usage of services by other sectors, and rising exports were important in boosting services growth in the 1990s, supply side factors including reforms and technological advances also played a significant role. The large growth potential of Indian services exports is well known, but the paper finds that there is also considerable scope for future rapid growth in the Indian service economy provided that deregulation of the services sector continues. The paper shows that employment growth in the Indian services sector has been quite modest, thus underscoring the importance of industry and agriculture also growing rapidly.

A number of studies have attempted to explain the fast growth in the share of services activity observed in cross country data. The literature draws a distinction between demand and supply factors (Kravis, 1982). On the supply side, the output share of services can be boosted by a switch to a more services-input intensive method of organizing production. Such a change in production methods can arise as a result of increasing specialization as the economy matures. Bhagwati (1994) calls this process of specialization splintering. Kravis (1982) points out that splintering can lead to growth in the share of services in GDP, even when GDP itself is not growing. On the demand side, an increase in the output share of services can arise from rapid growth in the final demand for services. This could be from domestic consumers with a high income elasticity of demand for services, or from foreign consumers with a growing demand for the country's service exports. Demand led growth of this type is likely to result, at least initially, in a rise in the prices of services, as well as a shift of resources into the production of services.

Services activity can also be stimulated by technological advances, whereby new activities or products emerge as a result of technological breakthrough—such advances are likely to be particularly relevant in the case of the IT and telecommunication sectors and to some extent in financial services (credit cards, ATMs etc.). Liberalization can also provide a boost to services. In India, important policy reforms were made in the 1990s which were conducive to the growth of services sector, such as deregulation, privatization and opening up to foreign direct investment (FDI). If the growth of services was previously inhibited by government controls, then policy changes may provide a positive shock that unleashes new activity and growth.

Services sector in India

The Indian economy does not completely conform to this international experience; it has shown a rapid and sustained growth since 1990 which can be attributed to high growth services sector. This rapid growth of the service sector is not unique to India; the point of departure is the fact that services sector has a low share in employment generation at around 25%. On average services grew more slowly than industry between 1951 and 1990. Growth of services picked up in the 1980s, and further accelerated in the 1990s, when it averaged 7.5 per cent a year, thus providing a valuable prop to industry and agriculture, which grew on average by 5.8 per cent and 3.1 per cent respectively.

This growth in services has been led by software and information technology (IT)-enabled services (including call centres, software design, and business process outsourcing). However, growth in services in India has been much more broad-based than IT. In fact, although IT exports have had a profound impact on the balance of payments, the sector remains a small component of GDP. Gordon (2004) shows that almost all service sub-sectors in India have grown faster than GDP over time, but the pick-up in growth in the 1990s was the strongest in business services, communication, and banking services, followed by hotels and restaurants and community services.

Employment in Services

Observers are skeptical about the developmental impact of the growth of the services sector on the presumption that modern services do not use significant amounts of unskilled and semi-skilled labour, the factor of production that India has in abundance. They downplay information-technology and communications-related service sector employment on the grounds that these activities are small and use little unskilled labour, the implication being that a labour-abundant economy cannot rely on them to move people out of low-productivity agriculture.

Evidence from other countries sheds indirect light on this question, Gordon (2004) finds that in Korea, while the share of traditional services in GDP has declined over time, its share in employment has not. Hybrid services have accounted for a growing share of GDP and an even more rapidly growing share of economy wide employment. The modern services have accounted for increased shares of both GDP and employment over time.

A striking feature of India's development is that in contrast to the substantial decline in the share of agriculture in GDP, there has been rather little change in the share of employment in agriculture (Bhattacharya and Mitra, 1990). Similarly, although services rose from 42 percent to 48 percent of GDP during the 1990s, the employment share of services actually declined by about one percentage point during the decade. Thus, while output generation has shifted to services, employment creation in services has lagged far behind.

India's relatively jobless service sector growth is unlike the experience of other countries, where the service sector has also tended to gain a larger share of employment over time. India, in fact, has an exceptionally low share of services employment, when compared with other countries. The normal pattern is thus for the share of services employment to rise faster than the share of output. This implies that labour productivity in services tends to fall as the service sector increases. In sharp contrast, since the labour share in services employment has been flat, labour productivity in Indian services has been increasing over time. In addition, the increase in labour productivity in Indian services has not been due to an increase in the relative capital intensity. This suggests that other factors have been at work in raising labour productivity, which could include the growth of services being concentrated in subsectors that are more dependent on skilled labour than on unskilled labour or capital. This trend has no doubt been reinforced by technological improvements, as well as by efficiency gains resulting from liberalization (RBI, 2002).

Widening Inequalities Across Sectors

The tremendous growth of services sector has led to a widening of inequalities amongst sectors. Consider the following table:

Sector	Year	Employment share	Output share	Share percent	Standardized labour product		
Agriculture	1950-51	74.7	55.9	0.74832664	1		
	1972-73	73.9	46	0.622462788	0.83180627		
	1993-94	64.7	31.3	0.483771252	0.64647071		
	2009-10	53.1	14.6	0.274952919	0.36742367	1	
Manufacturing	1950-51	10.1	14.3	1.415841584	1.89201013		
	1972-73	11.3	20.3	1.796460177	2.40063641		
	1993-94	14.8	27.6	1.864864865	2.49204661		
	2009-10	21.5	28.1	1.306976744	1.74653243	4.75346	1
Services	1950-51	15.2	29.8	1.960526316	2.61988043		
	1972-73	14.8	33.7	2.277027027	3.04282502		
	1993-94	20.5	41.1	2.004878049	2.6791483		
	2009-10	25.4	57.3	2.255905512	3.01460003	8.2047	1.726049

Source: Central Statistical Organization: National Accounts Statistics
National Sample Survey Organization: Surveys on employment

This table shows the data for sectoral shares in output and employment from 1951 to 2010. Output in the sector is divided by the sectoral share in employment to obtain a crude measure of per labour productivity in the sector; that is to say if 74.7 per cent of work force produces 55.9% of output, per person contribution to output in agricultural sector is 0.7483. This measure of productivity is then standardized by taking agricultural productivity per head in 1951 as numeriare. Since the employment share in agriculture has not decreased by as much as the decrease in output share, more people in agriculture are producing less output, this is also reflected by the standardized labour productivity, which declined from 1 in 1951 to 0.3674 in 2009-10.

Conclusions

The fact that growth in services sector has largely been 'jobless' cannot be denied. Further it needs to be noted that this growth has lead to an increase in poverty and in a widening of gap amongst sectors. The intensity of poverty in the agricultural sector seems to have worsened. This can be substantiated using Sen's concept of relative poverty. Since poverty and inequality are very significant, both functionally and intrinsically these trends are uncomforting and need to be undone. In other words labour productivity in other two sectors needs to converge to the levels of services sector. This calls for productivity augmenting investments by the state in manufacturing and more so in agriculture. These investments can come in the form of spreading literacy and imparting skills, making available easy institutional credit, developing infrastructure etc. Also it needs to be noted that services sector still have a lot of scope for expansion in India, the expansion would be more welcoming if formal sector and organized employment, for that universalisation of education is necessary.

References

Acharya, Shankar : Services not the Real Saviour? in Shankar Acharya (editors), *India's Economy, Some Issues andAnswers,*Academic Foundation, New Delhi, 2003, pp. 38-48.

Bhagwati, Jagdish : "Splintering and Disembodiment of Services and Developing Nations," *World Economy,* Vol. 7, No. 2, 1984, pp. 133-43.

Bosworth, Barry, Susan M., Collins and Arvind, Virmani : "Sources of Growth in the Indian Economy", in, *India Policy Forum 2006-07,* Vol-3, 2007, pp. 1-50.

Central Statistical Organisation : *National Accounts Statistics: Sources and Methods,* New Delhi: Government of India, 1989.

Central Statistical Organisation : New Series on National Accounts Statistics (Base Year 1993-94), New Delhi: Government of India, 1999.

Central Statistical Organisation : Report of the Working Group on Workforce Estimation for Compilation of National Accounts Statistics with Base Year 1999-2000, New Delhi: Government of India, 2004.

Central Statistical Organisation : National Account Statistics, New Delhi: Government of India, 2005.

Central Statistical Organisation : New Series on National Accounts Statistics (Base Year 1999-2000), New Delhi: Government of India, 2006.

Eichengreen, Barry and Poonam Gupta : 'Two Waves of Services Growth', *NBER Working Paper* no. W14968 May, 2009.

Eichengreen, Barry and Poonam Gupta : "The Service Sector as India's Road to Economic Growth" *NBER, Working Paper* no. 16757 Feb, 2011.

Gordon, Jim and Poonam Gupta : 'Understanding India's Services Revolution.' *IMF Working paper* WP/04/171 (September) 2004.

Kravis, Irving B. : 1985, 'Services in World Transactions,' in *Managing the Service Economy: Prospects and Problems,* ed. By Robert P. Inman, Cambridge: Cambridge University Press, 1985.

Reserve Bank of India, Report on Currency and Finance, Mumbai: Reserve Bank of India, 2002.

Virmani, Arvind: Bhartiya Rate of Growth: The Role of Services, Planning Commission, New Delhi, Government of India, 2002.

7

राजस्थान का कृषक वर्ग – दशा और दिशा

डा. राम पाण्डे

सृष्टि के प्रारम्भ में जब सब भूमि गोपाल की थी, तब कोई अटक नहीं थी, जमीन का कोई मालिक नहीं था परन्तु जब एक व्यवस्था प्रारम्भ हुई, समाज को परिवार, समूह और समुदाय में व्यवस्थित किया गया तो भूमि पर मालिकाना हक प्रारम्भ हुआ। खेतिहर लोग कृषक या किसान समूह में बंध गये, मानव एक समूह बनाकर रहने लगा। गाँव व्यवस्था का आरम्भ हुआ।

गाँव की ज़िन्दगी आत्मनिर्भर थी। एक वर्ग कृषि करता था, दूसरे वर्ग उसकी सहायता करते थे, बढ़ई कृषि में काम आने वाले औजार व हल-बैल तैयार करता, चमार कुएँ से पानी निकालने का चरस तैयार करता, लोहार औजार बनाता, कुम्हार बर्तन। गाँव के अन्य लोग जुलाहा, कोरी कपड़ा बनाता, भंगी सफाई व्यवस्था देखता, बलाई या मीणा चौकीदारी का काम देखते। नट भोपा इत्यादि मनोरंजन पक्ष देखते। इन सभी को किसान अपनी पैदावार में से हिस्सा देता। सब सुखी थे। इसी बीच राजा और जागीरदार वर्ग का उदय हुआ। कृषकों पर तरह-तरह के कर लगाये गये। राजस्थान का किसान लगभग 85 प्रकार के करों का बोझ सहन कर रहा था। सामन्तवाद के इस उदय से ग्रामीण आत्मनिर्भर व्यवस्था में कोई अंतर नहीं हुआ और उसे भी आत्मसात कर लेने की कोशिश की गई। इसी का परिणाम था कि भारत विशेषकर, राजस्थान का सामंतवाद यूरोप, रूस और चीन की तरह का सामन्तवाद नहीं था, और लोग उनके (सामन्तों के) दास या सर्फ नहीं थे अपितु स्वतन्त्र थे, लेकिन भारत में जब अंग्रेजी शासन व्यवस्था आ गई तो उसने राजस्थान के राजाओं को संधियों के माध्यम से ऐसा जकड़ा कि ग्रामीण आत्मनिर्भर व्यवस्था भंग होने लगी। किसान व आम ग्रामीण कष्ट भरा जीवन जीने लगे, फलस्वरूप सन् 1897 से कृषक आन्दोलन प्रारम्भ हुए और स्वतंत्रता प्राप्ति

व राजस्थान निर्माण (1950) तक चलते रहे। इनमें 1897 में प्रारम्भ हुआ बिजौलिया किसान आन्दोलन देश का पहला अहिंसात्मक आन्दोलन था जो महात्मा गांधी के किसान आन्दोलन से बहुत पहले हुआ था। मूल नायक विजय सिंह पथिक था। (अभी हाल ही में अरूप कुमार के शोध से यह पता चलता है कि असम में 1884 में अंग्रेजों के विरुद्ध किसान आन्दोलन हुआ था)।

देश स्वतंत्र हुआ। राजस्थान का निर्माण हुआ। राजस्थान की सरकार ने 1950 में भूख से मुक्ति हेतु एक कानून पारित किया और 1955 में जो भूमि सुधार कानून बना उसने जमींदारी जागीरदारी उन्मूलन कर किसान को जमीन का मालिक बना दिया। राजस्थान में देश के अन्य प्रदेशों की तरह बड़ा भूहड़प नहीं हुआ, जिसके कारण नक्सलवाद जैसी घटनायें यहाँ नहीं हुई। परन्तु किसान की उन्नति और विकास के लिय भी कुछ विशेष नहीं हुआ। ग्रामीण अर्थव्यवस्था भंग होने से सामाजिक तौर पर सागड़ियों (बन्धक मजदूरों) का जो वर्ग बन गया था, यह वर्ग गाँव के कारीगरों व गैर कृषि कार्य में दक्ष लोगों का था। उसके उन्मूलन हेतु 1961 में सागड़ी उन्मूलन एक्ट पास हुआ। इससे समाज में एक नई संस्कृति ने जन्म लिया। किसान अब जागीरदार या जमींदार से स्वतंत्र होकर भूमालिक हो गया था और सागड़ी उन्मूलन में एक नई सांस्कृतिक चेतना को बल मिला। लेकिन इससे समाज में कृषक वर्ग अभी भी लाभ की स्थिति में नहीं था। वह खेतिहर के साथ-साथ पशुपालक भी था और दोनों कार्य एक-दूसरे के पूरक थे।

श्वेत क्रान्ति के माध्यम से लोगों, विशेषकर किसानों की आमदनी बढ़ाने का इरादा और संकल्प सरकार ने किया। देशी गाय की जगह विदेशी जर्सी गाय ने ले ली और देशी गाय नकारा मानकर जगह से हटा दी गई। देशी गाय जर्सी गाय के मुकाबले दूध तो कम देती थी परन्तु उसका दूध अधिक पौष्टिक, उसके बछड़े खेती के लिये तैयार होते थे, उसके गोबर का खाद अच्छा बनता था। वह बन्द हो गया। राजस्थान के नागौर और परवतसर के बछड़े सबसे अच्छे बैल माने जाते थे, वे गायब हो गये, खेतों में जो हल चलते थे उनका स्थान ट्रैक्टर ने ले लिया। काम तो कम समय में होने लगा, परन्तु इसके साथ ही किसान के पास खाली समय बढ़ गया और उस खाली समय के उपयोग का कोई प्रबन्ध नहीं था। इसलिये किंकर्त्तव्य विमूढ़ की स्थिति हो गई। राजस्थान के आदिवासी

क्षेत्रों में इसका बड़ा विपरीत प्रभाव पड़ा और श्वेत क्रान्ति के बावजूद कई क्षेत्र तो दुग्धविहीन भी हुए।

इस खाली समय को भरने का प्रयास पेड़ों की कटाई और लकड़ी बेचने के रूप में होने लगा। जब अरावली के पहाड़ हरे-भरे होते थे तो जीवन की एक सुरीली तान उठा करती थी वह नदारद होने लगी। सरकार में चिंता जागी तो हरित क्रान्ति याद आई, जो हालांकि पूरे देश में ही लागू होनी थी परन्तु राजस्थान में उसे लागू करने में समझ से काम नहीं लिया गया और पेड़ लगाओ की होड़ लग गई। मारवाड़ में रेगिस्तान के बढ़ते प्रभाव को रोकने में कारगर मानकर इजरायली बबूल को बो दिया, जिससे पेड़ बड़े तो नहीं हुए उल्टी जमीन की उर्वरता पर प्रभाव पड़ा। इजरायली बबूल के अलावा यूकेलिप्टस यानि सफेदा भी बो दिया। यूकेलिप्टस को पानी बहुत चाहिये। जमीन को उर्वरक बनाने के लिये परम्परागत खाद की जगह रासायनिक खाद आ गये जो प्रारम्भ में तो उपज को बढ़ाने लगे, लेकिन धीरे-धीरे उर्वरता पर भी विपरीत असर डालने लगे।

खेती के विकास के लिये उर्वरता के साथ-साथ किसान को आवश्यकता होती है सिंचाई की। पहले सिंचाई के साधन कुएँ, तालाब, बावड़ी, नदी इत्यादि थे, नदियों में बाँधों का निर्माण भी किया गया, जिनसे नहरों के जरिये किसानों के खेतों की सिंचाई होनी थी। ग्रामीण विकास का सिलसिला ऐसा चला कि नदी, नालों पर एनीकट बन गये, बाँधों में जाने वाला परम्परागत बहाव बंद हो गया। फलस्वरूप कुछ बांध भी सूखे की चपेट में आ गये। यहाँ सबसे बड़ा उदाहरण जयपुर के रामगढ़ बाँध का है जहाँ आज एक बूँद भी पानी नहीं है। एनीकट से बहाव के रास्ते बन्द होने का फायदा माफिया और रसूखदार लोगों ने उठाया और जो नदी, नाले, पानी नहीं आने के कारण सूख गये थे वहाँ अवैध कब्जे कर लिये, किसान सिंचाई के लिये ताकता ही रह गया। किसानों की इस दशा और रोष का फायदा राजनैतिक दलों ने उठाया और कृषक आन्दोलनों की झड़ी लगने लगी। इनमें भोपालगढ़ (जोधपुर), गंगानगर, गड़साना और भरतपुर के किसान आन्दोलनों का जिक्र किया जा सकता है। अंततः इन आन्दोलनों से ज्यादा कुछ प्राप्ति किसान को नहीं हुई।

राजस्थान नहर जो इंदिरा गांधी नहर के नाम से भी जानी जाती है पाकिस्तान की सरहद से लगने वाले जिलों के लिये वरदान साबित हुई है

परन्तु उसके निर्माण में जिन मानकों का ध्यान रखना चाहिये था उनकी अनदेखी हुई और सरहद के उस पार की जमीन भी उसका लाभ लेने लगी, तथा अपनी जमीन जो नहर से बिल्कुल सटी हुई है, वह फोसरी भी होने लगी है। इस ओर प्रशासन को ध्यान देना चाहिये। खेतिहर मजदूरों को राहत देने हेतु सरकार ने भू सीलिंग कानून लागू किया। इसमें सरकार मात्र 1.74 लाख एकड़ जमीन लेने में कामयाब तो हुई मगर ये जमीन या तो नदी नालों के किनारे के बीहड़, ऊट पटांग, कन्दराओं की है या फिर पथरीली जमीन है जिसके विकास के लिये कई प्रकार के साधनों की आवश्यकता है।

सफेद कॉलर वर्ग बढ़ता देखकर किसान के मन में भी विचार कौंधा। जमीन की पैदावार का कोई भरोसा न देखकर उसका मन अपने बच्चों को सफेद कालर वर्ग में शामिल करने का हुआ। वह अपनी जमीन भी बेचकर अपने बच्चों को पढ़ाने भेजने लगा। सोचा उसके बच्चे भी इंजीनियर, तकनीशियन या कार्पोरेट बन जायेंगे। शिक्षा माफिया ने फायदा उठाया। उससे शिक्षा संस्थानों की बहार आ गई, जहाँ राजस्थान में सरकारी क्षेत्र में मात्र 15 विश्वविद्यालय हैं वहाँ निजी क्षेत्र में 45 विश्वविद्यालय है। पता नहीं किसानों के ये बच्चे अभिजात वर्ग में जगह पायेंगे या नहीं परन्तु बहुत से किसानों की जमीनें बिक जायेंगी। इससे बड़े-बड़े शहरों व गाँवों में भी अपराध संख्या बढ़ने लगी है। गाँवों से शहरों की तरह दौड़ने की होड़ में गाँवों की संस्कारिता को भी भंग किया है और सामाजिक समीकरण भंग हो रहा है।

बड़े नगरों का बढ़ता आकार भी एक समस्या बनने लगा है। पड़ोस के किसानों की जमीन या तो सरकार लेकर मुआवजा दे रही है और या भूमाफिया औने पौने दाम में खरीद रहा है। अपनी जमीन देकर बदले में मिले पैसे से अब किसान ऐश कर रहा है। गाड़ी, मोटर साइकिल और शराब में वह इस पैसे को समाप्त कर रहा है और गाँव से शहर की तरफ दौड़ लगा रहा है। जिसमें गाँव का समीकरण तो भंग हो ही रहा है, शहर में भी नई-नई समस्याओं का उदय हो रहा है। प्रश्न उठता है इन सबसे छुटकारा कैसे हो या इनका निराकरण कैसे हो? क्या कानून से इसका निराकरण संभव है? शायद नहीं तो फिर समाज के प्रबुद्ध वर्ग को खड़े होकर दृढ़ निश्चय से ही इसका निराकरण संभव करना होगा। महात्मा गांधी के हिन्द स्वराज्य की तरफ मुड़ना होगा। क्या एक सबके लिये और सब एक के लिये की संस्कृति लौटाई जा सकेगी? पता नहीं।

संदर्भ

1. राम पाण्डे : *एग्रेरियन मूवमेंट इन राजस्थान*, दिल्ली, 1974, पुनःमुद्रित जयपुर, 1999।
2. राम पाण्डे : *लैण्ड रिफॅार्म्स एण्ड सोशल चेन्ज*, जयपुर, 1983
3. राम पाण्डे : *एन अप्रेजल ऑफ लैण्ड रिफॅार्म्स, राजस्थान*, जयपुर, 1985
4. राम पाण्डे : *ए कलचरल ट्रान्सफोरमेशन इन रूरल राजस्थान*, 1989

8

Estimation of Multi-Dimensional Poverty Index for Bhalswa Resettlement Colony in Delhi : Comparison of Local and National Estimates

Shirin Akhter

Introduction

Traditionally, poverty estimates were based on income and/or consumption expenditure survey data. More recently, data from the Demographic and Health Surveys (DHS) were used in estimating poverty. In India, the official estimates of poverty are derived by the Planning Commission based on consumption expenditure data collected by the National Sample Survey Organization (NSSO) in its quinquennial round (since 1973-74) the poor are also identified by a Below Poverty Line (BPL) Survey carried out by the District Rural Development Authority (DRDA) of each state with guidelines from the Ministry of Rural Development, Government of India.

Data and Methodology

Poverty, however is a multidimensional phenomenon and any one parameter seems to be insufficient to capture 'poverty'. For instance, the traditionally used measure of poverty, income, fails to capture the multiple aspects that constitute poverty and deprivation such as poor health, lack of education, inadequate living standard, lack of cash or assets, disempowerment, poor quality of work and threat from violence. Therefore, income as the sole indicator of well-being is inappropriate and should be supplemented by other attributes or variables, calling for a multidimensional measure that incorporate a range of indicators to capture the complexity of poverty. This paper is an attempt to calculate the MPI for Bhalswa resettlement colony in Delhi, and compare it with other poverty measures and see if these comparisons yield similar results.

Data for this paper has been collected from primary survey of 55 households, comprising 316 members, selected randomly from the Bhalswa resettlement colony in Delhi. Secondary data from OPHI is used to make comparisons with India. The MPI is used as given by the UNDP's 2010 Human Development Report, where the MPI reflects both the incidence (H) of poverty i.e. the proportion of the population that is multi-dimensionally poor and the average intensity (A) of their deprivation i.e. the average proportion of indicators in which they are deprived. The MPI is calculated by multiplying the incidence of poverty by the average intensity across the poor. A person is identified as poor if he or she is deprived in at least 30 percent of the weighted indicators. Other poverty measures used are poverty lines at $1.25 and $2 a day.

Literature Review

The need for a multidimensional approach to the measurement of inequality in well-being has been emphasized, among others, by Kolm (1977), Atkinson and Bourguignon (1982), Maasoumi (1986) and Tsui (1995). Further, well-being is intrinsically multidimensional, following Sen (1985, 1992) well-being is to be seen from the view point of 'capabilities' and 'functionings', where functionings deal with what a person can ultimately do and capabilities indicate the freedom that a person enjoys in terms of functionings. In the capability approach functionings are closely approximated by attributes such as literacy, life expectancy, etc. and not by income per se. An example of multidimensional measure of well-being in terms of functioning achievements is the Human Development Index suggested by UNDP (1990). It aggregates at the country level functioning achievements in terms of the attributes life expectancy, per capita real GDP and educational attainment rate.

Ravallion (1996) argued that four sets of indicators can be defended as ingredients for a sensible approach to poverty measurement. These are: (i) real expenditure per single adult on market goods, (ii) non-income indicators as access to non-market goods, (iii) indicators of intra-household distribution such as child nutritional status and (iv) indicators of personal characteristics which impose constraints on the ability of an individual, such as physical handicap. In other words, a genuine measure of poverty should depend on income indicators as well as non-income indicators that may help in identifying aspects of welfare not captured by incomes.

The basic needs approach advocated by development economists regards development as an improvement in an array of human needs and not just as growth of income, Streeten (1981). There exists a debate about the importance of low incomes as a determinant of under-nutrition, Lipton and Ravallion (1995). Finally, well-being is intrinsically multidimensional from the view point of 'capabilities' and 'functionings', where functionings deal with what a person can ultimately do and capabilities indicate the freedom that a person enjoys in terms of functionings, Sen (1985, 1992). In the capability approach functionings are closely approximated by attributes such as literacy, life expectancy, etc. and not by income per se. An example of multidimensional measure of well-being in terms of functioning achievements is the Human Development Index suggested by UNDP (1990). It aggregates at the country level functioning achievements in terms of the attributes life expectancy, per capita real GDP and educational attainment rate.

In the multidimensional framework instead of visualizing poverty or deprivation using income or consumption as the sole indicator of well-being, the index is formalized in terms of functioning failures, or, more precisely, in terms of shortfalls from threshold levels of attributes themselves. Then various aggregation rules which permit to quantify the overall magnitude of poverty are examined using these shortfalls.

Multi-dimensional Poverty Index (MPI)

MPI was developed by Alkire and Santos (2010a) for the 2010 Human Development Report (UNDP, 2010). They choose 10 variables for their MIP under the same three headings; health, education and living standards as the UNDP's Human Development Index (HDI). There are two variables for health (malnutrition, and child mortality), two for education (years of schooling and school enrollment), and six for deprivation in living standards (namely, cooking with wood, charcoal or dung; not having a conventional toilet; lack of easy access to safe drinking water; no electricity; dirt, sand or dung flooring and not owning at least one of a radio, TV, telephone, bike or car). Poverty is measured separately in each of these 10 dimensions. The equally-weighted aggregate poverty measures for each of these three main headings are then weighted equally (one-third each) to form the composite index, also echoing the HDI. A household is identified as being poor if it is deprived across at least 30% of the weighted indicators. While the HDI uses aggregate country-level data, the Alkire-Santos MIP uses household-level data, which are then aggregated to the country level. Alkire and Santos constructed their index for more than 100 countries.

Calculation of MPI

MPI is calculated as follows:

MPI = H × A

Where,

H: Percentage of people who are MPI poor (incidence of poverty)

A: Average intensity of MPI poverty across the poor (%)

Indicators used,

The following ten indicators are used to calculate the MPI

Education (each indicator is weighted equally at 1/6)

1. **Years of schooling**: deprived if no household member has completed five years of schooling
2. **Child school attendance**: deprived if any school-aged child is not attending school up to class 8

   Health (each indicator is weighted equally at 1/6)
3. **Child mortality**: deprived if any child has died in the family
4. **Nutrition**: deprived if any adult or child for whom there is nutritional information is malnourished

   Standard of Living (each indicator is weighted equally at 1/18)
5. **Electricity**: deprived if the household has no

electricity

6. **Sanitation**: deprived if the household's sanitation facility is not improved (according to MDG guidelines), or it is improved but shared with other households
7. **Drinking water**: deprived if the household does not have access to safe drinking water (according to MDG guidelines) or safe drinking water is more than a 30-minute walk from home round-trip
8. **Floor**: deprived if the household has a dirt, sand or dung floor
9. **Cooking fuel**: deprived if the household cooks with dung, wood or charcoal
10. **Assets ownership**: deprived if the household does not own more than one radio, TV, telephone, bike, motorbike or refrigerator and does not own a car or truck.

Categorization: A person is considered poor if they are deprived in at least 30% of the weighted indicators. The intensity of poverty denotes the proportion of indicators in which they are deprived.

Ravallion (2011) criticizes this measure on the data requirements of the Alkire-Foster index, following Ravain data requirements of the said MPI entail that relevant dimensions of poverty invariably be left out in practice. Consider first the material goods entering the Alkire-Santos MIP; this is a rather narrow set of goods, leaving out a great many things that people do in fact consume. Thus their measure leaves out a great many of the multiple dimensions poverty. Further, the Alkire-Foster approach is criticized on the grounds of the options being constrained by the fact that one must obtain all the data for the same sampled household. So they must all come from the same survey but most surveys do not cover all the things one would like to know in a comprehensive assessment of poverty. This restricts the set of dimensions that can be included in the MPI.

Results

As discussed, the MPI reflects both the incidence (H) of poverty and the average intensity (A) of their deprivation. The MPI is calculated by multiplying the incidence of poverty by the average intensity across the poor. A person is identified as poor if he or she is deprived in at least 30 percent of the weighted indicators. The following table shows the multidimensional poverty rate (MPI) and its two components: incidence of poverty (H) and average intensity of deprivation faced by the poor (A).

Multidimensional poverty headcount (H)	0.704225 70.42254
Intensity (breadth) of deprivation (A)	0.399854 39.98538
Multidimensional poverty index (MPI)	0.281587 28.1587

Comparison Of MPI with Other two poverty measures is given as under:

Multidimensional poverty index (MPI)	0.281587
Head count ratio at $1.25	0.332278
head cunt ratio at $2	0.411392

The following table reports various descriptive statistics for India:

Multidimensional poverty headcount (H)	0.554
Intensity (breadth) of deprivation (A)	0.535
Multidimensional poverty index (MPI)	0.296
Head count ratio at $1.25	0.42
Head count ratio at $2	0.76

According to the MPI, for the sample poverty is 28.16, while percentage of poor at $1.25 and $2 per capita per day is 33.23% and 41.14% respectively; comparing this with values for India, we see that, MPI is 29.6% and HCRs are 42 and 76% respectively.

Analysis of Results

Comparing the results for the sample with that of India, we can see that though MPI is almost same for both, intensity of deprivation is higher for India while head count is much higher for the sample; more over percentage of poverty is higher for the national sample.

Intensity of deprivation being lower for the sample can be explained by the fact that sample has been collected from Delhi and all most all the indicators used by MPI for measuring living standard are present.

Conclusions

Given the fact that the sample was drawn from a low-income colony, with all respondent households engaged in low-paying unorganized and informal sector jobs, the estimated values of both, poverty headcount and MPI are far lower than expected. This could be understood as the reference poverty-lines ($1.25, 2 resp.) being too low to translate into well-being, due to which, even those households that are deemed above poverty line, fail to afford reasonable levels of education, health, housing etc. Further, the reported size of the household and number of children (3-5) is often smaller than the actual, a problem typical to reporting of family-size demographics among the poor (Sabina and Foster, 2009), because of which the actual level of deprivation often gets under-reported due to 'hidden-dependents' (apart from dependent relatives, particularly parents living in villages who are not included in the family size, but draw sustenance form the reported household income) who substantially reduce the per-capita access and availability of both household income and resources.

A low value for MPI (28.16) can be explained by the public provisioning of electricity, sanitation and potable water in the resettlement colonies, and by the fact that the quality of these resources is ignored by the MPI. Further, since Poverty in India is largely concentrated in the rural sector, with little or no public provisioning of these resources, the dummy response variables for access record a substantially higher value of deprivation in the rural sector as well as for India as a whole, while given the quality of the resources available in the resettlement colonies, the respondents covered in this survey are hardly better-off compared to the non-access average Indian poor, particularly for housing and sanitation.

Limitations

Poverty indeed being a multi-dimensional concept, and the MPI limited in both scope practical applicability, measurement of social levels of absolute and relative deprivation require the construction of more representative and robust indices.

Finally, poverty, either Income headcount or MPI, fails to reflect on many an aspect of deprivation and thus fail to do complete justice to the broader problems of overall well-being and Human-development.

Ignorance of Gender Inequality esp. within the households, adds to the problem of under-valued estimates for both HCI and MPI, since the general access of women to household income and nutrition (esp. non-working women) and other household assets (both working and non-working women) is lower among women. Further, deprivation among the elderly in the poor, esp. elderly women is found to be much higher than the household average by most of the contemporary research papers. No reference to the same by the index further compounds the practical reliability of the index.

Limitations of the questionnaire-design used by UNDP (and used by this paper) MPI, including and respondents' unwillingness to report true values of income, and child mortality due to image issues and social perceptions (Bourguignon and Chakravarty, 2003) also cause reporting errors. Finally, ignorance about what 'nutritional deprivation' actually means leads to erroneous response and estimation biases.

Acknowledgments

I express my gratitude to Prof. Suresh Aggarwal, Department of Business Economics, University of Delhi, for his valuable guidance and support. I also thank my mother, Mrs. Nasreen Naqvi, for valuable inputs on the subject. Gratitude is also due to my friends Richa Chintan (JNU) and Simin Akhter Naqvi (colleague and fellow researcher) for help with procurement and processing of the data.

References

Atkinson, A. and F. Bourguignon : 'The Comparison of Multidimension Distributions of Economic Status', *Review of Economic Studies,* 49, 183-201, 1982.

Alkire Sabina and James Foster : Counting and multidimensional poverty measures, OPHI Working, Paper No 7.5, 2009.

Bourguignon, F. and Chakravarty, S.R.: The measurement of multidimensional poverty, *Journal of economic inequality*, vol. 1, issue 1, 25-49, 2003.

Klasen, S.: Measuring poverty and deprivation in South Africa, *Review of Income and Wealth,* 46 (1), 33-58, 2000.

Ministry of Health and Family Welfare (MOHFW). (2005). National Rural Health Mission (2005-12). Department of Family Welfare, Govt. of India, New Delhi, India.

Kolm, S.C.: Multidimensional Egalitarianisms, *Quarterly Journal of Economics,* (1977), 91, 1-13.

Maasoumi, E.: The Measurement and Decomposition of Multidimensional Inequality, *Econometrica,* (1986), 54, 771-779.

Martin, R.: Multidimensional Indices of Poverty, Picy Research Working Paper, World Bank (2011).

Sen, A.K.: Poverty: An Ordinal Approach to Measurement, *Econometrica,* (1976), 44, 219-231.

Sen, A.K.: Commodities and Capabilities, North-Holland, Amsterdam, 1985.

Sen, A.K.: *Inequality Reexamined,* Harvard University Press, Cambridge, MA, 1992.

Streeten, P.: *First Things First: Meeting Basic Human Needs in Developing Countries,* 1981.

Sundaram, K. : On identification of households below poverty line: Some comments on the proposed methodology, *Economic and Political Weekly,* 38 (9), 896-902.

UNDP, Human Development Report (1990), Oxford University Press, New York.

UNDP, Human Development Report (2010), Oxford University Press, New York.

9

Problems Due to Traditionalism and Conservativism of Society: Status of Women in India

K.S. Saxena

In our Indian society, man and women are considered two wheels of life, though woman has to play a multifaceted role in the form of mother, wife, sister, and a source of inspiration etc. Mahatma Gandhi said woman is the companion of man, gifted with equal mental capacities. She has the right to participate in very minutest detail in the activities of man and she has an equal right of freedom and liberty with him. She is entitled to a supreme place in her own sphere of activity as man is in his. This ought to be the natural condition of things and not as a result only of learning to read and write. By sheer force of a vicious custom, even the most ignorant and worthless men have been enjoying a superiority over women which they do not deserve and ought not to have. Many of our movements stop half way because of the condition of our women.

In India, women have played a very significant role in every walk of life. During the freedom movement in India, Rani Laxmi Bai of Jhansi, Ba Kasturba, Sarojini Naidu, Vijaya Laxmi Pandit and others struggled and fought for the independence of the country. It is an irony that in spite of their outstanding contribution, women in our country are considered 'weaker section of our society.' In *Mahabharata*, women have been decorated as light of the House, mothers of the Universe and supporters of the earth and all its forests.[1]

During the Vedic and post-Vedic period also women actively played in the intellectual and social life of the country. As Dr. S. Radha Krishnan observed: 'Brahmin girls were taught vedic wisdom, girls of the Kshatriya community were taught the use of the bow and arrow. The Barhut sculptures represent skillful horsewomen in the army. Patanjali mentions the spear bearers (Saktikirs). Megasthenes speaks of Chandragupta's bodyguard of Amazonian women. Kautilya mentions women archers... In the houses as well in the forest universities of India, boys and girls were educated together. Atreyi studied under Valmiki along with Lava and Kusa, the sons of Rama.'[2]

During the medieval period Indian women, to some extent, lost their earlier status, but even then women like Razia Begum, Chand Bibi, Tara Bai, Ahilya Bai Holker left their great imprints. However, during this period 'Bhakti movement' spread all over the country and women like Mira Bai, Mukta Bai, Jana Bai and others contributed to the spiritual life of the country. With the advent of Islam, once again women like Jahanara, Begum Mumtaz and Noor Jahan enjoyed respectable positions in the country.

In the meantime, Sikhism, emerged. Sikhism also believes in the equality of men and women. Guru Nanak says, 'Within a woman is a man conceived, from a woman he is born, he is married to a woman and with her goes through

---

1. Baig, Tara Ali : *India's Women Power*, S. Chand & Co., New Delhi, 1976, p. 9.
2. Asaf Ali, Aruna : *The Resurgence of Indian Women*, Radiant Publishers, New Delhi, 1991, pp. 12-13.

life... why call her bad, she gives birth to kings. None may exist without a woman. Only the one, true God is exterior to woman.'[3] During the British rule 'Christianity' emerged as a new religion in India but it also accepts the equality between man and woman. The British rule led to a number of socio-religious reforms in the country. A remarkable development of the period was the participation of women in the civil disobedience movement under the guidance of Mahatma Gandhi. This was the beginning of women's political participation in modern India. The Constitution of independent India opened a new chapter granting equality to women in all walks of life.[4] Rabindra Nath Tagore observed: 'Women is the builder and moulder of nation's destiny. Though delicate and soft as a lily, she has a heart, far stronger and bolder than that of man... she is the supreme inspiration for man's onward march... she is, no doubt, her commanding personality, nevertheless is grimly solemn.'

But the structure of the family in our country, creates a lot of problems, specially for rural women. The social values that are built around it permeate all aspects of the personal and social life of Indian women. Consequently, women suffer discrimination right from birth. Given the pre-dominant preference for male children, female babies are usually unwanted. As a result, they are subject to conscious or unconscious negligence or even ill treatment. The incidence of malnutrition and deaths due to it is greater for females then for males. Studies indicate that it is not only in poorer families that female babies are discriminated against in terms of food and other resources. Discriminatory attitudes continue to govern the lives of

3. *Ibid.*, p. 28.
4. Articles 14-18, The Constitution of India.

girls as they grow up. The parental family plays a crucial role in the gradual conditioning of women in to an acceptance of their unequal status in Indian society. This is done by placing various socially-approved restrictions and regulations on the movement and behaviour of women. Traditional family norms require, girls to show deference and submissiveness to their parents and guardians and be guided by their decisions in all crucial matters. Restrictions on their mobility outside the family are dictated as much by what is deemed socially respectable as by any real fear of the insecurity of women on the streets.

This has an adverse effect on the educational opportunities for women. The drop out rate for girl students, at all levels, is higher than those for boys. In the rural areas and among the urban poor, the problem is more acute. A majority of girls do not join school at all, and of those who join, more than 70% drop out at the primary level itself. The parental family, also controls woman's right and choice of employment, her social and political equality, and finally marriage, with which both the woman and the power to exercise control over her are transferred to the husband's family. As a rule the process of conditioning is smooth and unobtrusive as the task is performed by the parental family and is tinged with the notion of protection. Over the years women themselves learn to acquiesce and adjust to established social norms. In cases, however, where there is an attempt on the part of women to deviate from clearly defines conduct, tensions arise often resulting in serious threats, including physical violence, to the women from their families.

Associated with marriage, the customary payment of dowry has become the most prevalent social evil in the country. The value of dowry, which itself is a status symbol, has increased manifold. The implications of these development for the status of women and the crimes against them is becoming increasingly evident with reports of dowry murders from all parts of the country. After marriage once inside's the husband's family women are subjected to more direct forms of coercion. In cases of joint families or otherwise, young women are expected to adjust and conform to the wishes of their husbands and in-laws, and to please the elders, both male and female. Any divergence, real or imaginary, from these roles can bring suffering on the woman, ranging from verbal abuse, mental torture and to beatings and physical torture.

In the case of married working women, the burden increases two-fold. Social values still deem it disrespectable for the male to assume an equal share in household responsibility. The expectation that the working woman should also fulfill the role of an ideal housewife results longer working hours and family tensions, thus placing greater physical and mental burdens on the woman. Besides, working outside the house does not necessarily bring about financial independence for women. The male heads continue to exercise control over women income. Tension arising out of all this may result in physical violence on women, which could mean beating, murder, or driving the women to suicide. Over the recent years, the phenomenon of unnatural deaths has registered a sharp increase. A brief look at the available statistics reveals significant facts. The largest category of unnatural deaths is by burning. Significantly, 90% of the victims are married women. Among these the percentage of young women (20-30 years) is the highest. Suicides of married women also show a disturbing trend of increase. Married women outnumber unmarried women.

Thus, the structure of the family, and the social norms and values that are around it, are thus completely against the democratic principles our Republic stands for. In fact a systematic violation of the rights of women is institutionalized in the prevailing family system. In fact that there are significant variations in the system and that in many parts and in some classes, women do not suffer the violation of their rights as severely as out lined, may be a mitigating feature. The variation is not so much from religion to religion as from class to class and from region to region. Historically certain parts of the country have developed relatively more democratic attitude towards women in the family than other parts have. Similarly, the economic and social status of the family also affects these attitudes within the family. Urban - rural difference is also more pronounced in the case of women.

The most worthy feature in this atmosphere of otherwise unrelieved gloom, is the increasing awareness among the public about the rights of women. In the last decade, a number of women's organizations fighting for their rights have come up in different parts of the country. Although based mostly in large cities and limited in numerical strength, these organizations are playing a pioneering role in increasing consciousness among different sections including the political parties and the media. But even as public consciousness is on the increase, paralleling it, the oppression of women is also on the increase. Whether it is scientific advances like 'Amniocentesis Tests' that are used for female foeticide or a spreading consumer culture, modernization has resulted in the further oppression of women. An alarming phenomenon is the revival of the practice of 'Sati' of which several incidents have been reported from U.P., M.P. and Rajasthan.[5] Crimes against women are on the increase. The infamous, Naina Sahni murder case (known as Tandoor case), death of Sarla Mishra, a youth congress leader of M.P. in suspicious circumstances, and a gruesome murder of Rajasthan University woman lecturer by her husband are some of the important incidents which evoked country-wide resentment.

These trends only mean that even now, women as a community are not allowed to live and function as independent human beings. They are born, grow up, marry and die, oblivious of their rights as human beings and citizens. Their ignorance about their rights has a social, if not a moral sanction. This results, often, tragically, in the perversion of the consciousness of the victims themselves. Thus we find mothers killing their own infant daughter and mother-in-law burning their daughter-in-law. Hence the women's rights movement and organizations must seriously take up such violations of the rights of women.

In this context, absence of a uniform civil code has been a great hurdle in improving the status of women in our society. As M.R. Masani, Hansa Nahta and Rajkumari Amrit Kaur, members of the Constituent Assembly, wrote in their minute, 'Out of the factors that has kept India back from advancing to nationhood has been the existence of personal laws based on religion which keep the nation divided in to watertight compartments in many aspects of life.'At this time the Hindu Code Bill was pending with the Constituent Assembly and the only hope was that it would be passed so that the vast majority of Hindu women would be ensured some rights. But the than Prime Minister allowed the Bill to be dropped as the general

5. Case of Roop Kanwar in Dist. Sikar (Raj.).

elections were ahead. Dr. B.R. Ambedkar, the than law minister was one of the most ardent advocates of the code bill and in protest he resigned. He wrote 'The Hindu Code Bill was the greatest social reform measure taken by the legislature in this country. No law passed by the Indian Legislature in the past or likely to be passed in the future, can be compared to it in point of significance. To leave inequality between class and class, between sex and sex, which is the soul of Hindu society untouched and to go on passing legislation relating to economic problems is to make a farce of our Constitution and to build a palace on a dung heap.'[6]

However, the ideal of a Uniform Civil Code was enshrined in the Directive Principles of State Policy.[7] These Directive Principles are guidelines for the government but are not justifiable, or enforceable in a court of law, though the Supreme Court has now taken a favourable view to implement Directive Principles. The demand for a Uniform Civil Code has been the demand of the people concerned about the oppression and exploitation of women in the name of religion. We have to see why it is related specially to women's status. There are certain features common in all personal law-including the reformed Hindu Personal law which perpetuates inequality between women and men :

(a) Under all the personal laws it is the man who is the head of the family in all circumstances (However now mother's name can also be mentioned in school's admission form).

(b) The line of succession is through the male line.

6. Quoted in *The Times of India*, dated March 8, 1986.
7. Chapter IV, Constitution of India.

(c) The woman, normally, has to live wherever the man decided after marriage.

(d) The right to divorce is far more lenient with the man under Christian and Muslim law but in interpreting the law Hindu also faces the same difficulties.

Women have been struggling to have one civil code in order to ensure that the family can be based on real consent between the parties and not to be enforced by considerations of property, family, honour or money. They want that the rights and interests of girls and boys be equally protected, the mother and father should have equal rights to guardianship of their children; that the woman's labour in house and her role in sustaining the family be recognized so that the matrimonial property be equally divided in case of separation or divorce, and that the women be given equal share in agriculture, ancestral and immovable property. The demand for a uniform civil code is also the demand of the dalits and the tribal people because Hindu Law which has been imposed upon them only furthers their subjugation though among lower castes and tribal people women have more equal rights with in the family which have been de-recognized as a result of Hindu Law.

Thus a demand for the uniform civil code is the demand for equal rights for women and men with in the family and for more equitable relations between the people from all communities. In fact women are struggling for their equal status in Indian society. It is an irony; the woman who was having a status of '*Yatra Naryastu Pujayante Ramante Tatra Devta*' is to struggle today for her status in Indian society. However, after independence, there is a lot of improvement in the status of women, but the 'raising of women's status as a whole in the country requires regional policies and micro-level, situation based programmes. It is not so much a question of bringing a woman's status at par with that of a man, but first to provide equal status to women belonging to all regions of the country.'[8]

The special attention given by the government to the needs of women and the special provisions regarding their role in the society 'make the Indian Constitution a 'social' document embodying the objectives of social revolution."[9] In this context, the Indian Parliament has enacted a number of laws to improve the position of women. These include Hindu Marriage Act, 1955; the Suppression of Immoral Traffic in Women and Girl's Act, 1956; the Dowry Prohibition Act, 1961; the Medical termination of Pregnancy Act, 1971; and the Commission of Sati (Prevention) Act, 1987 etc. But the mere enactment of these laws cannot change the status of women unless these are properly implemented. However, public opinion will also have to be moulded and in this context education can play a very important role. The national policy on education, if implemented properly can help in achieving a basic change in the status of Indian women, even the eighth plan had stressed on the need of educating the women specially to promote the education of scheduled caste and scheduled tribes women.

Status of women, in fact, can be divided into two individual and social. Women's socio-political rights, financial independence and right to property etc. relate to individual status while these like marriage and family life etc. fall in the purview of social status. Under the

---

8. Varma, Sudhir : *Women's Development : Policy and Administration*, Aalekh Publishers, 1992, p. 27.
9. Jain, C.K., : *Women Parliamentarians in India*, Surjeet Publications, Delhi, 1993.

Constitution of India,[10] right to education, right to franchise and right to freedom etc. have been guaranteed. It has also been laid down that state shall not discriminate against any citizen on grounds of religion, race, caste, and place of birth etc.[11] Equal opportunity in matters of employment has also been given under Article 16 of the Constitution. Similarly, right to freedom of speech has also been guaranteed without any discrimination of sex under Article 19 of the Constitution. Thus the social status of women has certainly increased in independent India. However the rural women, who are mostly illiterate, are still deprived off of their fundamental rights but the programming like free and compulsory primary education and the projects of community development have tried to improve their lot.

Female labour in India has also raised certain problems such as those of health, maternity, care of babies etc. The Government of India and the State Governments have made certain efforts to solve them. Women in India are now trying to improve their lot through various women's organizations, particularly through the All India Women's Conference, which perhaps has the largest women's membership. All India Women's Conference, in 1949, decided to take up the women's problem related to Hindu Code Bill, food campaign, cooperative societies, family planning facilities, health problems, educational work, and likewise other social-economic problems. This would certainly help in raising the status of women in India.[12]

---

10. Chapter III : The Constitution of India.
11. Art. 15 : The Constitution of India.
12. Quoted in Heptulla, Najma : The Unrepresented Electorate-Women in India Politics. *The Parliamentarian*, July, 1991.

In the post-independent India, the five Years Plans have also laid special emphasis over the all round development of women in India. No doubt in the earlier period, women's development programmes were not given top priority, but now there has been a significant change, particularly in the seventh plan, development programmes at the grass root level have been given more importance. Smt. Jayanthi Natarajan, speaking in the Rajya Sabha over the Women's Commission Bill observed:

'I condemn all kinds of atrocities against women and it is not a political issue... The attitude of men towards women and of boys towards girls even before their birth is one of the total domination and I want to state before you a few instances of their condition right from the time of their birth until the time of their death - the cause of their death through '*Sati*' the damnation, the servility and the total suppression of women which is going on in this country. There is, no dearth of laws. The point I am going to make is it is a question of implementation of the laws.

'The fact is that there must be a political will to implement the laws which are made in favour of women, to bring women forward in the national stream and to bring women out of the servile existence on which they live in this country. There has to be a political will on the part of the Government to implement these.

'I think it is very important that the Commission, should have powers, not just functions. The question of attitude should be there because right from the time we are born till the time we die, only thing before us is the object to be used. What you have written down as functions should rightly, include powers. Without saying what are the powers which they have to do it is difficult for the Commission to function. We need a sword arm. What is the sword arm? We need where? These people can go out and make sure that the rights of women are protected. If you only call them functions and we only make 2500 recommendations and none of them are implemented then Commission has to go with a begging soul to hundred different people asking them to implement them.'

However, there is no doubt that as in ancient India, so at in post-independent India, a number of distinguished women have actively participated in various spheres of national life, viz., in literature, education, dance, painting, films, television, music, sports, adventures, police, army, bureaucracies, executive, legislature, judiciary, culture, engineering and in the service of humanity.

Thus todays women have made a significant departure from the traditional roles and have entered in to active politics as well as in decision making process. In this context Smt. Indira Gandhi, the late Prime Minister observed: 'To be liberated, woman should feel free to herself not in rivalry to man but in the context of her own capacity. Women should be more interested, more alive and more active in the affairs of society not because they are women but because they constitute half the human race.'[13]

Now all the political parties in spite of some differences, have shown their interest and commitment on 33% reservation to women in all the legislative bodies. It is interesting to note that women have already got 33% reservation in *Panchayat* and Municipalities. This is another matter that due to their illiteracy and social background, they have not been very effective and vocal. For instance in many, even two-and -a half years after their election

13. Speaking on 72nd & 73rd Constitutional Amendment Bill, 1991.

as a *Sarpanch* and a member or chairperson of *Panchayat Samities* or *Zila Parishads*, the women have failed to assert themselves. In words of a dy. commissioner, 'Most of the women *Sarpanchas* are dummies. It will take some time for women to participate actively in the Panchayat Raj System.'

It is a fact that the husbands and sons of women sarpanchas go with her to official meetings. As a Block Development Officer said, 'We have to allow them to do so, otherwise the village work will suffer.' In rural areas women *sarpanchas* have been more or less reduced to rubber stamps. And some times, even this formality is completed by men. Women are made to observe purdah and are forbidden from going to the village *Chaupal*. Sarbati Devi, the then Chairperson of Hissar *Zila Parishad* said, 'women have not been allowed to move out of their homes in our society. They will naturally take some time.' She confessed that she was not allowed to have any say in official meetings as chairperson.[14] As such, still there is a need to improve their lot by social awakening and then only their status would improve.

A welcome development is that almost all the political parties-cutting across party line-have shown their commitment in raising the status of women in our country. The Indian National Congress, Bhartiya Janata Party, CPI, CPM, and Janata Dal etc. have all demanded to raise the status of women. No doubt a lot has been done to raise their socio-economic and political status, but still there is much to do. As the late Prime Minister. Smt. Indira Gandhi once said, 'If a handful of women go forward, become ministers or Judges, you should not think that women's status has gone up.'[15]

14. *Indian Express*, dated May 26, 1997.
15. Quoted in Jain, C.K.: *op. cit*. p. 25.

Now the days are gone when one used to say :

अबला जीवन हाय तुम्हारी यही कहानी।
आंचल में है दूध और आंखों में पानी।

The National Commission for Women (NCW) and the commissions and committees constituted at the state level has given a sense of security and boost to urban and rural women's morale. The NCW has tried to encourage urban and rural women with the slogan :

अबला नहीं कहा जा सकता, अब भारत की नारी को
राख समझना भूल बहुत है, छुपी हुई चिन्गारी को।

10

The Girl Child and the Nature; Twin Protection by Farmers : A Case Study

S. Chandni Bi

I

The modern period is an age of concrete farming inviting even the civil engineers from the European countries. India, being a developing country is eventful nation where more and more agricultural lands being converted into sky scrapers in the least time. Though this is one among the many problems that deter farmers from their job, still it is a major issue.

The other hurdles are like the ever growing high prices, low buying capacity of a section of the people, the increasing craze for the western food, low profits to the farmers, rising input costs, power scarcity, and the scanty rainfall over the couple of years. These reasons have made men to migrate to towns and cities. In many states particularly in states like Tamil Nadu, men engage themselves as lorry drivers, in mills and factories as daily wagers while many others take to gambling or addict to liquor resulting in permanent negligence of agriculture. Even in this stage both the state and the central governments have failed to pay their attention to the dying farmers and farming.

As a student of history, it is very natural for me to look back to the pages of ancient history that too in my Tamil land. From the literature of before Christ period a poet goes to the extent of warning the king that only if the paddy crops rise above, then the kings' crown will rise. To speak about the fame of farming the poet calls the farmers as the only people who carry out their profession with pride and self respect but the rest of the whole world revolves behind the farmers.

The sangam age (the first historical period) kings and chieftains gave much importance to nature and considered flora and fauna equally as human and protected them. The kings considered certain trees as their guardians and that trees were called as *kaval maram*, meaning policing trees. Even in their fights for land and supremacy these trees were protected, when they were cut that denoted the fall of the king himself.[1]

All law books right from the early period considered harming or destruction to nature as a punishable offence. Manu, the so called first law giver of India prescribed fines. When he speaks about trees, according to him,'.... a fine must be imposed for injuring all kinds of trees, in exact accordance with their usefulness'.[2] The difference in the value of fine is according to their products and position. Apart from this the expiation suggested was that the Vedic text must be repeated for a hundred times on cutting trees that bear fruit, and for cutting bushes, wines, creepers and plants which have blossoms.[3]

Even Kautilya (III.19), Yajnavalkya (II.227-229), Vishnu Dharma (S.V.55-59), all prescribe graduated fines for the destruction of trees, plants and branches, flowers and

1. *Purananuru* (a Sangam literature) speaks many times about such incidence.
2. *Manu Smruti*, pt-viii, p. 285.
3. *Ibid.*, pt. ix, p. 143.

fruits according to their usefulness and sanctity. Katyayana (p.793) provide fines for causing loss by injuring or felling not only trees but also shrubs and creepers.

Bhagavat Gita says that a fig tree (*Asvattha*) is the symbol of all life. It considered the fig tree as all varied lives of the globe and very genesis of life (Ch-XV, p-89). In Buddhism, the trees are compared to the disciples itself, who are the spreaders and upholders of the religion, and who are the real roots of the religion.[4]

The flora and fauna has been treated in equal terms with that of the human beings throughout all historical periods. The mother of a young girl tells her that the tree in front of their house was her younger sister, as when she was a child while playing she hid a seed in the earth, out of which the particular tree has grown. Thus the mother gives the interesting reason to call that tree in front of their house as her younger sister, goes one of the Sangam Age poems.[5]

Apart from literature, in practical life we have seen many communities practicing different customs and manners to save the nature. We have heard about the *chipko* movement started by the ladies to save the forest region by hugging the trees. We are aware of the *Bishnoi* community largely populated in Rajasthan and Haryana areas who share their mother's milk to the left out animals like Black Buck and deer. In Nagarkoil (Tamilnadu) there is a peculiar habit that in summers everyone should bath outside the house under a tree, irrespective of age and gender. This custom is followed even today.

In spite of all these painstaking tasks, the present condition of the farmers is pitiable. Still there are some

---

4. *Narrinai* (a Sangam literature), p. 13.
5. *The Sacred Books of the East*, vol. v-xxxv, p. 151.

promising model villages that cherish farming. Here is one such case study that we are going to study.

II

There is a village named Dharhara in the Bhagalpur district of Bihar State. It is at a distance of 30 kms. from the district capital Bhagalpur. It is a small village of 600 acres and with a population of 3500. There are nearly 400 families of mixed population, dominated by Brahmins and bhumihars.[6] This particular village is filled with fruit trees such as mango, litchi etc. The interesting story behind this is more fascinating.

It was in the modern times, the birth of girl child was seen as a burden and also it became a bad omen for the family. The main reason was that the family need a huge amount of money to give her in marriage taken in the form of dowry by the grooms' party due to which the bride's family had to undergo a lifelong trauma. Hence in most cases the family had to lose their land once for all. As a result the female child was considered as unwarranted. This situation was the same throughout India.

It was under such a situation only that someone had an idea to solve these twin problems of safeguarding the female child and also save agricultural land and cherish farming. That was to plant fruit bearing trees as soon as a girl child was born. The trees grow with them and the profit of the tree products will serve a source of income to spend for their marriage expense.

The origin of this practice in the village goes back to 1880 A.D. It was initiated by one Tulsi Singh followed by Munsi Singh and the third generation Banbari Singh. Now we have the fifth generation of Tulsi Singh in this

6. *Interviews* dt. 1-3 of August 2013 by the author.

village. In the present generation, the senior to whom the villagers' fingers are pointed to is one Mr. Bola. This man and one Nirmala Devi entered into wedlock by the year 1957. When Bola was approached to recall his memory, he started to travel back to the past. He narrated how people reacted to the birth of a female child in those days. All family members and relatives use to mourn the occasion for long time and will share the message with a tone of condolence.

But the situation in that particular village, Dharhara was different; though they did not jump in excitement they planted fruit trees. This habit was followed by our Bola, when he had the first girl child by 1961 he planted 30 mango trees in his farm land. Again the second child was also a she child and again he planted 50 litchi trees to celebrate the birth of his daughter. Now Mrs. Nirmala Devi is 73 plus.

Roopesh Kumar Singh, another native of the village, came forward to share his experience said to his knowledge he saw his three elder sisters got married from the income of the trees planted on the occasion of their birth and now the income is enjoyed by the family. Moreover he added that he too has planted fruit trees towards the birth of his own daughter. He also compared this custom as a fixed deposit in the bank.

Another villager Mr. Ram Saran had a complete different view to share. Since he had no daughters he never planted any trees, now laments why this custom was not for the sons too. He sorrowfully commented that none of his sons care for him and if trees were planted that would have served him to meet his ends.

This village Dharhara came to limelight only in 2010 when Bihar's chief minister Mr. Nitish Kumar identified and announced it as a 'Role model village'. He also donated two schools to this village as a compliment. Since then the arrangements were made to keep a census of girl child and an account of the trees planted. The Bihar government claims that the practice exists since 150 years in the village.[7]

Now days the villagers plant only ten trees for the birth of each girl child due to lack of land availability in the village. Generally only fruit trees like mango, litchi and jack-fruit are grown. Thus we could observe that the farmers of this particular village Dharhara help to maintain the ecological proposition of forestation and deforestation and also help to balance the men women ratio of the human population and win over the present twin problems of India.

---

7. *Ibid.*

11

The Participation of Peasant and *Biswedars* in the Peasant Movement : A Case Study of Patiala and East Punjab States Union (1948-56)

Dr. Mohammad Idris,
Dr. Haroon Nayam Khan

In recent years, social scientists have started studying agrarian society and the peasant movements. The peasant movements in India have played an important role in transforming the social economic structure before and after independence. PEPSU, a conglomeration of eight erstwhile Princely States of East Punjab, witnessed a violent but organized peasant movement against the traditionally well entrenched and highly exploitative *biswedari* system.[1]

Patiala and East Punjab States Union (PEPSU) was inaugurated on 15th July, 1948 by the then Deputy Prime Minister and Home Minister of India, Sardar Vallabh Bhai Patel. It was formed after combining eight erstwhile princely states of East Punjab. These were the states of Patiala, Nabha, Jind, Malerkotla, Kapurthala, Faridkot, Nalagarh and Kalsian. Maharaja Yadavindra Singh, the

1. Mohinder Singh: *Peasant Movement in PEPSU, Punjab*, New Delhi, 1991, p. ix.

prince of Patiala was given the office of the *Rajpramukh* of PEPSU, for the lifetime. In the same way, the Prince of Nabha was designated as the *Up-rajpramukh* of the Union.

As far as the sources for the present theme are concerned, there are still a handful of primary sources which have been explored by the students of history for the purpose of research. This, in no way means that there is any dearth of primary sources for the same, in the important among them being government records and files. The most noteworthy among them are *Reports on the Agrarian Reforms in* PEPSU published by the Ministry of states, PEPSU in 1952; PEPSU Government Gazetteers, PEPSU Legislative Assembly Debates etc. The literature and accounts written by the leaders and participants of the peasant movement are the sources of equal importance in studying the nature, aims and the causes and effects of the movements. The eminent among these sources are mentioned below :

1. *Agriculture Worker's Struggle in Punjab,* written by Master Hari Singh, 1980
2. *Agrarian Scene in British Punjab,* vol. I, by Master Hari Singh, 1983.
3. *Punjab Peasant in Freedom Struggle,* vol. II, by the same author, 1984.
4. *Kisanan Muzarian de Mittar Kaun* by Chhaju Mal Vaid.

It has been a sad practice among the historians working on Colonial and Post-colonial India, to ignore the writing of history of the Princely States of India. The states smaller in size and political relevance have been all the more ignored. A handful of secondary sources have been written on the smaller Princely States of East Punjab, which later constituted to form PEPSU. The worth mentioning works among them are *Peasant Movement* in PEPSU, Punjab written by Mohinder Singh in 1991 and *Peasant in India's Non-Violent Revolution* by Mridula Mukherjee in 2004.

In the light of the dearth of serious research on the peasant movement in the region, many events and aspects of the historical events have remained unnoticed. Thus a humble attempt is being made, in the present paper, to understand the nature and scope of the movement and the roles played by the three important factions in the same.

PEPSU was a region which witnessed one of the most serious and long drawn struggle between the peasant and the *biswedars*. The landlords in the local language were known as '*biswedars*'. The saplings of the peasant resentment against the *biswedars* and the government policies could be noticed as far back as 1850s. It this movement of time, the nature of the problems was totally different in comparison to the other area of the country. In the rest of India, peasants had to bear the exigencies of their *zamindars* and the British Government. The problems became more serious in the Princely States where the peasants had to bear three fold exploitation by *biswedars*, officials of the Princely Government and finally the princes and their relatives. The land settlement was also different to that existed in British India as in many of Princely States, Princes had become the land owners of large patches of land (sometimes running into thousands of acres). In many states they had acquired *Ala Malkiat* rights and the cultivating farmer, who was earlier the owner of the land, was now reduced to the status of *Adna Malik.* Thus the peasants in the Princely States suffered the severities of the faulty system of land settlement and land rights in a more serious and myriad way.

The beginning of the movement could be traced back to the second half of the nineteenth century in PEPSU.

It was the time when peasants were deprived of their proprietary rights; were rack rented and were ultimately reduced to rent paying tenants. With the growth of National movement in 1920s, the struggle took the shape of a mass movement. The peasant of the state began to protest against the oppressive feudal set up. The year 1937 marked the beginning of a militant peasant agitation, providing a backdrop to the movement. During 1948-52, the peasant movement assumed a highly militant character and it became so powerful that those having occupancy rights were finally given the proprietary rights of their land in 1953. This was followed by one more legislation act in 1956, due to which the region could claim to be the first in the country to pass an act on fixing a ceiling of 30 acres on the ownership of land.[2]

According to Mridula Mukherjee, the Peasant Movement in the erstwhile princely states of East Punjab and PEPSU passed through three subsequent phases. The first phase was the initial phase which started in the last quarter of the nineteenth century and lasted till 1937. Till this time, as in the centre, the moderate politics was in vogue, peasants also adopted peaceful and moderate ways to express their sorrows. But this could not go a long way in the rule of the Princes who were world renowned for their repressive policies and measures. Thus the second phase of the movement started which was quite reactionary in nature, had a wider participation of peasant and was more organized. This phase continued from 1937 to 1953. During this time the occupancy tenants, who constituted to be the major participants in the struggle got the right of proprietorship of the land which they were tilling since years. Thus they were now satisfied and left their

2. *Ibid*, p. ix.

participation had much decreased and the movement had slowed down and had rather become passive in nature by the time PEPSU merged into Punjab.[3]

In general, tenancy in PEPSU followed the pattern prevailing in the Punjab as the revenue settlements were formulated from time to time by the PEPSU State consonant with those of the Punjab province. But the pattern of relationship and the land rights were different in various states. The peasants in all the states, irrespective of some variations in the system of land rights and relationship, were facing the same kind of problems. The problems were confined to the claims put forward by occupancy tenants, group of special tenants and a proportion of tenants at will who represented that they had been deprived of occupancy or ownership rights which, in fact, belonged to them. Opposed to them there was a category of people, the landed Aristocracy, who asserted their rights of superior ownership. Yet another aspect of the problems was related to the grant of greater rights to the tenants at will, generally on the lines of legislation enacted in several states including Punjab.[4]

The *biswedars* had acquired the ownership of land by all fair and foul means. The cultivators, who were hitherto the owners of land, were now reduced to the status of tenants. In compensation to this loss, those who had lost the proprietary rights of their land were given the status of occupancy tenants. In the whole, the role of the Government and Government machinery must be critically considered. There was a strong offensive and

3. Mridula Mukherji: *Peasants in India's Non-Violent Revolution*, New Delhi, 2004, pp. 45-67.
4. *Report on Agrarian Reforms in PEPSU*, Ministry of States, Government of India, 1952, p. 4.

defensive alliance between *ahilkar* (official) and *biswedar* (landlord classes). The *ahilkar* who was not a *biswedar* generally converted into one and the *biswedar* found that it was necessary to obtain a support in the official camp to fulfill his ambitions.[5]

The circumstances, at the time of the formation of PEPSU, were largely in favour of the peasant and against any kind of oppressive and regressive policies. Some of the rurlers particularly those of Faridkot and Nalagarh, were recorded as *Ala Maliks* (superior landlords). Over the entire area of their state. In support to this, the cultivators were recorded as *Adna Maliks* (inferior landlords).[6] These *Adna maliks* could not be ejected from their land as they had its hereditary rights but they had lost all the claims on its proprietorship. On August 20, 1948, PEPSU Government announced the conferment of proprietary rights on inferior landowners. Being indicative of the change in the attitude and the policy of the government, this announcement gave sufficient hope to the tenants of gaining proprietary rights, if necessary through struggle.[7]

After independence, the landlords, fearing that the Congress Government would bring in radical legislations in favour of tenants, tried to evict their tenants forcibly on one pretext or the other.[8] The tenants resisted these attempts of the landlords. More importantly, the landlord-tenant relations were based on some unwritten codes

5. Major Popham Young : *Final Report of the Settlement of the Patiala State* (1900-08), 1909, p. 10.
6. *Report of Agrarian Reforms in PEPSU*, Ministry of States, Government of India, 1952, p. 20.
7. Mohinder Singh : *Peasant Movement in PEPSU, Punjab*, New Delhi, 1991, p. 47.
8. *The Tribune*, 10th October , 1950.

of conduct. Under the changed circumstances, for the protection of their interests, neither the landlords nor the tenants were prepared to abide by these unwritten rules. As a result of these factors the tenant-*biswedar* controversy assumed alarming proportions. In consequence to the above circumstances and the forcible implementation of various laws by the government officials, clashes between the police and peasants took place at Anupgarh, Mulewala, Dunakot, Gurthali and Kartar Singh Wala. Their prime slogan was 'no *batai*' and in these clashes they emerged out largely successful to foil the attempts of the police and the *biswedars* to realize *batai*. This victory of the peasants raised their prestige and morale too. The movement now spread to new areas and tenants at will also became its participants. Now villages like Dharamgarh, Dhandoli, Shafipur, Bakshi Singh Wala and Dale Singh Wala also became the active centre's of the struggle.[9]

The struggle between peasants and *biswedars* at village Kishangarh, located in district Bathinda, was a golden example of the success of peasants in the region. It was the important nucleic of the peasant movement in PEPSU. The whole struggle was against Bhagwan Singh and Syasat Singh, the *biswedars* of the village and they were also the Superintendents of Police and posted outside the village. The leaders of the tenants were Dharam Singh Fakkar and Jangir Singh Joga. They together raised the slogans of 'not a grain of *batai*' and 'not an inch of land'. This revolt showed the strength and zeal of the tenants in its full glory, as even the children and women participated in it. Later they were supplemented by the support of around 5000 tenants from nearby villages. The village was

9. Chajju Mal Vaid : *Muzarian Kisanan de Mittar Kaun*, published by the Tenant Committee, PEPSU, Ludhiana, 1949, p. 40.

seized by the police and the goondas of the *biswedars* but of no use. Later on the interference of the military and higher government authorities, the peasants allowed the opponents to enter the village. Kishangarh thus became a symbol of the movement and is quoted as an example of the heroic struggle of the tenants and *Muzaras* in PEPSU.[10]

The demands of the tenants were accepted to a large extent on 20th August, 1949 when the government issued an ordinance abolishing *Biswedari* in PEPSU.[11] This action could not calm down the tenants as all their demands were not fulfilled yet. So they continued their struggle in its full zest. In order to find a solution to the problems of the tenants the Government appointed two committees in 1950 and 1952 respectively. The findings of these two Agrarian reforms committees were in favor of the tenants.

The peasant movement which had emerged during the late 1930s was fully developed by 1952 as it had an organization, following and leadership. Now it had become the prime necessity of the government to solve the crises in order to bring peace in the region. Thus an attempt was made to reform the existing tenancy laws in the State. Three important acts were promulgated for this purpose.

1. The PEPSU Abolition of Ala Malkiat Rights Act, 1953 : it raised the inferior proprietors to the status of full proprietors.
2. The PEPSU occupancy Tenants (Vesting of Proprietary Rights)Act : it gave full proprietary rights to the occupancy tenants.

---

10. Mridula Mukherji : 'Communists and Peasants in Punjab : A Focus on the Muzara Movement in Patiala, 1937-53', *Studies in History*, vol. III, No. 142, New Delhi, 1981, p. 413.
11. *The Tribune*, 22 August, 1949.

3. The PEPSU Tenancy and Agriculture Lands Act, 1953 : raised the status of tenants-at-will to that of full proprietors. In addition to this the permissible limit for personal cultivation was fixed at one half of the total area owned by the land lord, subject to a maximum of 30 standard acres and a minimum of 10 standard acres.[12]

After the enacting of these acts, a large proportion of the occupancy tenants and the earlier *adna maliks* whose rights had been given back to them, did not show much interest in struggling with their other brethren who were still fighting for their rights. Thus the movement got weak after 1953.

Here the role of the government also needs to be analyzed. Though some fruitful acts were passed in favour of tenants, there still was a big gap between their enactment and application. Corruption and negligence on the part of the government machinery was nowhere lying hidden in this respect. Moreover, though after much delay, a law on ceiling of holdings was passed in 1956, the *Biswedars* mend it the way they liked, ejected the tenants by all means from their land, and in thousands of cases opted for the *benami* transfers of land. Thus the part played by the government remained a mixture of both positives and negatives for both the parties. Though formally the acts were passed for the betterment of the tenant, deep down in their essence, they held a soft corner for the landowning section of the society too which was clearly visible from the supportive behaviour of the government section to this powerful and rich section of the society.

---

12. *President's Rule in PEPSU* (March 1953-54), PEPSU Government, Patiala, 1954, pp. 4-5.

In conclusion, it might be said that the achievements of the peasant movement in PEPSU was a mixture of successes and failures. Some laws were passed in favour of the peasant which definitely improved their lot. These reforms paved way for the social and economic development of this section of the society in the future. But at the same time, the power and glory of the land lords did not fade away with this. They secured their land and status in the society by all means and in many cases supported by the government officials. But optimistically, a hopeful beginning was made and a path was set for the future bringing reforms in the same light.

12

हरियाणा में कृषि का विकास एवं परिवर्तन

मंजु पंघाल

किसी भी देश का विकास उसकी अर्थव्यवस्था पर निर्भर करता है। भारत का विकास भी हमेशा उसकी कृषि आधारित अर्थव्यवस्था पर निर्भर रहा है। भारत की स्वतन्त्रता से पहले यहां की लगभग 80% से भी अधिक जनसंख्या कृषि पर निर्भर थी और आज भी भारत की अधिकतर जनसंख्या कृषि व कृषि सम्बन्धी अन्य संगठनों से प्रत्यक्ष व अप्रत्यक्ष रूप से जुड़ी हुई है।

19वीं शताब्दी से पहले तक विश्व के अन्य देशों की तरह भारतीय कृषि भी पिछड़ी हुई थी। लेकिन औद्योगिक क्रांति व कृषि क्रांति आने के पश्चात् विश्व के अन्य देशों के साथ-साथ भारतीय कृषि में भी विकास हुआ। उत्तर-आधुनिक काल में आई हरित क्रांति के परिणामस्वरूप भारत में कृषि के विकास की गति ओर तेज हो गई। हरित क्रांति का सबसे अधिक प्रभाव भारत के उतर-पश्चिम में स्थित हरियाणा क्षेत्र पर पड़ा, इसका कारण यह था कि यह क्षेत्र हरित क्रांति का केन्द्र रहा है।

हालांकि भारत के राजनैतिक नक्शे में हरियाणा क्षेत्र का एक राज्य के रूप में उदय 1 नवम्बर 1966 को हुआ लेकिन इस क्षेत्र को, भारतीय संस्कृति व कृषि में विशेष योगदान के कारण प्राचीन काल से ही जाना जाता है। आधुनिक हरियाणा क्षेत्र के उत्तर में शिवालिक की पहाड़ियां, दक्षिण में अरावली की पहाड़ियां, पूर्व में यमुना नदी और पश्चिम में थार का मरुस्थल स्थित हैं।[1]

---

1. चतर सिंह : *सोशल एण्ड इकॉनोमिक चेंज इन हरियाणा*, दिल्ली (2004), पृ० 1

प्राचीन काल से ही इस क्षेत्र की अर्थव्यवस्था कृषि पर आधारित रही है। कृषि ही यहां के लोगों का सबसे पुराना व महत्वपूर्ण व्यवसाय था। यहां की लगभग 90 प्रतिशत से भी ऊपर जनसंख्या अपने जीवनयापन के लिए कृषि पर निर्भर थी।[2] लेकिन खेती करने के तरीके व साधन पुराने थे। किसान खाद, फसलों को अदल-बदल कर बोने, गुणात्मक बीजों के प्रयोग और कृत्रिम सिंचाई से परिचित नहीं थे[3] जिस कारण उत्पादन कम होने की वजह से ग्रामीण जीवन बिल्कुल सादा था।

मध्यकाल में कुछ मुस्लिम शासकों ने भारत के अन्य भागों की तरह हरियाणा में भी कृषि के विकास में विशेष योगदान दिया। मुस्लिम शासकों द्वारा कृषि के विकास में विशेष रुचि लेने के कारण भूमि व राजस्व सुधारों, नई सिंचाई योजनाओं और कृषि अनुसन्धान का फायदा हरियाणा को अधिक मिला क्योंकि यह क्षेत्र राजधानी दिल्ली के अधिक नजदीक था, जिसने इस क्षेत्र की ग्रामीण जनता पर एक चिरस्थायी प्रभाव डाला। ग्रामीण अर्थव्यवस्था का विकास हुआ। ग्रामीण जीवन अब प्राचीनकाल से अधिक समृद्ध हो गया था।[4] हालांकि इस काल में मुगल साम्राज्य के अन्य भागों की तरह हरियाणा में भी कृषि से संबधित कोई वैज्ञानिक व तकनीकी विकास नहीं हुआ परन्तु अमरूद, अनान्नास, आलू, तम्बाकू और पपीता जैसी नई फसलों की पहचान हुई। कृषि उत्पादन के बढ़ने से जहां औद्योगिक माल और विभिन्न प्रकार के व्यापार में उन्नति हुई वहीं इससे विभिन्न प्रकार के व्यवसायों के रास्ते भी खुल गए।[5] गाँवों में कृषि उत्पादों एवं जरूरतों पर आधारित अनेक हस्तकरघा और छोटे स्तर के उद्योग स्थापित हुए।

इस काल के कुछ शासकों की सहायता व सुधारों के बावज़ूद भी किसानों की स्थिति विशेष अच्छी नहीं थी। इसका कारण यह था कि किसानों के उत्पादन का बहुत बड़ा भाग राज्य के लिए भू-राजस्व व अन्य कर देने में

---

2. के॰सी॰ यादव : *हरियाणा इतिहास एवं संस्कृति*, भाग II, न्यू दिल्ली (2000), पृ॰ 49
3. गडगिल, डी.आर. : *द इन्डस्ट्रीयल इवोल्यूशन ऑफ इंडिया इन रीसेन्ट टाइम्स*, 1860-1939 (1971), पृ॰ 2
4. रन्धावा, एम.एस. : *ए हिस्ट्री ऑफ एग्रीकल्चर इन इंडिया* : वोल्यूम II, न्यू दिल्ली (1982), पृ॰ 10-11
5. *उपरोक्त*, पृ॰ 203-208

चला जाता था। एक छोटी सी रकम ही उनके पास बचती थी। ज्यादातर किसान साहूकारों से लिए गए ऋण में फंसे हुए थे इस प्रकार इस काल में किसानों की अर्थव्यवस्था अच्छी न होने के कारण ग्रामीण विकास की गति धीमी ही रही।

भारत में ब्रिटिश शासन के दौरान देश के अन्य भागों की तरह हरियाणा में भी कृषि के विकास पर यूरोप में आई कृषि और औद्योगिक क्रान्तियों का प्रभाव पड़ा। नए कृषि औजार, तकनीक, बीजों की विभिन्न किस्मों और कुछ नई फसलों का आरम्भ हुआ। व्यापार व वाणिज्य के विकास, विकसित सिंचाई सुविधाओं, यातायात व संचार के साधनों के विकास से कृषि को कुछ लाभ पहुँचा। इसके साथ ही वाणिज्यीकरण, प्रथम और द्वितीय विश्व युद्धों और ब्रिटिश सरकार द्वारा करवाये गए भूमि सुधारों ने भारत के अन्य क्षेत्रों की तरह हरियाणा मे भी कृषि सम्बन्धी उत्पादन और फसलों की किस्मों को बढ़ाने में सहायता की।[6] लेकिन यूरोप के ज्ञान व तकनीक का यह खज़ाना केवल पढ़े-लिखे भारतीयों तक ही पहुँच पाया।

हरियाणा का क्षेत्र ब्रिटिश शासकों की नजर से दूर ही रहा। जहां भारत के अन्य भागों में सिंचाई व्यवस्था, सड़कें, शिक्षण संस्थान, उद्योग और व्यापार जैसी नई विकासात्मक परियोजनाएं अपनाई गई, वहीं हरियाणा को इन सब से वंचित रखा गया। इस तरह अंग्रेजों द्वारा इस क्षेत्र की अर्थव्यवस्था का मुख्य आधार रही कृषि को पूरी तरह नकार दिया था। साथ ही अकाल, सूखा व महामारी जैसी आपदाओं ने भी इस क्षेत्र की अर्थव्यवस्था को बिगाड़ने में अहम् भूमिका निभाई।[7] इतना ही नहीं प्रथम एवं द्वितीय विश्वयुद्धों, ब्रिटिश अफसरों के शोषणात्मक कार्यों, महलवाड़ी व्यवस्था और भू-राजस्व की नकदी में बढ़ती मांग[8] आदि ने हरियाणा के किसानों को पूरी तरह बर्बाद कर दिया। ग्रामीण व किसान ऋणों के भारी बोझ से दब गए,[9] क्योंकि ब्रिटिश प्रशासन द्वारा जरूरत के समय गरीब ग्रामीणों को नाममात्र की ही सहायता दी गई।

---

6. *हरियाणा स्टेट गज़ैटियर्स*, वोल्यूम II, पृ॰ 33
7. सैटलमैन्ट रिपोर्ट्स रोहतक, पृ. 44-49, सैटलमैन्ट रिपोर्ट्स करनाल डी.सी. पृ. 23-25, सैटलमैन्ट रिपोर्ट्स हिसार, डी.सी., पृ॰ 180-181
8. कोतावस्की, जी. : *एग्रेरियन रिफोर्म्स इन इंडिया*, न्यू दिल्ली (1964), पृ॰ 1-2
9. इम्पीरियल गजैटियर्स ऑफ इंडिया, पंजाब, वोल्यूम II, पृ॰ 257

पूरी तरह कृषि पर निर्भर ग्रामीण जीवन अस्त-व्यस्त हो गया। ऐसे में विश्व-युद्धों के समय हरियाणा के गरीब व भूखे मरते किसानों के आगे ब्रिटिश सेना में भर्ती होने के अतिरिक्त कोई रास्ता नहीं था।[10] करनाल परगने[11] में तो जब गरीब किसान भू-राजस्व नहीं दे पाए तो कुछ गांवों के बहुत सारे लोग अपने घर और जमीनें छोड़ कर भाग गए। इसी प्रकार की कष्टदायक स्थिति सोनीपत परगने के लोगों को भी सहनी पड़ी जब 1842 ई. में इस परगने के कुछ गांव पूरी तरह रेगिस्तान में बदल गए थे।[12] लेकिन उन्नीसवीं शताब्दी के उत्तरार्ध से हरियाणा की अर्थ व्यवस्था में परिवर्तन आना शुरू हो गया था। विशेष रूप से स्वामी दयानन्द सरस्वती के आर्य समाज द्वारा कृषि व्यवस्था, सामाजिक-धार्मिक स्तर को सुधारने, शिक्षा के विकास, छूआछूत को दूर करने और स्त्रियों के सामाजिक स्तर को सुधारने के भरपूर प्रयास किए गये। 20वीं शताब्दी के शुरू तक आर्य समाज कृषि सम्बन्धी विकास के लिए हरियाणा की एक महत्वपूर्ण शक्ति बन चुका था। इस संस्था ने यहां के कृषक समुदाय को अपनी जरूरतों के लिए जागृत कर दिया था।

इसके साथ ही आज के हरियाणा के हर प्रकार के विकास में सर छोटू राम के अथक प्रयासों का बहुत योगदान रहा है। इन्हें कृषक वर्ग के पुनरुत्थानवादी के रूप में जाना जाता है। उन्होंने किसानों को पारम्परिक पिछड़ेपन से बाहर निकाला।[13] उन्हीं के प्रयासों से 1938 में द पंजाब लैंड रिवेन्यू (अमैन्डमैन्ट एक्ट) व द पंजाब रजिस्ट्रेशन ऑफ मनीलैंडर्स एक्ट तथा 1940 में द रिलीफ ऑफ इन्डैब्टनैस एक्ट XXI पास हुए। जिनके कारण एक लम्बे समय के पश्चात् न केवल इस क्षेत्र के किसानों को भूमि सुधारों से लाभ प्राप्त हुआ बल्कि किसानों को साहूकारों से लिए गए ऋणों से भी राहत मिली।[14]

---

10. के॰सी॰ यादव : *हरियाणा : इतिहास और संस्कृति*, वोल्यूम II, न्यू दिल्ली, (2003), पृ॰ 185
11. सैटलमैन्ट रिपोर्ट्स करनाल, पृ॰ 7
12. मदनगोपाल : *सर छोटू राम-ए पोलिटिकल बायोग्राफी*, दिल्ली (1977), पृ॰ 65-66
13. *उपरोक्त*
14. चतर सिंह : *सोशल एण्ड इकानामिक चेंज इन हरियाणा*, दिल्ली (2004), पृ. 10

स्वतन्त्रता के पश्चात् जहां भारत में कृषि से सम्बन्धित महत्वपूर्ण सुधार हो रहे थे, वहां यह भी सत्य है कि हरियाणा का यह क्षेत्र जो पंजाब राज्य का एक भाग था, अभी भी पिछड़ा हुआ था। इसे भारत सरकार द्वारा शुरू की गई विभिन्न परियोजनाओं, सेवाओं, कृषि, सिंचाई व अन्य संसाधनों में कोई हिस्सा नहीं मिल रहा था। यहां के लोगों द्वारा शान्तिपूर्ण किए गए एक लम्बे संघर्ष के पश्चात् आधुनिक हरियाणा 1 नवम्बर 1966 को अपनी राजनैतिक पहचान के साथ एक अलग राज्य के रूप में अस्तित्व में आया।[15] इसी समय से इस क्षेत्र में हर प्रकार के विकास और समृद्धि का युग आरम्भ हो गया, इसी के परिणामस्वरूप कृषि उत्पादन में भी वृद्धि हुई। ग्रामीण विकास के लिए सड़कों का निर्माण, विद्युतीकरण और अन्य ऊर्जा संसाधनों का विकास, कृषि सम्बन्धी सेवाओं व बाजारों का विकास आदि से सम्बन्धित बहुत-सी सरकारी नीतियां और योजनाएं बनाई गयी। प्रशासनिक कार्यों व राजनीतिक प्रभाव के कारण भूमि सम्बन्धी सुधारों, मूल्य निर्धारण संबंधी लाभकारी नीतियां, क्रेडिट सप्लाई और अन्य कई प्रकार की सहायता छोटे व अत्यल्प आय वाले किसानों को देनी सम्भव हुई। इन कृषि सम्बन्धी तकनीकों, सेवाओं और सार्वजनिक नीतियों ने किसानों को आत्मनिर्भर बनाने में सहायता की। इस कारण आज यह क्षेत्र राष्ट्रीय स्तर पर खाद्य फसलों का एक प्रमुख योगदानकर्ता है।

हरियाणा में कृषि के परिवर्तन व विकास से आई हरित क्रान्ति का प्रभाव यहां के लोगों के सामाजिक व सांस्कृतिक जीवन पर भी पड़ा और उनके जीवन स्तर और रहन-सहन में भी बदलाव आया। आजादी से पहले गांवों में जिन लोगों को दो वक्त की रोटी नसीब नहीं होती थी, जिनके पास पहनने को कपड़े और रहने को मकान नहीं थे, आज वे रोटी, कपड़ा और मकान की समस्याओं से मुक्त हैं। जिनके पास टूटी-फूटी साइकिल भी नहीं थी, आज उनके पास मोटर-साइकिल हैं। जो किसान मुश्किल से हल-बैल जुटा पाते थे, उनके पास आज अपना ट्रैक्टर है। विवाह-शादियों में जो सूखी हल्दी का टीका लगाते-लगवाते थे, आज वे हजारों-लाखों का दहेज लेते-देते हैं।

इसमें संदेह नहीं है कि आज गांव भी शहरों की तरह प्रगति की राह पर चल पड़े हैं। आज ग्रामवासियों के कदम स्कूल-कालेज की दहलीज तक पहुँच रहे हैं। खादी ग्रामोद्योग, लघु ग्रामोद्योग, कुटीर उद्योग, किसान सेवा

15. *हरियाणा : संवाद* (मासिक पत्रिका), अप्रैल-मई (2006), पृ॰ 40-41

सहकारी समिति, स्वरोजगार योजना, अल्पसंख्यक कल्याण विभाग, भूमि विकास बैंक, क्षेत्रीय ग्रामीण बैंक आदि संस्थाओं ने जरूरतमंद लोगों को आर्थिक सहायता प्रदान कर इन्हें काफी खुशहाल बना दिया है। सरकार गांवों से गरीबी हटाने के लिए तथा इन्हें खुशहाल बनाने के लिए, बजट में सर्वाधिक धन ग्राम विकास कार्यों के लिए रखती है।

यहां ध्यान देने की बात है कि हरियाणा में कृषि के बदलाव और हरित क्रान्ति का प्रभाव एक ओर इनके जीवन व रहन सहन पर तो पड़ा ही लेकिन इसके साथ-साथ इससे समाज में कुछ विरोधी तत्व भी उदित हो रहे हैं। दूसरी ओर कृषि की नई तकनीक और ज्ञान का अधिक फायदा बड़े किसानों को ही हुआ ये किसान सामान्यतः प्रभावशाली वर्गों से सम्बन्धित होने, अधिक शिक्षित होने एवं जागरूक होने के कारण विकासात्मक संस्थाओं तक आसानी से पहुँच गए और इनका फायदा उठा गए। जबकि ग्रामीण क्षेत्रों के कम आय वाले व छोटे किसान, कृषि मजदूर, अनपढ़ महिलाएं और दस्तकार जैसे कमजोर वर्ग-जोत के विघटन, जनसंख्या की अधिकता, अशिक्षा एवं अन्य सामाजिक, आर्थिक तत्वों के कारण अब भी कमजोर हालात में हैं। इस प्रकार कृषि के विकास के बावजूद ये वर्ग सामाजिक चिंता का विषय बना हुआ है। अतः केन्द्र व राज्य सरकार द्वारा इनकी स्थिति को सुधारने के लिए इस ओर अधिक प्रयास करने चाहिएं।

13

मारवाड़ में किसानों की सामाजिक एवं आर्थिक स्थिति

जोगाराम सारण

मारवाड़ राजस्थान के पश्चिमी भाग में स्थित है। इसकी लम्बाई ईशान कोण से नैऋत्य कोण तक 320 मील और चौड़ाई उत्तर से दक्षिण तक 170 मील है।[1] मारवाड़ में जोधपुर, बाड़मेर, जालौर, पाली तथा नागौर जिले सम्मिलित हैं। आजकल यह क्षेत्र 24 अंश 36 कला उत्तर अक्षांश से लेकर 27 अंश 52 कला उत्तर अक्षांश तथा 70 अंश 6 कला पूर्व देशान्तर से 75 अंश 24 कला पूर्व देशान्तर तक है और इसका क्षेत्रफल 35016 वर्ग मील है।[2]

यहां की जमीन मुख्य रूप से रेतीली है। यहां पर जाट, राजपूत, मुसलमान, कलबी, बिश्नोई, अनुसूचित जाति-जनजाति, ब्राह्मण, चारण, सुथार, नाई, ढ़ाढ़ी, रबारी आदि जातियां मुख्य रूप से निवास करती हैं। यहां का प्रमुख व्यवसाय खेती करना है। पशुपालन यहां का दूसरा मुख्य व्यवसाय है।

किसान उसे कहते हैं जिसका अपनी जमीन पर खेती करने का अधिकार होता है और वह अपने और अपने परिवार के श्रम के आधार पर सारे कृषि कार्य करता है। उसके उत्पादन का मुख्य उद्‌देश्य अपने परिवार के उपभोग की जरूरतों को पूरा करना, पशुओं के लिए चारा जुटाना और अगली बुवाई के लिए बीज का प्रबन्धन करना होता है। चूंकि वह अपनी जरूरत की

---

1. पं॰ विश्वेश्वरनाथ सेठ : *मारवाड़ का इतिहास*, पृ॰ 13
2. *उपरोक्त।*

सभी वस्तुओं का उत्पादन नहीं कर सकता है, इसलिए पैदावार का एक भाग बेचकर पैसा जुटाता है और अपनी इच्छित वस्तुओं और सेवाओं को प्राप्त कर अपने उपभोग में विविधता लाता है।[3]

चूंकि किसान की न कोई जाति होती है और न कोई धर्म, खेती करने वाला ही किसान कहलाता है। मारवाड़ क्षेत्र में खेती करने वाली मुख्य जातियां जाट, बिश्नाई, कलबी, सीरवी आदि हैं। ये जातियां प्रारम्भिक काल से ही कृषि व पशुपालन पर निर्भर रही हैं।

रियासत काल में किसानों की सामाजिक एवं आर्थिक स्थिति

इस काल में किसानों में संयुक्त परिवार प्रथा प्रचलित थी। दो-तीन पीढ़ी तक एक साथ ही रहते थे। संयुक्त परिवार होने के कारण घर बड़े तथा एक-एक घर में 15-20 तक झोंपे होते थे। बाजरे की रोटी, राब, दही किसानों का मुख्य भोजन था। मोठ की दाल, ग्वारफली, काचर, सांगरी, हिलारिया की सब्जी चाव से खाते थे। आमतौर पर मारवाड़ के किसान शाकाहारी थे।[4] पहनावे में किसान पगड़ी को सबसे अधिक महत्व देते थे। यह सम्मान का प्रतीक मानी जाती थी। घुटनों तक धोती एवं शरीर पर अधोवस्त्र पहनते थे। किसान स्त्रियां भेड़ की ऊन से 'धाबला' बनाकर पहनती थी। वह चटख रंग की कांचली व कुर्ती पहनती थी। महिलाएं गहने की शौकीन थी। वह नख से शिख तक गहने पहनती थी। वह बिछुए, हमेल, झांझर, गुलीबंध, हंसली, कंठी, बोर, झुमका, मोहनमाला, बाली, तुरपती, झुबझुबी, नथ, सेठ आदि जेवर और हाथीदांत की चूड़ियां पहनती थी।[5] पुरुष कानों में गोखरू, मुरकी, लूंग तथा गले में अपने देवता का फूल पहनते थे। गहने को भूखे का आसरा और धाय का श्रृंगार माना जाता था।[6]

हिन्दू धर्म के सोलह संस्कारों में से कुछ संस्कार किसानों में प्रचलित थे। मृतक का आमतौर पर अग्नि संस्कार होता था किन्तु जसनाथी एवं बिश्नोई सम्प्रदाय के लोग शव को गाड़ते थे। मृत्युभोज उस समय का प्रमुख एवं प्रतिष्ठा का अनिवार्य उपक्रम था। मृत्युभोज करना किसान अपना प्रमुख

---

3. जाट समाज सांचोर, स्मारिका 2008 में मकाराम चौधरी का लेख
4. जोगाराम सारण : *बाड़मेर के जाट गौरव*, पृ॰ 14-15
5. *जाट समाज* पत्रिका, आगरा 1998 में नरेन्द्र मूटियाड़ा का लेख
6. जोगाराम सारण : *वहीं*, पृ॰ 15-16

कर्त्तव्य मानते थे। गुड़ एवं लापसी मृत्युभोज का प्रमुख भोजन था। सामान्य रूप से ये किसान दरिद्र होते थे। पर किसी व्यक्ति पर कुछ भगवान की कृपा से कुछ सुविधा हो भी जाए तो वे अपने यहां दावत में लड्डू नहीं बना सकते थे। शक्कर का प्रयोग एवं लड्डू जागीरदार ही बना सकते थे।[7] हलवा 'रावला चौधरी' ही बना सकते थे। मृत्युभोज के अवसर पर किसबियों को दान दिया जाता था। औसर-मौसर में किसानों को ऐसा जकड़ा कि एक-एक औसर-मौसर में बीस-बीस हजार रुपये लगने लगे। रिश्वतों तथा महाजनों के बही खातों से किसान बर्बाद होने लगे।[8] किसान का बच्चा कर्ज में ही जन्म लेता था तथा बूढ़ा होकर कर्ज में ही मरता था।

बाल विवाह उस समय की दूसरी बड़ी कुरीति थी। विवाह योग्य एक लड़की के साथ अन्य नाबालिग लड़कियों का विवाह कर देना आम बात थी। यहां मृत्यु भोज के अवसर पर लड़कियों की शादी करना किसान अपना धर्म समझते थे। किसानों में नाता प्रथा प्रचलित थी। नाता करने वाला विधवा को चूड़ा या जोड़ा पहनाकर अपने घर ले जाता था। देवर अपनी भाभी से नाता कर सकता था। परन्तु नाते में बड़ा भाई छोटे भाई की विधवा को नहीं ला सकता था।[9]

आपसी विवाद पंचायत द्वारा निपटाये जाते थे। जो पंचों का निर्णय नहीं मानता वह जाति से बाहर कर दिया जाता था। किसान महिलाओं में पर्दा प्रथा नहीं थी। उन्होंने महिलाओं को सामाजिक अधिकार दिये। किसान महिला धर्म लोक लाज को आंचल में संजोये खेत खलिहान में स्वच्छंदतापूर्वक काम करती थी। खेत जोतने, बोने अथवा काटने में वह अपने पति-पुत्रों का साथ देती थी। बेटी की पहली संतनोत्पत्ति पीहर में होती थी। पुत्र जन्म को अत्यधिक महत्व दिया जाता था।

किसानों का बिश्नोई सम्प्रदाय जाम्भोजी का अनुयायी था। जाट वीर तेजाजी, जसनाथजी एवं रामदेव जी के भक्त थे। आई माता सिरवी जाति की कुल देवी थी।

---

7. आचार्य गोपाल प्रसाद कौशिक : *चौ॰ मूलचन्द अभिनन्दन ग्रन्थ*, पृ॰ 50
8. लक्ष्मी नारायण मिश्र : *चौ॰ गुल्लाराम स्मृति ग्रंथ*, पृ॰ 202
9. व्यास एवं गहलोत, *राजस्थान की जातियों का सामाजिक एवं आर्थिक जीवन*, पृ॰ 110

अफीम का उस समय अत्यधिक प्रचलन था। इसे शुभ माना जाता था। विवाह, रेहाण, तीज-त्यौहार एवं समझौते में अफीम पिया जाता था। किसानों में शराब का प्रचलन नहीं था। चिलम या हुक्के का अत्यधिक उपयोग किया जाता था। किसानों में छोटे-छोटे आपसी झगड़े मिल-बैठकर सुलझा लिये जाते थे। दंड अपराध के अनुसार दिया जाता था। हत्या, बलात्कार, तलाक या गंभीर अपराध के मामलों में अपराधी को समाज से बहिष्कृत भी किया जाता था। आखातीज किसानों का प्रमुख त्यौहार था। तीन दिन तक बाजरे का खीच और गुड़ की गुड़याणी बनाई जाती थी। आखातीज पर किसान अगले वर्ष के अकाल सुकाल की भविष्यवाणी शगुन देखकर करते थे।[10] होली-दीपावली, गोगा नवमी के त्यौहार भी किसान हर्षोल्लास से मनाते थे। ब्राह्मण लोग किसानों के साथ भेदभाव करते थे। यहां उनकी रसोई का बना भोजन नहीं करते थे बल्कि कच्ची सामग्री-आटा, गुड़, घी, तेल, दाल आदि ग्रहण करते थे।

यहां खेती पूर्ण रूप से वर्षा पर निर्भर थी। इस क्षेत्र में अनिश्चित वर्षा तथा सिंचाई के साधानों के अभाव के कारण एक ही फसल होती थी। व्यवसायी जातियां सुनार, नाई, दर्जी, कुम्हार काम के बदले किसानों से बाजरी लेते थे। यहां पर ऊन व सूत की बुनाई होती थी। सूत से धोती व खत्थे तथा ऊन से लुंकार, बरड़ी, पट्टू, कोट व धाबला बनाये जाते थे।

हर तीसरे व चौथे वर्ष यहां अकाल पड़ता था। नकद रुपये नहीं के बराबर थे। उस समय चांदी के रुपये चलते थे। जागीरदारों द्वारा किसान के शोषण की तो अनंत कथाएं हैं। भाग्य तो उसका दैवाधीन रहा और शरीर के मालिक होते थे राजा, सामंत, साहूकार, अधिकारी, अहलकार, भिक्षुक आदि।[11] फसल काटने तक तो उसके साथ अच्छा व्यवहार रखा जाता और फसल कटकर खलिहान में पंहुचती तो अनाज निकालना भी उसके लिए मुश्किल हो जाता था। कभी कुड़की लेकर महाजन पंहुच जाता तो कभी जागीरदार के कणवारिये।[12]

उस वक्त किसान का कोई धणी-धोरी नहीं था। जागीरदारों ने अन्नदाता की पीठ पर लगान व हासल का भारी बोझ लाद रखा था। दुनिया का पेट पालने

10. जोगाराम सारण : *वही*, पृ० 17
11. लक्ष्मी नारायण मिश्र : *वही*, पृ० 161
12. लक्ष्मी नारायण मिश्र : *वही*, पृ० 200

वाला किसान दाने-दाने को मोहताज था। तन ढकने के लिए कपड़ा नहीं, रहने को छत नहीं, शिक्षा तो दूर की बात, गांवों में पक्के मकान के नाम पर शोषण का प्रतीक रावला गढ़ या बोहरे की हवेली अवश्य दिखती थी।[13]

किसानों की दशा अत्यधिक दयनीय थी एवं उन स्थितियों से उबरने को कोई रास्ता नहीं मिल रहा था। वे सामंतवादी और साम्राज्यवादी भार को अपना भाग्य समझकर ढो रहे थे। किसान क्रमशः अंग्रेज, महाराज व जागीरदारों के तिहरे शोषण के शिकार थे।[14]

जागीरदार स्वयं कोई कार्य नहीं करते थे। वे किसानों को जमीन बटाई पर देते थे। भू-लगान के रूप में पैदावार का एक तिहाई से लेकर आधा भाग तक उनसे लेते थे। बटाई के अलावा किसानों से अनेक प्रकार की लाग-बाग ली जाती थी। लाग-बाग के अतिरिक्त किसानों को बेगार (मुफ्त काम) भी देनी पड़ती थी। जागीरदार के स्वयं के काम के वक्त या जोधपुर से सरकारी अफसरों के आगमन पर किसानों से बेगार अनिवार्य रूप से ली जाती थी।[15]

कुल मिलाकर आजादी से पूर्व रियासत काल में किसान वर्ग सामाजिक रूप से अर्द्ध दास तथा आर्थिक रूप से पंगु था।

चेतना की ओर बढ़ते कदम

मारवाड़ के किसान नेता जब दूसरे राज्यों के लोगों के सम्पर्क में आए तो उन्हें शिक्षा, जागृति जैसी बातें समझ में आई। बलदेव राम मिर्धा, मूलचन्द सियाग, चौधरी रामदान सरीखे किसान जागृति के अग्रदूतों ने शिक्षा का महत्व, अशिक्षित किसानों के समक्ष रखा। मारवाड़ के जोधपुर, नागौर, बाड़मेर, मेड़ता आदि स्थानों पर किसान छात्रावासों की स्थापना की तथा ग्रामीण क्षेत्रों में पाठशालाएं खोली।

इसी समय अक्तूबर, 1925 में कार्तिक पूर्णिमा को पुष्कर में अखिल भारतीय जाट महासभा का वार्षिक जलसा हुआ जिसकी अध्यक्षता भरतपुर महाराजा किशनसिंह ने की। इस जलसे में युक्त प्रांत (अब उत्तर प्रदेश),

---

13. भागीरथ सिंह नेण : *किसान केसरी बलदेव राम मिर्धा*, पृ॰ 15
14. डॉ॰ बृजकिशोर शर्मा : *राजस्थान में किसान एवं आदिवासी आन्दोलन*, पृ॰ 118
15. डॉ॰ रामगोपाल शर्मा : *राजस्थान में प्रजामण्डल आन्दोलन*, भाग-2, पृ॰ 55

पंजाब, दिल्ली के अलावा राजपूताना के हर कोने से जाट सम्मिलित हुए। इस जलसे का जो चमत्कारिक प्रभाव जाटों पर पड़ा, वह यह था कि वे हीन नहीं हैं और न उन्हें हीन इरादे रखने चाहिएँ।[16] मारवाड़ में किसान आन्दोलन का नेतृत्व जाटों ने किया। शिक्षा के प्रचार एंव किसानों को शिक्षित करने के लिए 4 अप्रैल 1927 ई॰ को चौधरी गुल्लाराम के रातानाड़ा स्थित मकान में जाट बोर्डिंग हाउस की स्थापना की।[17] इसके बाद बाड़मेर, नागौर, मेड़ता व अन्य स्थानों पर किसान छात्रावासों की स्थापना की गई।

इधर जिस समय किसान नेता शिक्षा के प्रचार में लगे हुए थे, उस समय जोधपुर राज्य में जागीरदारों के जुल्म बढ़ रहे थे।[18] चंडालिया, मलार, भुण्डाना, डाबडा आदि अनेक स्थानों पर किसानों की हत्या कर दी गई। उनके घरों को लूटकर आग लगा दी गई लेकिन किसानों ने संघर्ष जारी रखा।

26 जनवरी 1950 को संविधान लागू किया गया। मिर्धा बलदेव राम के नेतृत्व में किसानों ने जागीरदारी प्रथा को खत्म करने का आन्दोलन जारी रखा। कांग्रेस नेता गोविन्द वल्लभ पंत एवं मारवाड़ किसान सभा के अध्यक्ष बलदेवराम मिर्धा के बीच समझौता के समय किसान सभा ने कांग्रेस में विलय की सहमति दी, तो कांग्रेस ने प्रथम आम चुनाव से पूर्व जागीरदारी प्रथा समाप्त करने का निर्णय लिया।[19] इसके तहत 15 नवम्बर 1951 को 'राजस्थान भूमि सुधार एंव जागीरों का पुनर्गठन अधिनियम 1952' राजस्थान गजट में प्रकाशित कर राष्ट्रपति को स्वीकृति के लिए भेज दिया, जो 18 फरवरी 1952 को लागू हुआ। इसके बाद भूमि के मालिक किसान हो गये।

मारवाड़ में किसानों की वर्तमान सामाजिक एवं आर्थिक स्थिति

देश की आजादी के पश्चात् अन्य लोगों की भाँति मारवाड़ के किसानों को राजनीतिक रूप से वोट की ताकत मिल गई। उन्हें अपना जनप्रतिनिधि चुनने का अधिकार मिल गया। नाथूराम मिर्धा, परसराम मदेरणा, पूनमचन्द

16. डॉ॰ विक्रमादित्य चौधरी : *राजस्थान में किसान आन्दोलन*, पृ॰ 101
17. रिपोर्ट श्री जाट बोर्डिंग हाउस जोधपुर, पृ॰ 1-2, *चौधरी मूलचन्द अभिनन्दन ग्रंथ*, पृ॰ 114-115
18. डॉ॰ विक्रमादित्य चौधरी : *राजस्थान में किसान आन्दोलन*, पृ॰ 106
19. महेश कुमार चौधरी : *मालाणी के महामना चौधरी रामदान*, पृ॰ 84-85, रघुवीर सिंह एवं यशोराज शास्त्री : *श्री बलदेव राम मिर्धा*, पृ॰ 89-92

बिश्नोई, भगराज चौधरी जैसे कई किसान प्रतिनिधि राजस्थान विधानसभा व भारत की संसद में किसानों की आवाज उचित मंच से उठाते रहे शिक्षा के क्षेत्र में भी किसान वर्ग ने आशातीत सफलता प्राप्त की है। किसान वर्ग से ताल्लुकात रखने वाले कई युवा भारतीय प्रशासनिक सेवाओं एवं राजस्थान प्रशासनिक सेवाओं में चयनित हुए। सवाईसिंह चौधरी (नागौर), लाभुराम सियाग (बाड़मेर), जोगाराम जांगिड (बाड़मेर), आरूषि चौधरी (नागौर), जोगेन्द्र पूनिया (बाड़मेर) भारतीय प्रशासनिक सेवाओं में चयनित होकर किसान वर्ग की बढ़ती शिक्षा की साख भर रहे हैं।

सामाजिक रूप से किसानों में काफी बदलाव आया है। अबाध रूप से बढ़ती जनसंख्या पर भी काफी हद तक रोक लगी है। किसान वर्ग के लोग छोटे परिवार के महत्व को समझ रहे है किन्तु बाल विवाह, मृत्युभोज जैसी कुरीतियां मारवाड़ के किसानों में बदस्तूर जारी हैं। बाल विवाह से उत्पन्न बेमेल विवाह ने तलाक की संख्याओं को बढ़ाया है। रिश्तों का टूटना आम बात हो गई है जो सामाजिक ढांचे को बिगाड़ रहा है। शिक्षा के स्तर, सुंदरता, अभिमान और धन के कारण रिश्ते-विवाह धड़ल्ले से बिखर रहे हैं। सामाजिक व्यवस्था आधुनिकता के सामने बेबस नजर आ रही है। सरकार द्वारा सामाजिक पंचायती व्यवस्था को अलोकतांत्रिक और असंवैधानिक मानने की वजह से लोगों में समाज का भय खत्म हो गया है।

मृत्युभोज की बीमारी अभी मिटी नहीं है बल्कि और अधिक खर्चीली हो गई है। औसर-मौसर के अवसर पर 10 लाख रुपये तक का खर्चा होने लगा है। हालांकि समाज सुधारकों यथा राजस्थान जाट महासभा के संरक्षक डॉ॰ ज्ञानप्रकाश पिलानिया आदि के सद्प्रयासों से इसमें सुधार अवश्य हुआ है। तीन-तीन दिन तक होने वाला मृत्युभोज एक दिन में सिमटकर रह गया है।

मृत्युभोज न करने, न भोज खाने को किसान समाज के कई लोगों ने खेमा बाबा के मेले के अवसर पर बायतु में हाथ में गंगाजल लेकर शपथ ली थी।[20] इसी प्रकार समय-समय पर स्थानीय स्तर पर भी जातीय पंचायतें मृत्युभोज और बाल विवाह न करने के पक्ष में फैसले सुना चुकी हैं। ग्राम गरल इसका जीता जागता उदाहरण है।[21]

---

20. *जाट समाज* पत्रिका, 1999 का अंक
21. *राजस्थान पत्रिका* एवं *दैनिक भास्कर* का अंक

दहेज प्रथा, कन्या भ्रूण हत्या, नाता प्रथा किसान वर्ग में नये कोढ़ के रूप में अपने पांव पसार चुकी हैं। घरेलू सामान तक सीमित दहेज प्रथा का लेखा लाखों को पार कर चुका है। धन के लालची कीड़े कम दहेज लाने की वजह से बहुओं को परेशान करते हैं। आत्महत्या या हत्या की घटनाओं में दहेज के कारण वृद्धि हुई है। कभी बालिका को देवी का अवतार मानने वाला किसान वर्ग कन्या भ्रूण हत्या की काली करतूतों की ओर कदम रख चुका है। हालांकि बालिका शिक्षा में जबरदस्त बढ़ोतरी हुई है। पिछले दो दशकों से बालिकाओं ने शिक्षा और सह-शैक्षिक गतिविधियों में अपार प्रगति की है। आरुषि चौधरी (नागौर), विधि चौधरी (नागौर) भारतीय प्रशासनिक सेवा में तथा सविता टी॰ चौधरी (पाली) राजस्थान प्रशासनिक सेवा में चयनित होकर औरों के लिए प्रेरणा स्रोत बनी हैं। शिक्षक, एएनएम आदि पदों पर तो किसान वर्ग की बालिकाओं की बाढ़ सी आ गई है।

नशा प्रथा में अफीम-डोडा के साथ युवा वर्ग में शराब की लत बढ़ी है। धूम्रपान, गुटखा-जरदा, पान-मसाला के प्रयोग में वृद्धि चिन्तनीय है। हालांकि समय-समय पर इन नशों के खिलाफ जन-जागरण अभियान चलाये जाते रहे हैं। नशा छुड़वाने के लिए शिविरों के आयोजन भी किये जाते रहे हैं।

किसान वर्ग के लोगों की संस्कृति में भी बदलाव आया है। वेशभूषा में धोती-साफे का स्थान पैन्ट-शर्ट ने ले लिया है। साफा तो समाप्त होने के कगार पर है।

किसान कार्यों में मशीनों का प्रभाव बढ़ा है। बैल-ऊंट का स्थान ट्रैक्टर ने ले लिया है। मशीनों के कारण कार्य तेजी से होने लगे हैं। किसान के सिर से जागीरदार का भार तो उतर गया है किन्तु साहूकार के बोझ से अभी भी दबा हुआ है। अकाल अभी भी मारवाड़ का पीछा नहीं छोड़ रहा है। कृषि उत्पादन के लिए जितना परिश्रम किया जाता है उसके अनुपात में यहां पैदावार और आमदनी नहीं है। आज किसान शोषित है, बेबस है, खेती में अधमरा हो गया है।[22]

खेती पर जनसंख्या का जो दबाव बढ़ा है, उसका नकारात्मक परिणाम यह हुआ है कि लोगों का खेती से मोह भंग हो रहा है। इसके कारण किसानों के जीवन स्तर में गुणात्मक सुधार न आना, सरकार के योजनाकारों का सही

22. *तेजाजी एक्सप्रेस,* मार्च 2003

योजना न बनाना आदि है।[23] हमारे देश में किसानों एवं गांवों को प्रबुद्धजन आवश्यक बुराई मानते हैं। किसानों एवं गांवों से उन्हें कोई हमदर्दी और लगाव नहीं होता है। मजबूरी में किसान उनकी आधारभूत आवश्यकताओं की पूर्ति का साधन है। किसानों को आधे दिन पानी, बिजली, खाद, बीज के लिए लाठियां झेलनी पड़ती है। कृषि फसल बीमा की राशि भी समय पर नहीं मिलती है।[24]

पूरी कृषि व्यवस्था मौसम पर निर्भर होने की वजह से सूखा, अतिवृष्टि, पाला, कीट-प्रकोप और शीतलहर का शिकार होती रहती है। जिसकी वजह से अर्थव्यवस्था तो प्रभावित होती है, साथ ही किसान की आर्थिक स्थिति भी डगमगा जाती है। प्राकृतिक आपदाओं, कीट व्याधि की वजह से फसलें चौपट हो जाती हैं। ऐसे में किसान का आत्मविश्वास टूटता ही है। वहीं छोटे किसान सेठ साहूकारों के चंगुल में फंस कर और अधिक कर्जदार हो जाते हैं।[25] किसानों को न तो समय पर बीज और बुवाई के लिए कृषि ऋण उपलब्ध हो पाता है और न ही पर्याप्त समय पर विद्युत, किसानों को न तो बीमा सेवाओं का पर्याप्त लाभ मिल पाता है न ही उन्हें मानक स्तर के बीज खाद, कीटनाशक, सिंचाई के लिए पर्याप्त बिजली व डीजल मिल पाता है।[26]

मारवाड़ का किसान सदियों से तिहरी गुलामी में पिसता रहा है। देश में मारवाड़ रियासत के विलय के साथ ही किसान राजनीतिक रूप से आजाद हो गया। राजस्थान टिनेन्सी एक्ट के प्रावधानों के तहत वह अपनी जोत का मालिक बन गया किन्तु किसान की आर्थिक दशा में क्या सुधार हुआ, यह विचारणीय विषय है। छोटी होती जोत, बंजर भूमि, वर्षा आधारित खेती, पर्याप्त पानी व बिजली की उपलब्धता न होना, समय पर बीज, खाद एवं बुवाई के लिए पर्याप्त ऋण उपलब्ध न हो पाना, किसान की दुर्गति का कारण है। रही सही कसर सेठ साहूकार निकाल देते है। किसान कर्ज तले दबता चला जाता है।

---

23. *जाट परिवेश*, सितम्बर 2012, पृ॰ 23
24. *जाट एक्सप्रेस*, 25 जून 2010
25. *किसान की कलम*, मार्च 2012, पृ॰ 2
26. *किसान की कलम*, मार्च 2012, पृ॰ 2

किसान को अपनी पैदावार का वाजिब दाम नहीं मिलना भी गंभीर समस्या है। जब सोने का भाव तीन हजार रुपये प्रति तोला था, तब बाजरे का मूल्य 300 रुपये प्रति क्विंटल था। आज सोने का भाव 36,000 रुपये प्रति तोला है तो बाजरे का भाव 1,400 रुपये प्रति क्विंटल है। सोने का भाव 18 गुना बढ़ गया परन्तु किसान की उपज बाजरे का भाव साढ़े चार गुना ही बढ़ा। यह किसानों के साथ धोखा नहीं तो क्या है? पिछले वर्ष के अन्त में ग्वार का भाव 30,000 रुपये प्रति क्विंटल हो गया था चूंकि किसानों ने सारा ग्वार कोइ व्यवस्था न होने के कारण पहले ही 4,000 से 8,000 रुपये प्रति क्विंटल के हिसाब से बेच दिया। सारा मुनाफा दलाल और बिचौलिये ले गये। दूसरे साल मारवाड़ के किसानों ने ग्वार की बम्पर खेती की। किसानों ने बीज के लिए ग्वार 350 रुपये प्रति किलो की दर से खरीदा। लटाई के बाद किसान ग्वार को कृषि मंडी ले गया तो व्यापारियों ने उसे 5,000 से 7,000 रुपये प्रति क्विंटल के हिसाब से ही खरीदा। अब किसान स्वयं को ठगा सा महसूस कर रहा था।

आज के समय में एक उद्योगपति पांच पैसे में तैयार होने वाली सुई की कीमत स्वयं निर्धारित करता है, फिर पांच माह तक सर्दी, गर्मी, वर्षा में अपने हाड़ गलाने वाले किसान को अपनी जिंस की कीमत का निर्धारण करने का अधिकार क्यों नहीं ? उसकी पैदावार का मूल्य निर्धारण कृषि मंडी में व्यापारी करता है तो किसान आर्थिक रूप से समृद्ध कैसे होगा?

किसानों के जो जनप्रतिनिधि किसानों की आवाज व्यवस्थापिका में उठाने के वादे कर वोट मांगकर संसद या विधानसभा में जाते हैं वे वहां जाकर किसान को भूल जाते हैं। किसान पर महंगाई की मार बढ़ती जा रही है। किसान को पैदावार का वाजिब दाम नहीं मिल पा रहा है।

किसानों की आर्थिक व सामाजिक दशा सुधारने हेतु सुझाव

1. किसान की परिभाषा तय की जाए। किसान वह है जो अपनी जमीन को स्वयं जोतकर अन्न पैदा करता है।[27] करोड़ों की फैक्ट्रियों के मालिक, बड़े अधिकारी, राजनेता व धर्मगुरुओं के नाम हजारों बीघा जमीनें हैं, जिन्हें यह भी पता नहीं कि मेरा खेत कौनसा है ? वे भी कृषि आय के नाम मिलने वाली छूट का लाभ उठा लेते हैं।

---

27. रामनारायण चौधरी : *किसानों के कंस*, पृ॰ 106

2. कृषि में काम आने वाले सामान-बीज, खाद, औजार, कीटनाशकों पर विकसित राष्ट्रों में मिलने वाली सुविधाएं दी जाएँ। इन पर सब्सिडी बाजार मूल्य पर दी जाए न कि मुद्रित मूल्य पर।

3. कृषि भूमि पर खेत जोतने वाले का मालिकाना हक हो। जागीरदारी या जमींदारी प्रथा नहीं हो। इससे देश में बेरोजगारी घटेगी। किसानों को शोषण से मुक्ति मिलेगी और उत्पादन भी बढ़ेगा।

4. कृषि जिन्सों की कीमतों पर सरकार का नियंत्रण हो, न कि मण्डी के दलालों एवं व्यापारियों का। किसान को लागत मूल्य में 25 प्रतिशत मुनाफा जोड़कर जिन्स का मूल्य निर्धारित किया जाए।

5. किसान के पूरे परिवार का बीमा हो। बीमा व्यवस्था को सरल बनाया जाए ताकि समय व धन की बचत हो।

6. फसल का बीमा इस प्रकार से किया जाए कि इसे प्राकृतिक आपदा की स्थिति में भी किसी प्रकार का नुकसान न झेलना पड़े। वर्तमान में फसल बीमा योजना भीख योजना के समान है।[28]

7. नौकरशाही पर लगाम लगे। वे अन्नदाता से मधुर शब्दों में बात करें। शिकायत के लिए रजिस्टर का संधारण कर पावती रसीद किसान को दें।

8. कृषि से सम्बन्धित चीजों कृषि उपकरण, बीज, खाद की व्यवस्था स्थानीय स्तर पर करायें। मारवाड़ जैसे इलाकों में जिला मुख्यालय पर पहुंचने के लिए सैकड़ों किलोमीटर का फासला तय करना पड़ता है। जैसे बाड़मेर जिला मुख्यालय पर पहुँचने के लिए डोली, अराबा के किसानों को 200 किमी॰ तथा बाखासर के किसानों को 175 किमी॰ का सफर तय करना पड़ता है। इसके लिए जिलों का पुनर्गठन कर छोटे जिले बनाये जायें।

9. व्यापारियों की मनमानी पर अंकुश लगे। एक फिल्म अभिनेता या क्रिकेट स्टार ट्रेक्टर का विज्ञापन कर करोड़ों रुपये कमा लेता है। यह रकम उस उत्पाद में जोड़कर किसान से वसूल की जाती है। इस पर रोक लगाई जानी चाहिए।

---

28. *वही*, पृ॰ 108

10. किसान वर्ग शिक्षा पर ध्यान दें। शिक्षा रोजगारपरक होनी चाहिए। तकनीकी संस्थानों विशेषकर ग्राम-सम्बंधी तकनीकी शिक्षा की अधिकाधिक स्थापना हो। बालिका शिक्षा पर विशेष ध्यान हो।

11. परम्परागत खेती एवं खेती के तरीकों के स्थान पर नई फसलें, व्यापारिक फसलें तथा आधुनिक तरीके से खेती को बढ़ावा देने की व्यवस्था हो।

12. सामाजिक कुरीतियों को खत्म कराने के लिए सरकार कारगर उपाय करे। बाल-विवाह, मृत्युभोज, दहेज, कन्या भ्रूण हत्या पर व्यापक पैमाने पर जनजागृति अभियान चलाए और कानून का कठोरता से पालन कराया जाये।

13. नशा, अपराधीकरण पर समाज व सरकार लगाम कसे।

14. किसान उन जनप्रतिनिधियों को चुनकर भेजें जो किसान के हित की बात करें।

15. अंधविश्वास को त्यागकर विज्ञान की ओर बढ़ें।

16. किसान अपनी सांस्कृतिक विरासत को बनाए रखने का प्रयास करें।

17. छोटे-मोटे झगड़े आपस में मिल-जुलकर सुलझाएं।

14

विधवा पुनर्विवाह करवाने में जाति-पंचायतों की भूमिका : पश्चिमी राजपूताना के विशेष संदर्भ में एक अध्ययन (1850-1940)

सुमेस्ता

19वीं शताब्दी में ढहते हुए मध्यकालीन सामंतीय ढाँचे व अंग्रेजों के साथ सन्धियों से राजपूत शासकों व सामंतों की आर्थिक स्थिति निश्चित रूप से कमजोर हो चुकी थी। परन्तु फिर भी राजपूत अपनी तथाकथित शान को बरकरार रखने के लिए इस स्थिति को जानते हुए भी समझने की कोशिश नहीं कर रहे थे, और बहुत सी कुरीतियों के शिकार भी थे। दूसरी तरफ समाज के अन्य सामाजिक वर्गों की आर्थिक स्थिति तो अत्यधिक खराब थी। लगातार पड़ते अकाल व सूखे से पहले से ही कमजोर आर्थिक स्थिति के कारण पश्चिमी राजपूताना-बीकानेर, जैसलमेर और जोधपुर राज्य के विभिन्न सामाजिक वर्गों की आर्थिक हालत और भी खराब हो चुकी थी। ऐसे में तथाकथित निम्न जातियों (जाट, गूजर, माली, रेबारी, सुनार इत्यादि) के लिए अपना जीवनयापन करना अत्यधिक कठिन हो गया था। साथ ही उनमें अनेकों कुरीतियों यथा विधवा विवाह का न होना, बाल विवाह, बेमेल विवाह, स्त्रियों की खरीद-फरोख्त, इत्यादि ने घर कर लिया था। समीचीन है कि इन कुरीतियों के केन्द्र में महिलाएँ ही शिकार रही।

इस माहौल में 20वीं सदी के प्रारम्भ में विभिन्न जातियों में जाति पंचायतों का गठन हुआ, जिन्होंने अपनी-अपनी जातियों में समाज सुधार के लिए प्रयास किये। इन जातीय सभाओं में मुख्य रूप से अखिल भारतीय चारण सभा, अग्रवाल हितकारिणी सभा, मीणा राजपूत महासभा, प्रान्तीय कायस्थ सभा, वैश्य महासभा, राजस्थान जाट क्षत्रिय महासभा, मारवाड़ जाट कृषक सुधारक

सभा इत्यादि ने 20वीं शताब्दी के आरम्भ में राजस्थान में विभिन्न जातियों में सुधार के प्रयास किये। इन जातीय सभाओं ने अन्य सामाजिक कुरीतियों के उन्मूलन के साथ-साथ विधवा पुनर्विवाह पर भी बल दिया। परन्तु इसका अर्थ यह नहीं है कि 20वीं सदी से पहले पश्चिमी राजपूताना में जातीय पंचों व पंचायतों की कोई भूमिका नहीं थी। विभिन्न जातियों में जाति पंचों ने समय-समय पर अपनी जातियों में दखल बनाकर रखी हुई थी तथा यहाँ तक कि कुछ जातियों में विधवा-पुनर्विवाह प्रचलन में भी था तो उसमें इन पंच व पंचायतों की अहम भूमिका होती थी।

इस शोध-पत्र द्वारा विवेच्य काल में पश्चिमी राजपूताना में विभिन्न जातियों में विधवाओं की स्थिति, जाति-पंचायतों एवं जातीय सभाओं द्वारा विधवा पुनर्विवाह करवाने के लिए लोगों को जाग्रत करने के तरीकों व विभिन्न विधवा आश्रमों के माध्यम से विधवा विवाह करवाने में जाति पंचायतों की भूमिका का अध्ययन करने का प्रयास किया गया है।

विधवाओं की स्थिति

विदित है कि विधवाओं की स्थिति केवल पश्चिमी राजपूताना में ही नहीं बल्कि राजपूताना के सभी राज्यों में अत्यधिक शोचनीय थी। समाज की तथाकथित उच्च जातियों (राजपूत, ब्राह्मण, महाजन इत्यादि) में विधवा पुनर्विवाह पूर्णतः प्रतिबन्धित था और विधवाओं का जीवन किसी नरक से कम नहीं था।

यह जानना महत्त्वपूर्ण है कि समाज में बाल विवाह व बेमेल विवाह का प्रचलन था। अतः स्वाभाविक था कि जहाँ कम उम्र की बालिकाओं का विवाह होता था तो वहां विधवाओं की संख्या भी अधिक होती थी। तीन से चार वर्ष की उम्र तक अधिकांश बालिकाओं का विवाह तय कर दिया जाता था। कई बार तो छः महीने की लड़की की सगाई तय कर दी जाती थी।[1] ब्रिटिश रिकार्ड्स के अनुसार 1923 ई० में विभिन्न आयु वर्ग की विधवा स्त्रियों की स्थिति निम्नानुसार थी[2]-

---

1. *जोधपुर सनद परवाना बही,* न० वि० सं० 1832, पृ० 96, राजस्थान राज्य अभिलेखागार (इसके बाद रा० रा० अ०), बीकानेर
2. *आर्य मार्तण्ड,* 24 जुलाई 1923, रा० रा० अ०, बीकानेर

आयु	विधवाओं की संख्या
1 माह से 12 तक आयु वर्ग की विधवाएँ	17,014
1 से 2 वर्ष तक आयु वर्ग की विधवाएँ	859
2 से 3 वर्ष तक आयु वर्ग की विधवाएँ	1807
3 से 4 वर्ष तक आयु वर्ग की विधवाएँ	8273
4 से 5 वर्ष तक आयु वर्ग की विधवाएँ	17,703
5 से 10 वर्ष तक आयु वर्ग की विधवाएँ	84,240
10 से 15 वर्ष तक आयु वर्ग की विधवाएँ	2,23,032

1941 की जनगणना रिपोर्ट के अनुसार राजपूताना में 9500 लड़कियों का विवाह 5 वर्ष या उससे भी कम उम्र में कर दिया जाता था।[3] उच्च वर्ग में 19वीं सदी के उतरार्द्ध व 20वीं सदी के तृतीय दशक तक स्थिति लगभग यही रही। इन वर्गों में विधवा से विवाह करने पर हत्या तक करवा दी जाती थी। उदाहरणत: जोधपुर के राजा मानसिंह के गुरु आयस लक्ष्मीनाथ ने पारिवारिक प्रतिष्ठा के विरुद्ध रतीराम (लक्ष्मीनाथ का शिष्य) द्वारा विधवा से विवाह करने पर उसकी हत्या करवा दी।[4]

तथाकथित निम्न जातियों में विधवाओं की स्थिति तथा विधवा पुनर्विवाह प्रचलन में जाति पंचों व पंचायतों की भूमिका

दूसरी तरफ यदि तथाकथित निम्न जातियों की महिलाओं व विधवाओं की स्थिति का जायज़ा लिया जाये तो यह कहना गलत नहीं होगा कि इन सामाजिक वर्गों में भी महिलाओं की स्थिति इतनी अच्छी नहीं थी। परन्तु इनमें विधवा पुनर्विवाह प्रचलन में था। जिसमें निश्चित रूप से जाति पंचों की भूमिका अहम होती थी। जो विशेष कारणों से अपनी-अपनी जातियों में विधवा पुनर्विवाह करवाते थे।[5]

---

3. मारवाड़ मरदुमशुमारी रिपोर्ट, 1941, पृ॰ XI-XVII, रा॰रा॰अ॰, बीकानेर
4. राजपूताना एजेन्सी रिकार्ड न॰ 228, फाइल न॰ 14 सी, जोधपुर 1841 कलक्शन न॰ 7, पृ॰ 186-89, रा॰रा॰अ॰, बीकानेर
5. *सनद परवाना बही जोधपुर* न॰, वि॰सं॰ 1823, हस्तलिखित, रा॰रा॰अ॰, बीकानेर, कागद री बही बीकानेर न॰ 6 वि॰ सं॰ 1840, हस्तलिखित, रा॰रा॰अ॰, बीकानेर, मरदुमशुमारी रिपोर्ट, मारवाड़ सन् 1891 ई॰, रा॰रा॰अ॰, बीकानेर

राजस्थान राज्य अभिलेखागार में उपलब्ध कागज की बहियों व सनद बहियों से पता चलता है कि लौकिक भाषा में इसे 'नाता', 'पल्लै लगाई', 'घर में घालना', 'गांठ बँधई', 'चूड़ी पहराई' इत्यादि नामों से जाना जाता था।[6] 'पल्लै लगाई' प्रथा में विवाहिता को देवर के साथ ओढ़नी ओढ़ाकर व चूड़ी पहनाकर सम्मान सहित पुनर्विवाह किया जाता था।[7] नाता प्रथा में स्त्री स्वयं की इच्छा से पति के होते हुए भी, उसमें कोई शारीरिक दोष होने पर पुनर्विवाह कर सकती थी।[8] घर में घालना प्रथा में कोई भी व्यक्ति किसी भी विवाहिता स्त्री को जानबूझकर अपने घर में रख लेता था।[9]

पुनर्विवाह की उक्त प्रथा जाति पंचों द्वारा नारी को एकाकी कष्टपूर्ण वैधव्य जीवन का परित्याग कर उसके जीवन को सामान्य बनाने व समाज में व्यवस्था कायम रखने के लिए बनाई गई एक वैकल्पिक व्यवस्था थी।[10] 'नाता' प्रथा के नियमों की अनुपालना करवाने व समाज में उत्पन्न वैवाहिक विवादों का निवारण करने में जाति पंचायतों की अहम भूमिका थी। इन नियमों का उल्लंघन करने पर भिन्न-भिन्न प्रकार के दण्डनीय प्रावधान थे, यथा घर ज़ब्त कर लेना, न्यात से बाहर कर देना, बिरादरी को भोजन करवाना, अर्थदण्ड इत्यादि।[11]

इसके अलावा जाति-पंचायतें विधवा पुनर्विवाह में जो सबसे महत्त्वपूर्ण कार्य करती था वह थी स्त्रियों के अधिकारों व सम्मान की रक्षा करना, व उनके जीवनयापन की व्यवस्था करवाना। कोई भी पीड़िता अपनी बिरादरी की पंचायत के सामने अपना पक्ष रखकर न्याय की मांग कर सकती थी।[12] पंचायत इसे सुलझाने का पूरा प्रयास करती थी।

---

6. *कागदों की बही बीकानेर,* वि॰स॰ 1840, न॰ 7, सनद के कागद, रा॰रा॰अ॰, बीकानेर
7. *कागद री बही बीकानेर,* न॰ 13, वि॰सं॰ 1861, पृ॰ 13बी व 26बी, रा॰रा॰अ॰, बीकानेर
8. *कागद री बही बीकानेर,* न॰ 12, वि॰सं॰ 1859, पृ॰ 208ए, रा॰रा॰अ॰, बीकानेर
9. *पेशकशी रे लेखे री बही,* बीकानेर, वि॰स॰ 1833, पृ॰ 125, रा॰रा॰अ॰, बीकानेर
10. मरदुमशुमारी रिपोर्ट मारवाड़, सन् 1891 ई॰, रा॰रा॰अ॰, बीकानेर
11. मरदुमशुमारी रिपोर्ट, 1891, पृ॰ 42-43, रा॰रा॰अ॰, बीकानेर
12. *कागद री बही नं॰ 10,* वि॰सं॰ 1854, पृ॰ 147ए, रा॰रा॰अ॰, बीकानेर-सहीराम चौधरी आसा चौखाणी सिंहाग जोग भातुमल मीग रे गोसु सहारण रे परिणीयो थो सु, पछै बड़े भाई री बहु घर में घाल लीवी, ईय न काढ़ दीवी, सु आपरे पीहर रहती, हमे ईयरा माँ-बाप घक (मर) गया, सु पुकार आई छे हमे इये ने घर में मेली (साथ) राखे, रोटी कपड़ो दीजो, न दीयो तो तलब हुसी, गुनगारी लागसी सावण वद-1

इस प्रकार के विवाह में अपनी स्वयं की पत्नी होते हुए भी देवर अपनी भाभी से 'नाता' कर लेता था तो ऐसी स्थिति में अगर उसकी प्रथम पत्नी को कष्ट होता था तो जाति पंचायतें उसके पति पर अर्थदण्ड लगाकर उसे चेतावनी देती थीं। ऐसा न करने पर स्त्री को अन्यत्र 'नाता' करने की छूट दे दी जाती थी।[13]

इस प्रकार के विवाहों में जाति-पंचायतों की भूमिका बहुत अधिक रुचिपूर्ण लगती है। जाति-पंचायतें इतनी उदारता से कार्य करती थीं कि कुछ विशेष परिस्थितियों में स्त्रियों द्वारा 'बैर'[14] की राशि चुका देने पर उन्हें स्वतन्त्र रहने या अन्यत्र कहीं स्वयं अपनी मर्जी से नाता करने की छूट प्रदान कर देती थीं।[15]

जाति पंचायतें 'बैर' की रकम निर्धारित करते समय उस परिवार की आर्थिक स्थिति का ख्याल रखती थी।[16] पंचायत के मुखिया लोग नाते की वैधता के रूप में फारगती का कागज भी तैयार करके देते थे, जो बैर की रकम चुकाने, बाल-बच्चे, धन-दौलत व अन्य सम्पत्ती के ज़िक्र का बतौर सबूत होता था।[17]

यदि उस महिला के पूर्व पति से बच्चा होता था तो उसे जाति-पंचायतों के निर्णयानुसार पूर्व पति के घर ही भेज दिया जाता था[18] तथा धन-सम्पत्ति

---

13. शर्मा, जी॰एन॰ : *राजपूत स्टडीज,* आगरा, पृ॰ 175
14. बैर एक प्रकार की क्षतिपूर्ति राशि जो मुश्त पति के परिवार वालों से सम्बन्ध विच्छेद के रूप में दी जाती थी। इसे पंचायत व पूर्व पति का परिवार आपस में बाँट लेते थे।
15. *सनद परवाना बही* न॰, वि॰स॰ 1832, पृ॰ 7, रा॰रा॰अ॰, बीकानेर
16. *कागद री बही* न॰ 30, वि॰सं॰ 1881, पृ॰ 117, कागद बही न॰ 12, वि॰स॰ 1859, पृ॰ 70, रा॰रा॰अ॰, बीकानेर

    1-गाँव पांचू रे जाट मेधे गोंधू रे नाते रा 411-देसर सर रे जाखड़ नातो कीयो तेरे कागद रा फागुण सुद 6 नायवो तेरी रे चण्ड जीवण री बेटी चण्ड रूपले रें पलै लगाई तेरी रीठ रा 10 आना खजांची साहचन्द रे जमा लागा चैतसुद-7 (कागद, बही न॰ 4)
17. मरदुमशुमारी रिपोर्ट, सन् 1891, पृ॰ 44, रा॰रा॰अ॰, बीकानेर
18. *फॉरेन एण्ड पॉलिटिकल कन्सलटेशन,* मई 1877, कॉन्स न॰ 273-80, राष्ट्रीय अभिलेखागार (इसके बाद एन॰ए॰आई॰), नई दिल्ली

पर मालिकाना हक इस स्थिति में उसका (उक्त नाता करने वाली स्त्री का) नये पति के घर में ही होता था।

यह प्रथा राजपूतों के एक थोक में भी मिलती है जिन्हें नातारायत राजपूत कहा जाता था तथा इनके यहाँ नाता 'करेवा' नाम से जाना जाता था। कहावत भी है कि "नातारायत की तीजी पीढ़ी गढ़ चढ़े।"[19] राजस्थानी बातों में भी राजपूतों द्वारा विधवा से विवाह के प्रसंग मिलते हैं।[20]

इसके अलावा नाथों में भी पुनर्विवाह होता था।[21] इससे स्पष्ट है कि समाज सुधारक संस्थाओं जैसे आर्य समाज आदि का प्रभाव अब उच्च जाति में भी होने लगा था।

20वीं सदी के पूर्वार्द्ध में विभिन्न जातीय सभाओं की स्थापना तथा विधवा पुनर्विवाह

19वीं सदी के अंतिम दशकों में आर्य समाज व वाल्टरकृत राजपूत हितकारिणी सभा (1888 ई० में) के द्वारा राजपूतों व सामन्तों तथा चारणों में सामाजिक कुरीतियों को दूर करने के प्रयास किये गये। इसी का अनुसरण करते हुए विभिन्न जातियों के कुछ प्रबुद्ध लोगों ने जातियों की सभाओं का गठन किया व सामाजिक कुरीतियों के विरुद्ध उन्हें जागरूक करने के प्रयास किए।

1921 ई० में स्थापित अखिल भारतीय चारण सभा ने राजपूताना सहित गुजरात, मालवा व कच्छ क्षेत्र में चारण समुदाय के लड़के-लड़कियों को शिक्षित करने, विधवा पुनर्विवाह करने की मंजूरी दी तथा साथ ही टीका व रीत, मृत्युभोज इत्यादि अन्य सामाजिक कुरीतियों को प्रतिबन्धित करने का ऐलान किया।[22] उपरोक्त उद्देश्यों की प्राप्ति के लिए प्रान्तीय स्तर पर गठित

---

19. मरदुमशुमारी रिपोर्ट, मारवाड़ की कौमों का इतिहास, ई० 1891, पृ० 44। गहलोत, जगदीश, मारवाड़ राज्य का इतिहास, महाराजा मानसिंह पुस्तक प्रकाशन, जोधपुर, 1991, 12 मई जोधपुर स्थापना दिवस, पृ० 355-56
20. सिखरो बहैलवै गयो रहे (हस्त प्रति० अ०सं०पु० बीकानेर) (अनूप संस्कृत पुस्तकालय) सोनगिरै मालदे री (हस्त प्रति), अ०स०पु०, बीकानेर
21. मारवाड़ सेन्सस रिपोर्ट भाग-2, पृ० 245, 251, राजस्थान हिस्ट्री कांग्रेस, वाल्यूम XIV, बीकानेर सेंसस 1984
22. *चारण त्रैमासिक पत्रिका,* वि०स० 1997/सन् 1940 ई०, नं० 2, पृ० 1-5, वि०सं० 1996/1941 ई०, पृ० 43

सभाओं में पश्चिमी राजपूताना में मारवाड़ प्रान्तीय चारण सभा कार्य कर रही थी तथा इस सभा ने जोधपुर व बीकानेर में चारण समुदाय में विधवा पुनर्विवाह करवाने के भरपूर प्रयास किये।[23]

इस दिशा में अगला प्रयास 1924 ई॰ में जयपुर में स्थापित अग्रवाल हितकारिणी सभा का रहा।[24] इस सभा ने अग्रवाल समाज से सामाजिक कुरीतियों के उन्मूलन के लिए शिक्षा के प्रसार पर बल दिया। विधवा पुनर्विवाह का प्रचलन न होने सहित अन्य सामाजिक बुराइयों पर साप्ताहिक सभायें व संगोष्ठियाँ करके विचार-विमर्श किया तथा इन सभाओं व संगोष्ठियों में अपने समुदाय के लोगों को बाहर से भी आमन्त्रित किया जिसमें बीकानेर व जोधपुर से भी प्रतिनिधियों ने भाग लिया।[25]

इसी प्रकार मीणा राजपूत महासभा की स्थापना 1931 ई॰ में जयपुर में की गई तथा पश्चिमी राजपूताना के बीकानेर, मारवाड़ (जोधपुर) तथा जैसलमेर में इसकी स्थापना की गई सभा ने बाल-विधवाओं की बढ़ती संख्या पर चिंता ज़ाहिर करते हुए विवाह के लिए लड़कियों के लिए कम से कम 13 वर्ष की आयु सीमा तय की तथा विधवा-विवाह के लिए प्रचार किया।[26]

अखिल भारतीय कायस्थ सभा की प्रान्तीय शाखाएँ राजपूताना में 1891 ई॰ से ही कार्य कर रही थी। इन शाखाओं ने राजपूताना के अन्य राज्यों के साथ-साथ जोधपुर, बीकानेर व जैसलमेर राज्यों में भी अपने समाज के लिए सामाजिक और आर्थिक उन्नति के लिए कार्य किए।[27]

अखिल भारतीय वैश्य महासभा की स्थापना मेरठ में 19वीं सदी के अंत में स्थापित की गई थी। इसकी शाखाएँ राजपूताना के अन्य राज्यों व पश्चिमी

---

23. *वही*
24. जयपुर रिकाड्र्स, महकमा खास, जी-20, फाइल नं॰ 33, पार्ट-1, रा॰रा॰अ॰, जयपुर (ब्रांच)
25. जयपुर रिकाड्र्स, महकमा खास, जी-20, फाइल नं॰ 145, रा॰रा॰अ॰, जयपुर (ब्रांच)
26. जयपुर रिकाड्र्स, महकमा खास, जी-20, फाइल नं॰ 152, पार्ट-2, रा॰रा॰अ॰, जयपुर (ब्रांच)
27. माथुर, पी॰सी॰ (सम्पादित), *सोशल एंड इकानोमिक डायनामिक्स ऑफ राजस्थान पोलिटिक्स बिफोर एंड आफ्टर,* 1947, आलेख पब्लिशर्स, जयपुर, 1947, पृ॰ 97

राजपूताना में की गई। इन शाखाओं ने वैश्य समाज के विकास के लिए शिक्षा और वाणिज्य पर जोर दिया।[28] इस सभा का उद्देश्य था कि आप अपने समाज को शिक्षित कीजिए तथा उनको आर्थिक रूप से सशक्त कीजिए इससे अन्य सामाजिक कुरीतियाँ अपने आप समाप्त हो जायेंगी। इन्होंने वैश्य समाज के लड़के-लड़कियों के लिए शैक्षणिक संस्थान खोले। परिणाम यह हुआ कि इन शैक्षिणक संस्थाओं में पढ़े-लिखे लड़कों ने एक संगठन बनाकर "वैश्य हितकारिणी" पत्रिका निकालनी आरम्भ की जिसमें वैश्य समाज में बढ़ते बाल व बेमेल विवाहों एवं इस वजह से बढ़ती बाल विधवाओं की संख्या व विधवाओं की दुर्दशा की जमकर आलोचना की तथा विधवाओं को पुनर्विवाह करने की अनुमति देने की वकालत की। इसका परिणाम यह हुआ कि 2 अप्रैल 1936 को वैश्य सभा के वार्षिक अधिवेषन में जो प्रस्ताव पास हुआ उसमें लड़कियों के लिए विवाह की कम से कम उम्र 14 वर्ष तथा लड़कों की आयु 18 वर्ष निर्धारित की गई।[29]

समीचीन है कि जाटों में विधवा पुनर्विवाह पहले से ही प्रचलन में था तथा क्षेत्रीय स्तर पर छोटी-छोटी पंचायतों द्वारा इसे करवाने व नियमों का पालन करवाने के उदाहरण भी मिले हैं किन्तु हिन्दू समाज में यह कार्य हीनता से देखा जाता था। अतः जब 1911 ई० में स्थापित अखिल भारतीय जाट महासभा का अक्तूबर 1925 ई० में पुष्कर में वार्षिक अधिवेशन हुआ और इस महाजलसे में राजपूताना के पश्चिमी भाग बीकानेर, मारवाड़ (जोधपुर) के प्रतिनिधि भाग लेकर इस अधिवेशन से वापिस लौटे तो उन्होंने पश्चिमी राजपूताना में अशिक्षा व सामाजिक कुरीतियों को दूर करने के उद्देश्य से जगह-जगह स्कूल खोले। दूर-दराज के छात्रों को भी इन स्कूलों में प्रवेश के लिए प्रोत्साहित किया तथा इन स्कूलों के विद्यार्थियों व समाज सुधारकों ने भजन मण्डलियों व उपदेशकों के रूप में गाँव-गाँव में जाकर तथा पशु मेलों में जाकर लोगों को अन्य सामाजिक कुरीतियों के साथ-साथ विधवाओं को सम्मान देने, उनके 'नाता' और 'पल्ले लगाई' को सामान्य विवाहों की तरह मानने का आग्रह किया और लोगों को जागरूक करने के प्रयास किये।[30]

---

28. जयपुर रिकाड्र्स, महकमा खास, जी-फाईल नं॰ 156, 1936, रा॰रा॰अ॰, जयपुर (ब्रांच)
29. *वही*
30. रिपोर्ट ऑन दी मारवाड़ जाट कृषक सुधारक सभा, फरवरी 1942, पृ॰ 17-18, रा॰रा॰अ॰, बीकानेर

सन् 1938 ई॰ में जोधपुर में मारवाड़ जाट कृषक सुधारक सभा की स्थापना हुई तथा इस सभा के माध्यम से जाटों ने बेमेल व बाल विवाह तथा इसके परिणामस्वरूप बाल विधवाओं की बढ़ती संख्या पर चिंता ज़ाहिर करते हुए लोगों को इन कुरीतियों के प्रति चेताने के प्रयास किये।[31] इसी प्रकार के कार्य बीकानेर रियासत (चुरू) में स्थापित सर्वहितकारिणी सभा ने भी किये तथा जाटों में सामाजिक कुरीतियों को दूर करने में महत्त्वपूर्ण योगदान दिया।[32]

इस प्रकार इस बात का आकलन तो यहाँ किया जा सकता है कि विवेच्यकाल में पश्चिमी राजपूताना के किन-किन सामाजिक वर्गों में विधवा पुनर्विवाह प्रचलन में था तथा किन में पूर्णतया प्रतिबन्धित था। साथ ही यह कहना भी कुछ आसान हो जाता है कि विभिन्न जाति-पंचायतों व जाति सभाओं की पुनर्विवाह आरम्भ करवाने में कितनी महत्त्वपूर्ण भूमिका रही। परन्तु इसका अर्थ यह कदापि नहीं लिया जा सकता कि पश्चिमी राजपूताना के जिन वर्गों में उपरोक्त पंचों-पंचायतों व सभाओं के माध्यम से विधवा-पुनर्विवाह के जो प्रयास किये गये वे समाज के सभी वर्गों या किसी वर्ग विशेष में स्वत: स्वीकार्य हो गये थे, तथा विधवाओं की कठिनाइयाँ समाप्त हो गई थीं। ऐसा कतई नहीं हुआ। जहाँ समाज का एक तबका इन पंच-पंचायतों, जातीय सभाओं, आर्य समाज के प्रयासों व कुछ हद तक कुछ रियासती शासकों द्वारा इस दिशा में उठायें गये कदमों से आश्वस्त होकर भविष्य के लिए उम्मीद लगाये हुए था, वहीं समाज के अन्दर रूढ़िवादी मानसिकता वाले तत्व अपने आप को अपनी झूठी मान-मर्यादा का रक्षक बताकर इसका विरोध कर रहे थे। परिणामस्वरूप विधवाओं की स्थिति में कोई आमूलचूल परिवर्तन नहीं हुआ। इसका ज्वलंत उदाहरण सन् 1975 ई॰ में वर्तमान राजस्थान राज्य के जोधपुर जिले में आखातीज के दिन 10,000 बाल विवाह हुए, जो कि आरम्भ से ही विधवाओं की बढ़ती संख्या का एक अहम कारण रहा है।

---

31. बीकानेर रिकाड्र्स, होम डिपार्टमेन्ट (बीकानेर स्टेट), कॉन्फिडेन्शियल, फाईल नं॰ सी-3, 1932, रा॰रा॰अ॰, बीकानेर
32. *इण्डियन एक्सप्रेस,* दिनांक 26 मार्च 1976, Editorial, When to Marry.

15

मारवाड़ क्षेत्र के सामाजिक-आर्थिक परिवर्त्तनों में जाट-किसानों की भूमिका

मोनिका

जाट समुदाय आधुनिक काल में उत्तरी-पश्चिमी भारत के क्षेत्रों-पंजाब, हरियाणा, उत्तर प्रदेश, राजस्थान और दिल्ली में प्रमुख जाति के रूप में विद्यमान है तथा इन क्षेत्रों के सामाजिक, आर्थिक बदलावों में प्रमुखता से इस जाति द्वारा महत्वपूर्ण भूमिका समय-समय पर निभाई गई है। आज इस समुदाय ने सभी दृष्टिकोणों से प्रमुख स्थिति प्राप्त की है परन्तु यह स्थिति तथा इन बदलावों में इस समुदाय की भूमिका, उसकी पहचान उसी अवस्था में नहीं रही है अपितु पूर्व आधुनिक काल में इस समुदाय की पहचान व अस्मिता का समय-समय पर रूपांतरण ऐतिहासिक बदलावों के साथ होता रहा है। यद्यपि ऐतिहासिक दस्तावेज के अभाव में इस प्रक्रिया को एकीकृत निरन्तरता की प्रक्रिया के साथ रेखांकित करना काफी मुश्किल है परन्तु पूर्व आधुनिक काल में भिन्न-भिन्न क्षेत्रों में जाटों की भूमिका को ऐतिहासिक बदलावों के सन्दर्भ में नये उपजते सांस्कृतिक, धार्मिक पद्धतियों, व्यवसायों में उतार-चढ़ाव आदि गतिविधियों के संदर्भ में समझा जा सकता है। यह तथ्य स्पष्ट स्वीकार करना होगा कि जाटों की सामाजिक स्थिति, अस्मिता, पहचान निरन्तर बदलावों से गुजरती रही है। यद्यपि ऐतिहासिक रचनाओं, पर्याप्त स्रोतों के अभाव में अनेक इतिहासकारों द्वारा जाट समुदाय की ऐतिहासिकता को प्राचीनतम दिखाने के प्रयास रहे हैं परन्तु यह स्पष्ट है कि स्थानीय स्तर पर इस वर्ग की भूमिका अलग-अलग कालों में अलग-अलग रूप में रही है जिसकी खोजबीन से जाटों के इतिहास की अधिक तर्कपूर्ण ढंग से समझ बनाई जा सकती है। इतिहास के पन्ने इस तथ्य के साक्षी है कि जाट शक्ति हमेशा से ही अतीत

के बदलावों को अपने सामर्थ्य से नई दिशा देने वाली रही है। जाट शक्ति ने मध्यकाल में पश्चिमी राजस्थान के क्षेत्र में परिवर्तनकारी शक्ति के रूप में अपनी उपस्थिति दर्ज करवाई है।

पश्चिमी राजस्थान का क्षेत्र पूर्व मध्यकाल में महत्वपूर्ण ऐतिहासिक बदलावों का साक्षी रहा है विशेषकर मध्यकालीन भारत में राज्य निर्माण के संदर्भ में इस प्रक्रिया को समझने में। पश्चिमी राजस्थान के लिए प्रचलित शब्द-मारवाड़ का अर्थ ही 'मौत की भूमि' है जो यहां के संघर्षमय जीवन को स्पष्ट करता है।[1] मारवाड़ शब्द सीधे तौर पर एक गर्म, रूखे, प्रतिकूल, रेतीले, जलविहीन प्रदेश का पर्याय था, जहाँ मानव के लिए अपने जीविका के प्रारम्भिक साधनों कृषि और पशुपालन को चलाना काफी कठिन था तथा स्वयं मानव अस्तित्व को खतरा बना रहता था। कम वर्षा, गर्म, शुष्क, रेतीले तूफान, अपर्याप्त जल, अनुपजाऊ भूमि से मारवाड़ के क्षेत्र में कृषि कार्य सीमित रूप में रहा है। अकाल, सूखा ज्यादा पड़ता है। ऐसी आपदाओं से संघर्ष करने के लिये कृषक व पशुपालक समाज के लिए साधनों का अभाव सदैव रहता रहा[2] परन्तु इन प्रतिकूल परिस्थितियों में भी जाटों ने यहाँ मानवीय कठिनाइयों के साथ पूर्व में पर्याप्त संघर्ष किया।

ऐतिहासिक दृष्टि से जाटों का मध्यकाल में जो वर्णन हुआ वह उन्हें सिंध क्षेत्र के आसपास ऐसे सामाजिक वर्ग के रूप में दिखाता है जिसे परम्परागत ढाँचे में काफी नीचे गिना जाता था। यद्यपि हमारे पास यह स्पष्टता से दिखाने के स्रोत अभी अधिक नहीं है कि जाटों का राजस्थान के क्षेत्र में कब आगमन हुआ परन्तु यह तथ्यपूर्ण है कि मारवाड़ के क्षेत्र में जाटों का आगमन पूर्व मध्यकाल में उत्तर की ओर से हुआ तथा उन्होंने यहां की स्थानीय मेर जाति को खदेड़ते हुये अपने आप को स्थायी रूप से बसाया।[3] मध्यकाल में जाट जाति की राजस्थान के उत्तरी-पश्चिमी क्षेत्रों में महत्वपूर्ण जाति के रूप में

---

1. कर्नल जेम्स टॉड : *राजस्थान का इतिहास* (अनु०) बलदेव प्रसाद मिश्र एवम् ज्वाला प्रसाद मिश्र, (सं०) राय मुंशी देवी प्रसाद, भाग-2, जिल्द चतुर्थ, यूनिक ट्रेडर्स, चौड़ा रास्ता, जयपुर, 1987, पृ० 1108
2. जगदीश गहलोत : *राजस्थान का सामाजिक जीवन,* हिन्दी साहित्य संस्थान, जोधपुर, 1974, पृ० 108-109
3. मुंशी देवी प्रसाद : *मर्दुमशुमारी राजमारवाड रा,* बीकानेर अभिलेखागार, 1899, पृ० 48, 57

उपस्थिति स्वीकार की जाती है जिसने अपने प्राथमिक व्यवसायों-पशुपालन और कृषि के साथ इस क्षेत्र के सामाजिक व आर्थिक क्षेत्र में महत्वपूर्ण भूमिका निभाई है।

इतिहास लेखन में यद्यपि जाट जाति की व्यापक भूमिका का उल्लेख है परन्तु स्थानीय स्तर पर जाटों की भूमिका, उनके संक्रमण, स्थानीय जनजातियों से जाटों के समबन्ध और उनसे उपजी विशेष परिस्थितियों पर इतिहास मौन है।

आरम्भिक मध्यकाल में पश्चिमी राजस्थान का क्षेत्र महत्वपूर्ण परिवर्तनों के दौर से गुजर रहा था। सामाजिक और आर्थिक रूपांतरण की प्रक्रिया में नए क्षेत्रों का कृषिकरण, नई जातियों का बनना, जनजातियों से राज्य की ओर संक्रमण तथा नए शासकों का उभार प्रमुख थे। जाटों के आगमन से पहले पश्चिमी राजस्थान एक वीरान, पिछड़ा, अभावपूर्ण क्षेत्र था जहाँ की मरूभूमि की तपन, जल संसाधनों की कमी तथा लूटमारी ने जीवनदायिनी शक्तियों को सीमित कर दिया था। इन कष्टव्यापी क्षेत्रों को इसीलिए जांगल प्रदेश के नाम से जाना जाता था। मानव निवास के लिए जटिल परिस्थितियों के विरुद्ध संघर्ष ने इस क्षेत्र के लोगों को हर विपरीत परिस्थिति का सामना करने में सक्षम एवं संघर्षशील बना दिया। इस दुर्गम क्षेत्र में अधिकांश जाट जाति के किसान रहते थे, जो जीवन संघर्ष के प्रतिरूप थे।[4] जाट जैसी परिश्रमी जाति के मारवाड़ में आगमन को महत्वपूर्ण बदलावों से जोड़कर देखना चाहिए। इन क्षेत्रों में कृषि विस्तार की सम्भावनाओं को जाटों ने जागृत किया तथा जहाँ कहीं सम्भव हुआ उपजाऊ मिट्टी की उपलब्धता तथा जल की उपस्थिति से प्रतिकूल परिस्थितियों में कृषि कार्य को बढ़ाया। जाट किसान चारे, पानी व काम की तलाश में मालवा, मेवाड़, गुजरात तक पलायन करते रहे इससे उपजाऊ क्षेत्रों का विकास हुआ।

12वीं शताब्दी के बाद नागौर के क्षेत्र में जाटों का आगमन हुआ जिससे इस क्षेत्र में कृषि पर आधारित अर्थव्यवस्था का पोषण कर नये-नये क्षेत्रों का उपनिवेशीकरण हुआ। नागौर में जाटों की सबसे अधिक बस्ती थी।[5] नौवीं

---

4. कैलाशनाथ व्यास, देवेन्द्रसिंह गहलोत : *राजस्थान की जातियों का सामाजिक एवं आर्थिक जीवन,* जगदीश सिंह गहलोत शोध संस्थान, जोधपुर, 1992, पृ॰ 108
5. करणी सिंह : *दि रिलेशन्स ऑफ दि हाउस ऑफ बीकानेर विद दि सेन्ट्रल पॉवर्स,* मनोहर पब्लिकेशन, नई दिल्ली 1974, पृ॰ 74

से तेरहवीं शताब्दी के बीच जब राजस्थान का क्षेत्र विशेषकर मारवाड़ में जनजातीय तत्वों का कृषि कार्यों में संक्रमण चल रहा था तो जाट इस प्रक्रिया में प्रमुख भूमिका निभा रहे थे तथा इस प्रक्रिया में स्थानीय जनजातियों-भील, मेर, मेवो को अधीनस्थ किया जा रहा था।[6] बारहवीं व तेरहवीं शताब्दी में तुर्कों के आगमन के पश्चात पंजाब के क्षेत्रों में रहट का प्रयोग बढ़ने से खेतों में पानी की उपलब्धता बढ़ी। मारवाड़ के जाटों ने भी इसे ग्रहण किया जिससे अधिक से अधिक संख्या में जाट कृषि कार्यों से जुड़े और कृषि क्षेत्र को बढ़ाने में उल्लेखनीय भूमिका निभाई।[7] नागौर और मेड़ता का क्षेत्र राजस्थान में पशुपालन के प्रमुख केन्द्र के रूप में प्रसिद्ध हुआ। आज भी नागौरी बैलों को सर्वोत्तम गिना जाता है।

हम 13वीं व 14वीं शताब्दी में उत्तरी-पश्चिमी राजस्थान के आस-पास के क्षेत्रों में जाटों की बस्तियों व गाँवों को पूर्ण विकसित रूप में पाते है। यह बसावट एकाएक न उभरकर इतिहास के पूर्व कालों में संक्रमण प्रवास से उपजी क्योंकि पूर्व मध्यकाल में यह क्षेत्र मेर, मेव, गुर्जर व भील जनजातियों से भरा था। पूर्णतः गोत्र पर आधारित बसावट इस तथ्य को समझने में सहायता करती है कि पूर्व मध्यकाल में यह प्रक्रिया आरम्भ हुई जो चलती रही। बीकानेर राज्य के आस-पास का बहुत सा इलाका जाटों के अधिकार में था। इन क्षेत्रों में जाटों के अनेक गोत्रों का विकास हुआ जो विभिन्न क्षेत्रों के स्थायी वासी बन चुके थे। बीकानेर का जो क्षेत्र जाटों के अधीन था वह जाटों की निम्नलिखित शाखाओं के अंतर्गत था[8]-

---

6. जी॰ एन॰ शर्मा : *सोशल लाइफ इन मीडिवल राजस्थान,* लक्ष्मी नारायण अग्रवाल, आगरा, 1968, पृ॰ 227
7. पेमाराम : *मध्यकालीन राजस्थान में धार्मिक आन्दोलन,* अर्चना प्रकाशन, अजमेर, 1972, पृ॰ 37
8. बी॰ डी॰ चट्टोपाध्याय : 'द इमरजैन्स ऑफ राजपूत एज हिस्टोरिकल प्रोसेस इन अर्ली मिडिवल राजस्थान' के. सोमर, जे॰एल॰ इर्डमैन, लौड्रिक रूडोल्फ (सं॰) *आइडिया ऑफ राजस्थान,* मनोहर पब्लिकेशन, दिल्ली, 1994, पृ॰ 163-166

क्र॰ सं॰	नाम	जाट शक्ति के गाँवों की संख्या	मुख्य गाँव	प्रमुख व्यक्ति का नाम
1.	गोदारा	360	लधाड़िया तथा शेखसर	पांडू
2.	सारन	360	भाड़ग	पूला
3.	कस्बां	360	सीधमुख	कंवरपाल
4.	पूनिया	360	बड़ीलूंधी	कान्हा
5.	सीधगा	140	सूई	चोखा
6.	सेहूवा	84	धानसी	अमरा

राजस्थान में किसान और जाट परस्पर पर्यायवाची हैं। आरम्भ में इनका मुख्य व्यवसाय पशुपालन था। इस क्षेत्र में नये-नये क्षेत्रों का उपनिवेशीकरण करके ये कृषि कार्यों की ओर उन्मुख हो रहे थे।[9] अब तक जाटों ने मुख्य कृषक समुदाय की मान्यता प्राप्त कर ली थी। जाट सामान्य पशुपालन और कृषि व्यवसाय में अग्रसर होकर भी भारत की वीर जाति के रूप में विशेष स्वाधीनताप्रिय थे।[10] जाटों ने यद्यपि अनुपजाऊ भूमि को कृषि योग्य बनाया तथा कृषि क्षेत्रों का विकास किया फिर भी मारवाड़ के क्षेत्र में जाट किसानों की आर्थिक-सामाजिक स्थिति अच्छी नहीं थी। रेगिस्तानी भूमि में वर्षा कम होने के कारण अकसर अकाल पड़ते रहते थे और किसान खेती या पशुधन के सहारे अपना जीवन-निर्वाह करते थे।

इसके कारण मारवाड़ में किसानों को आर्थिक व सामाजिक दृष्टि से निम्न स्तर का समझा गया। यहाँ की रेतीली और उपजाऊ दोनों तरह की भूमि पर रहने वाला किसान जागीरदारों के अत्याचारों से पीड़ित था। उन्हें जागीरदारों की दया पर निर्भर रहना पड़ता था। जागीरदारों की विलासिता के कारण आमदनी में कमी आई। खर्च बढ़ने और आमदनी में कमी आने के कारण जागीरदारों द्वारा आय के नये साधन पैदा करने के बजाए किसानों पर अतिरिक्त बोझ डाला गया जिससे किसानों का शोषण बढ़ता गया। बेगार प्रथा भी किसानों

---

9. इरफान हबीब : द *एग्रेरियन क्राइसिज ऑफ मुगल इंडिया 1556-1707*, द्वितीय भाग, ऑक्सफोर्ड यूनिवर्सिटी प्रैस, दिल्ली 1999, पृ॰ 390-391
10. पी॰ डब्ल्यू पाउलेट : गैजेटियर ऑफ द बीकानेर स्टेट, पुनर्मुद्रित, बीकानेर, 1932, पृ॰ 4

के लिये बहुत बड़ी समस्या थी, जिसमें मुख्य रूप से जागीरदारों के खेतों को जोतना, उनकी फसल काटना, उनके सामान को ढोना और उनके घरेलू कार्य करना आदि प्रमुख थे।[11] किसानों पर लगान दिन-प्रतिदिन बढ़ता रहता था। लगान को चुकाने के लिए किसानों पर ऋण का बोझ बढ़ता गया। जो भी किसान लगान देने से मना करता था उस पर जागीरदारों द्वारा अनेक तरह के अत्याचार किये जाते थे -उसको मारपीट कर कोठरी में बंद कर देना, उसके पशुओं को फाटक में बन्द कर देना तथा बाद में उनको नीलाम कर देना, मारपीट करके घर और गाँव छोड़ने पर मजबूर करना, भूमि से बेदखल करना, ढाणियों पर सामूहिक हमले करना। किसानों को भूमि सम्बन्धी कोई अधिकार नहीं था, जिस कारण हमेशा किसान को अपनी भूमि से बेदखल होने का भय रहता था।[12]

आर्थिक के साथ-साथ सामाजिक क्षेत्र में भी किसानों को बहुत उपेक्षित समझा जाता था। जागीरदार उनको ओछे नामों से पुकारते थे और जूते निकालने की जगह उनको बैठाते थे। उन पर अनेक तरह के प्रतिबन्ध लगा रखे थे। किसान घोड़े पर नहीं चढ़ सकते थे, मिल के बने बारीक कपड़े नहीं पहन सकते थे, रंगीन पगड़ी नहीं पहन सकते थे, जागीरदार के सामने चारपाई पर नहीं बैठ सकते थे, स्त्रियाँ सोने के आभूषण नहीं पहन सकती थी, शादी के अवसर पर लड्डू नहीं बना सकते थे। रावले के सामने से छाता लगाकर नहीं निकल सकते थे, पक्के मकान नहीं बना सकते थे, निवाड़ की खाट नहीं बना सकते थे। इस तरह से किसानों पर अनेक प्रतिबन्ध लगाकर सामाजिक दृष्टि से भी उनको हीन समझा जाता था।[13]

मारवाड़ की जागीरों में शासन कार्य के लिए कोई कानून नहीं थे। जागीरदारों के अत्याचार, आर्थिक-सामाजिक दृष्टि से दबे-कुचले हुये किसानों के मन में जागीरदारों और सामाजिक-आर्थिक व्यवस्था के प्रति आक्रोश पैदा

11. कर्नल जेम्स टॉड : *बीकानेर राज्य का इतिहास,* बलदेव प्रसाद मिश्र एवम् ज्वाला प्रसाद मिश्र (सं०), राय मुंशी देवी प्रसाद, यूनिक ट्रेडर्स, चौड़ा रास्ता, जयपुर, 1998, पृ० 16
12. पेमाराम : *राजस्थान के जाटों का इतिहास,* राजस्थानी ग्रंथागार, जोधपुर, 2012, पृ० 42
13. विक्रमादित्य चौधरी : *राजस्थान में किसान आन्दोलन,* राजस्थान साहित्य संस्थान, जोधपुर, 2005, पृ० 211

हुआ। मारवाड़ की भ्रष्ट शासन व्यवस्था के खिलाफ किसानों में जागृति आई। उन्होंने महसूस किया कि अगर वे संगठित होकर सामूहिक प्रयास करें तो उनकी स्थिति में कुछ सुधार हो सकता है। क्योंकि उनके थोड़ा सा मना करने पर ही जागीरदारों को अपने किसानों से लगान वसूल करने में कठिनाई होने लगी थी। इन सभी बातों से प्रभावित होकर किसानों ने सामूहिक रूप से अनेक आंदोलन आरम्भ किये।

मारवाड़ के बाली व गोडवाड़ इलाकों में भीलों व गिरासियों का ऐकी आंदोलन (1922-23), मादा पशुओं की निकासी के विरुद्ध आंदोलन (1924), मारवाड़ हितकारिणी सभा का जागीरी इलाकों में किसानों के कष्टों को दूर करने हेतु आंदोलन (1929-31), मारवाड़ के खालसा इलाके में बिगोड़ी (नकद भूमिकर) में छूट हेतु किसानों का आंदोलन (1931-34), मारवाड़ के डिडवाना परगने में किसान आंदोलन (1934), किसानों में शिक्षा-प्रसार व कुरीति निवारण तथा उनकी तकलीफों को उजागर करने हेतु आंदोलन (1927-1941), मारवाड़ किसान सभा व मारवाड़ लोक परिषद द्वारा जागीरी किसानों की तकलीफों को दूर करने हेतु आंदोलन (1941-1949), आदि आंदोलनों ने किसानों के सामाजिक-आर्थिक जीवन को विशेष रुप से प्रभावित किया। इससे जाटों को अनेक नेता एवं सामाजिक कार्यकर्त्ता मिले। जाटों के जीवन स्तर में बदलाव हुआ। आंदोलनों के परिणामस्वरूप मारवाड़ में अनेक संगठन जैसे-मारवाड़ हितकारिणी सभा, मारवाड़ यूथ लीग, मारवाड़ प्रजामण्डल, सिविल लिबर्टीज यूनियन आदि उभर कर सामने आये और उन्होंने किसानों के हितों के लिये कार्य करना शुरू किया। इनमें सबसे महत्वपूर्ण सभा *'जाट कृषक सुधारक सभा'* थी। इस सभा के द्वारा मारवाड़ क्षेत्र में शिक्षा का काफी विकास हुआ। नागौर, मेड़ता, जोधपुर, बाड़मेर तथा मारवाड़ के कई शहरों में छात्रावास खोले गये। इस प्रकार अखिल भारतीय जाट महासभा द्वारा किसान बच्चों को पढ़ाने का एक व्यापक कार्यक्रम शुरू किया गया, जिससे शिक्षा की रोशनी मारवाड़ में चारों तरफ फैलने लगी।[14]

शिक्षा के साथ-साथ इस सभा का उद्देश्य कृषक जातियों में पारस्परिक मेल-जोल का भाव पैदा करना, कुरीतियों को हटाना व उनके खिलाफ उपदेशकों तथा भजन मण्डलियों तथा अन्य साधनों द्वारा प्रचार करना तथा

14. पेमाराम : *शेखावाटी किसान आंदोलन का इतिहास,* राजस्थानी ग्रन्थागार, जोधपुर, पृ॰ 31

किसानों के कृषि सम्बन्धी हकों की रक्षा करना था। इस सभा ने प्रचलित सामाजिक कुरीतियों जैसे बाल-विवाह, बेमेल-विवाह, शादियों में अधिक खर्च, मौसर (मृत्यु भोज), लड़ाई-झगड़े व मुकदमेबाजी, शराब, अफीम, तम्बाकू, चूड़ा प्रथा इत्यादि को हटाने के प्रयास शुरू कर किये। साथ ही किसानों की कठिनाइयों व उन पर होने वाले अत्याचारों की सूचना राज्य सरकार को देने तथा किसान व जागीरदार के मध्य संघर्ष में किसानों की सहायता करने की व्यवस्था भी की गई।[15]

मारवाड़ क्षेत्र से पशुओं, चारा, अनाज, घी जैसी चीजों की निकासी बंद हो गई। इन सबकी निकासी से सरकार को फायदा होता था और कृषक वर्ग को नुकसान क्योंकि किसानों से सभी वस्तुयें कम दाम पर खरीदकर उनको उचित मूल्य पर बाहर बेचा जाता था। किसानों को अब जमीन से भी बेदखल नहीं किया जा सकता था। राजस्थान सरकार ने इस समस्या के समाधान के लिए 21 जून 1949 ई० को जागीरदारों द्वारा अपने किसानों को अपनी जमीन से निकाल देने या उनसे उनकी जमीन छीन लेने की प्रवृत्ति पर रोक लगाने के लिए 'राजस्थान आर्डिनेन्स 1949' जारी किया जिसमें किसानों को बेदखली से पूरा संरक्षण दिया गया और यह व्यवस्था की गई कि 1 अप्रैल 1948 ई० को किसान के कब्जे में जितनी भूमि थी उसे अगर बेदखल कर दिया जाये तो कानूनी रूप से उसे वह जमीन वापिस मिल जायेगी।[16]

जागीरदार जो कि किसानों से मनचाहा कर वसूल करते थे, उनकी मनमानी को रोकने के लिए 'राजस्थान उपज लगान अधिनियम 1951 ई०' पारित किया गया। अब जागीरदार किसानों से ¼ भाग लगान अधिक से अधिक वसूल सकते थे। नकद लगान की सीमा तय कर दी गई जो निर्धारित भूराजस्व से अधिक नहीं हो सकती थी। 1955 ई० में राजस्थान टिनेन्सी एक्ट बनाकर जागीरदारों के स्थान पर किसानों को भूमि का मालिक बनाया गया। जागीरदारी प्रथा के समाप्त हो जाने से अब किसानों का शोषण करने वाला वर्ग समाप्त हो गया। किसानों को घोड़े की सवारी करने, सोने-चाँदी के आभूषण पहनने व पक्की हवेलियों में रहने की पूरी आजादी थी। इन सब प्रतिबन्धों के हटने से किसानों की आर्थिक व सामाजिक प्रतिष्ठा में वृद्धि हुई। किसान वर्ग का

---

15. विक्रमादित्य चौधरी : *राजस्थान में किसान आन्दोलन,* राजस्थान साहित्य संस्थान, जोधपुर, 2005, पृ० 106-107
16. पृथ्वीसिंह मेहता : *हमारा राजस्थान,* इलाहाबाद, 1950, पृ० 383

सम्मान बढ़ा। शिक्षा का प्रसार होने से बाल विवाह जैसी कुरीतियों में कमी आई, बाहर रोजगार के अवसर बढ़ने से न केवल आर्थिक दशा में सुधार हुआ, अपितु अच्छी नौकरियाँ प्राप्त करके मारवाड़ की किसान संततियों ने राज्य के और देश के विकास में योगदान देना प्रारम्भ किया। यह सब किसानों के प्रयास का ही फल था जिससे मारवाड़ का किसान सुख की सांस ले सका।

16

मेवाड़ का बिजोलिया किसान आन्दोलन

डॉ. मलिका बोहरा

देश में संगठित किसान आन्दोलन की शुरूआत सर्वप्रथम मेवाड़ के भीलवाड़ा क्षेत्र के बिजोलिया गांव से हुई थी।[1] उन दिनों बिजोलिया मेवाड़ राज्य का प्रथम श्रेणी का ठिकाना था, जिसका संस्थापक भरतपुर के जगनेर का निवासी अशोक परमार था, जो कभी मेवाड़ के महाराणा सांगा (1509-1528 ई.) के समय में उनकी सेवा हेतु चित्तौड़गढ़ आया था। सन् 1527 में महाराणा सांगा की ओर से बाबर के विरूद्ध लड़ा था। उसकी वीरता से प्रभावित होकर महाराणा ने उसे ऊपरमाल की जागीर प्रदान की थी। अतः ऊपरमाल जागीर का सदर मुकाम बिजोलिया था।

बिजोलिया के किसान धाकड़ जाट जाति के रहे हैं, जो बड़े मेहनती, कर्तव्यनिष्ठ, महत्वाकांक्षी तथा बहादुर थे, जिन्होंने कभी मराठों को यहां से बाहर निकाल फेंका था। बिजोलिया एक ऐसे स्थान पर था, जहां से किसान आवश्यकता पड़ने पर पड़ौसी क्षेत्रों में आ-जा सकते थे।

यहां किसान आन्दोलन के बीज उस समय बोये गये जब 1894 ई. में राव गोविन्ददास की मृत्यु के बाद राव किशनदास (कृष्णसिंह) नया जागीरदार बना। उस समय भारत में अंग्रेजी सत्ता की स्थापना हो चुकी थी। जैसा कि जब सन् 1857 में प्रथम स्वतंत्रता संग्राम हुआ तब यहां के राजाओं ने अंग्रेजों का साथ दिया था। वे अंग्रेजी सत्ता के पिट्ठू बन गये थे, इसलिए वे प्रशासनिक कार्यों में मनमानियां करते रहे। उनके अपने जागीरदार थे, जो अपनी-अपनी जागीरों में किसानों से भू-राजस्व एकत्रित करते थे तथा इन्हें रियासत को पहुंचाते थे। राव किशनदास के समय में जागीर प्रबन्ध तथा

1. बी.एल. पानगडिया : *राजस्थान में स्वतंत्रता संग्राम*, पृ. 24

किसानों के प्रति नीति में परिवर्तन आना शुरू हो गया। उसने पुराने कामदारों को हटाकर नये कामदार लगाये, जिन्हें किसानों से अधिकाधिक भू-लगान वसूलने का आदेश दिया तथा किसानों पर 84 प्रकार की लागतें थोप दी गई। साथ ही उपज का 1/2 भाग लगान के रूप में वसूला जाने लगा। जनता पर भी बैठ बैगार[2] ली जाने लगी, इस प्रकार बिजोलिया का किसान मेहनती होकर भी भूखा व कंगाल रहने लगा।

सन् 1897 में ऊपरीमाल के किसानों ने एक मृत्यु भोज के अवसर पर गिरिधारीपुर नामक गांव में जमा होकर लागतों व लगान को कम करने के उद्देश्य से अपने दो प्रतिनिधियों को उदयपुर भेजा, लेकिन नतीजा यह निकला कि महाराणा स्वरूपसिंह ने इस पर ज्यादा ध्यान नहीं दिया, जिससे किशनदास के हौसले बढ़ गये। उसने उदयपुर जाने वाले दोनों प्रतिनिधियों को दण्डित किया। इस प्रकार किसानों का यह प्रथम प्रयास विफल रहा।

दूसरी तरफ किशनदास ने ऊपरमाल के किसानों पर प्रत्येक लड़की की शादी पर 5 रुपया चंवरी कर लागू कर दिया, जिसका किसानों ने घोर विरोध किया। बाद में उसे उठा भी दिया गया। साथ ही भूमि लगान को कम कर 2/5 भाग कर दिया गया, जो किसानों की अप्रत्याशित विजय साबित हुई।

सन् 1906 में महाराणा फतहसिंह के समय में राव किशनदास की मृत्यु के बाद बिजोलिया का नया जागीरदार पृथ्वीसिंह बना। मेवाड़ राज्य के नियमानुसार पृथ्वीसिंह को बिजोलिया का उत्तराधिकारी स्वीकार करने से पूर्व उसे 'तलवार बंधाई' के रूप में महाराणा को एक बड़ी धनराशि देनी

---

2. 1. बैठ बैगार : बिना पारिश्रमिक दिये काम करवाना। राजस्थान में इस प्रथा का तेजी से प्रसार 19वीं सदी में हुआ था। इस हेतु रियासतों में समस्त पिछड़ी जातियों, चमार, नाई, कुम्हार, बढ़ई, दरजी इत्यादि को मुफ्त में अपनी सेवाएं देनी होती थी। 2. प्रकाश व्यास : *राजस्थान का सामाजिक इतिहास* (7वीं से 1950 ई. तक), पृ. 167-170।

थी, इसलिए उसने यह भार वहां के किसानों पर थोपकर 'तलवार बंदी'[3] जैसे लगान में एक ओर बढ़ोतरी कर दी, जिसका किसानों ने जमकर विरोध किया। इस समय किसानों का नेतृत्व साधु सीतारामदास, फतहकरण चारण तथा ब्रह्मदेव ने किया था। सन् 1913 में ऊपरमाल के किसानों ने भूमि को परती ही रखा तथा लगान नहीं दिया, जिससे उन्हें निर्वासित कर दिया गया। कई किसान कार्यकर्ताओं को जेल में ठूंस दिया। साधु सीताराम को रियासत की पुस्तकालय की नौकरी से हटा दिया। इसी बीच राव पृथ्वीसिंह की मृत्यु हो गई तथा उसका नाबालिग पुत्र केसरीसिंह जागीरदार बना। दूसरी तरफ साधु सीताराम ने 'मित्रमण्डल' की स्थापना कर किसानों में जागृति पैदा कर दी।

केसरीसिंह के अवयस्क होने से मेवाड़ रियासत ने मुंसरमात (कोर्ट ऑफ वाईस) बिठाई। अमरसिंह राणावत को मुंसरिम तथा डूंगरसिंह भाटी को नायब मुंसरिम नियुक्त किया[4] जो पूर्ववत लगान वसूल करते रहे। इसी बीच प्रथम विश्व युद्ध शुरू हो गया। इस युद्ध कोष में धन को जमा करना प्रत्येक जागीरदार के लिए आवश्यक था। अतः जागीरदारों ने ये बोझ किसानों पर लाद दिया, जिससे किसानों की माली हालत बिगड़ती गई। उस समय उन्हें विजयसिंह पथिक जैसा एक योग्य नेता भी मिल गया।[5] अतः वे उनके मार्गदर्शन में संगठित होकर आन्दोलन करने को तैयार हो गये।

विजयसिंह पथिक तथा बिजोलिया किसान आन्दोलन

इस आन्दोलन की प्रारंभिक सफलता का श्रेय विजयसिंह पथिक को जाता है। पथिक का पूर्व नाम भूपसिंह था। उनका जन्म उत्तरप्रदेश के बुलंदशहर जिले के गुलावठी गांव में चैत्र कृष्णा वि.सं. 1930 (सन् 1873) में हुआ था। उनके दादा सन् 1857 की क्रांति में मालागढ़ के नवाब की सेना का नेतृत्व

---

3. तलवार बंदी : मेवाड़ रियासत में जागीरदार की मृत्यु के बाद नये उत्तराधिकारी द्वारा मेवाड़ के महाराणा को दिया जाने वाला एक प्रकार का कर, जिसमें एक उत्सव का आयोजन होता था, जिसमें महाराणा व उनके दरबारीगण पधारते थे तथा जागीरदारों को शपथ देकर जागीरदार घोषित करते थे। इस अवसर पर नवीन जागीरदार को कई भेंट, उपहार, नज़राने हाथी-घोडे इत्यादि भेंट करने होते थे। **पाग लाग** नामक कर था, जो पगड़ी बांधने के उपलक्ष्य में जनता पर लगाया जाता था।
4. शर्मा एवं पावा : *राजस्थान का इतिहास*, पृ. 538
5. उपरोक्त।

करते हुए शहीद हुए थे। सन् 1907 में भूपसिंह विख्यात क्रांतिकारी शचीन्द्र सान्याल तथा रासबिहारी बोस के सम्पर्क में आये। बोस ने ही उन्हें राजस्थान में क्रांति की ज्वाला प्रज्ज्वलित करने के लिए खटवा के ठाकुर गोपालसिंह के पास भेजा था, परन्तु क्रांति की यह योजना असफल हो जाने से जब देशभर में कई क्रांतिकारी पकड़े गये तब उन्हें तथा गोपालसिंह सहित कई क्रांतिकारियों को टाढ़ागढ़ के किले में कैद कर दिया था, परन्तु वे चुपचाप यहां से निकल भागे। उन्होंने अपनी दाढ़ी बढ़ा ली व अपना नाम भूपसिंह से बदलकर विजयसिंह पथिक रख लिया। मृत्युपर्यन्त वे इसी नाम से जाने जाने लगे।

शुरूआती दौर में उन्होंने मेवाड़ के कांकरोली के पास एक स्कूल की स्थापना की। जहां उनका परिचय ठाकुर डूंगरसिंह भाटी व केसरीसिंह बारहठ के दामाद ईश्वरदान आसिया से हुआ। वहां से वे चित्तौड़ आये। यहीं हरिभाई किंकर द्वारा संचालित 'विद्याप्रचारिणी सभा' से जुड़ गये, जिसकी एक शाखा साधु सीताराम ने बिजोलिया में स्थापित की थी। इसी के वार्षिक अधिवेशन में उनकी मुलाकात साधुजी से हुई। उन्होंने ही उन्हें बिजोलिया किसान आन्दोलन का नेतृत्व संभालने के लिए आमंत्रित किया, जिसे उन्होंने सहज स्वीकार कर लिया बिजोलिया पहुंचे और उसे ही अपनी कर्मभूमि बना दिया। इस कार्य में उनको राजस्थान के लौह पुरुष माणिक्यलाल वर्मा से मदद मिली, जो उन दिनों ठिकाने के कर्मचारी थे। उन्होनें पथिकजी के विचारों से प्रभावित होकर ठिकाने की सेवा से इस्तीफा दे दिया तथा विद्याप्रचारिणी सभा के मंत्री बन गये। यहीं बिजोलिया में ही पथिक जी से पार्श्वनाथ के जैन मंदिर में दीक्षा ली व जीवनभर सेवा करते रहे।

पथिकजी के विश्वस्त साथियों में साधु सीतारामदास तथा माणिक्यलाल वर्मा का नाम अग्रणी है। जब ब्रिटिश सरकार को किसान संगठन की क्रान्तिकारी गतिविधियों का पता चला तो उनके इशारों पर मेवाड़ रियासत ने उनके विरुद्ध वारंट जारी किया। तब विजयसिंह पथिक अमाजी के खेड़ा गांव में आकर एक वीरान झोंपड़े में रहने लगे तथा इसी झोंपड़े को बिजोलिया किसान आन्दोलन की क्रांति का केन्द्र बना लिया। सन् 1917 में 'ऊपरमाल पंच बोर्ड' के नाम से संगठन स्थापित कर क्रांति का बिगुल बजा दिया। मन्ना पटेल को इस पंचायत का सरपंच बनाया गया। इस दिन हरियाली अमावस्या थी, इसलिए पथिक जी ने निम्न पंक्तियों से किसानों को आह्वान किया।

हरियाली अमावस सुखा, शुभ मुहर्त को जान लो,
स्वतंत्रता के हित अब, धर्मयुद्ध की ठान लो।

इस समय बिजोलिया के किसान मेवाड़ रियासत द्वारा थोपे गये कई प्रकार के करों से परेशान थे। उस पर प्रथम विश्वयुद्ध के लिए किसानों से चंदा वसूली की जाती थी जिसका किसानों ने घोर विरोध किया। इसी बीच ठिकानेदारों ने नारायण पटेल नामक एक प्रभावशाली किसान को जबरन बेगार देने को विवश किया। इंकार करने पर उसे बंदी बना लिया। ज्यों ही उसकी गिरफ्तारी का समाचार गांव में फैला तब लगभग 2000 किसान सत्याग्रह के लिए बिजोलिया में जमा हुए तथा उन्होंने ठिकानेदारों के विरुद्ध नारे लगाये। अंततः ठिकानेदारों ने नारायण पटेल को छोड़ दिया। इस प्रकार किसानों की धाक जम गई। वे पथिकजी के प्रति अधिक वफादार बन गये।

युद्ध का चन्दा एकत्रित करने के प्रयास में रुकावट डालने के आरोप में ठिकानेदारों ने दो किसान कार्यकर्ताओं साधु सीतारामदास व प्रेमचन्द मीणा को भी गिरफ्तार किया। उन पर राजद्रोह का आरोप भी लगाया तथा अभियोग चलाया। इस संदर्भ में 1300 किसानों के बयान लिये गये, जिनमें किसानों ने यही कहा कि यह आन्दोलन वे किसी के बहकावे में नहीं कर युद्ध के चन्दे के विरोध में कर रहे हैं। इसका कारण यह है कि उन पर पहले से ही कई तरह के कर लादे गये हैं, जिनकी वजह से वे भूखे नग्न रहने को विवश हैं। इस बात को पथिकजी ने पत्र के माध्यम से लोकमान्य तिलक तक पहुंचाया। तिलकजी ने महाराणा फतेहसिंह को पत्र लिखकर मेवाड़ के पूर्व महाराणाओं द्वारा देश के लिए किये गये बलिदान को याद दिलाया तथा किसानों को रिहा करने की मांग की, जिससे प्रभावित होकर महाराणा ने उक्त दोनों किसान कार्यकर्ताओं को रिहा कर दिया।

पथिकजी अब भी चुप नहीं बैठे। उन्होंने किसान संगठन को मजबूत बनाने के लिए अनवरत प्रयास किये तथा लोगों में आज़ादी के लिए मर मिटने के प्राण फूंके। राष्ट्रव्यापी नेताओं तथा राष्ट्रव्यापी समाचारपत्रों का सहारा लिया। महात्मा गांधी से सम्पर्क साधा व 'प्रताप' समाचारपत्र के सम्पादक गणेश शंकर विद्यार्थी से मिलने कानपुर गये। जब 1918 ई. में मुंबई में कांग्रेस का अधिवेशन हुआ तब वे गांधीजी से मिले। उनकी गैरहाजरी में माणिक्यलाल वर्मा व साधुजी ने आन्दोलन जारी रखा। इस बार किसानों ने परती जमीन का लगान नहीं देने का विरोध किया तथा परती भूमि को ही जोतना प्रारंभ किया,

लेकिन ठिकानेदारों ने पूर्ववत लगान वसूलने के प्रयास में किसानों पर जुल्म ढाना शुरू किया, जिसकी खबर मेवाड़ रियासत को पहुंची तथा अखबारों में भी खबरें छपने लगी, जिस पर मेवाड़ सरकार ने केवल जुती हुई भूमि पर ही लगान वसूलने के आदेश दिये। इस प्रकार यह किसानों की दूसरी विजय थी।

सन् 1919 में पथिकजी ने 'राजस्थान सेवा संघ' की स्थापना अजमेर में की तथा यहीं से बिजोलिया किसान आन्दोलन का संचालन शुरू किया। सन् 1919 के दिसम्बर माह में अमृतसर में आयोजित कांग्रेस अधिवेशन में पथिकजी ने भाग लेकर बिजोलिया का मामला उठाया, लेकिन देशी राज्यों के मामले में हस्तक्षेप न हो इस बात को ध्यान में रखते हुए गांधीजी तथा पं० मदनमोहन मालवीय ने इस प्रस्ताव का विरोध किया, लेकिन व्यक्तिगत रूप से दोनों ने मेवाड़ के महाराणा को समझाने का आश्वासन दिया। अत: बिजोलिया का यह आन्दोलन राष्ट्रीयस्तर के नेताओं की निगाह में आने से राष्ट्रीय स्तर का बन गया।[6]

उधर महाराणा ने ठाकुर राजसिंह की अध्यक्षता में एक कमीशन गठित किया तथा रमाकान्त मालवीय व तख्तसिंह को इसका सदस्य बनाया।[6] दूसरी तरफ माणिक्यलाल वर्मा की अध्यक्षता में 15 सदस्यों का प्रतिनिधिमण्डल बिजोलिया से उदयपुर गया। पंडित मदनमोहन मालवीय भी दिल्ली से उदयपुर गये। महाराणा ने आयोग की सिफारिशों व मालवीय जी की मंत्रणा दोनों को ठुकरा दिया तथा आन्दोलन को सख्ती से दबाने के आदेश दिये। इस समय महात्मा गांधी द्वारा चलाया जा रहा असहयोग आन्दोलन भी जोरों पर था। दूसरी तरफ बिजोलिया का यह आन्दोलन, जो बिजोलिया से भड़कता हुआ पड़ोसी क्षेत्रों बेंगू, पारसोली व दक्षिण पश्चिम की पहाड़ियों तक फैल गया। जिस पर महाराणा तिलमिला गया उसने इस हेतु खैरवाड़ा छावनी में स्थित 'मेवाड़ भील कोर' की मदद ली जिसके ए.जी.जी. (एजेन्ट टू दि गवर्नर जनरल) ने ठिकानों का दौरा किया।

उक्त दोनों आन्दोलनों को जोर पकड़ता देख ब्रिटिश सरकार भी चिन्तित हो गई तथा स्थिति से निपटने के लिए कि कहीं किसान आन्दोलन असहयोग

---

6. शंकर सहाय पद्मजा : *बिजोलिया किसान आन्दोलन का इतिहास*, पृ. 106–107

आन्दोलन से न जुड़ जाय इस हेतु ए०जी०जी० होलेण्ड को वहां भेजा। होलेण्ड के प्रयासों से किसानों व जागीरदारों के बीच समझौता हुआ। इस समझौते के अनुसार (1) किसानों पर लगाई 35 लागतें समाप्त कर दी गयी तथा लगान कम कर दिये गये। (2) ठिकानों पर कार्यरत कामदार हीरालाल व फौजदार तेजसिंह को हटा दिया गया। (3) किसानों पर लगाये अभियोग वापस ले लिये गये। (4) किसानों की हड़प ली गई जमीने वापस लौटा दी गई। (5) 3 साल के भीतर बिजोलिया की जमीन का बंदोबस्त कर के लगान जिन्स की बजाय नकद लेना स्वीकार किया, जो फसल पकने के एक माह बाद लिया जायेगा, यह तय हुआ। चित्तौड़ी मुद्रा को अंग्रेजी सिक्कों में बदलने के लिए जो बट्टा लिया जाता था, अब उसे बंद कर दिया गया।

उक्त समझौता बिजोलिया के किसानों की तीसरी विजय थी। लेकिन उक्त समझौते के परिणाम ज्यादा दूरगामी सिद्ध न हुए। इसका कारण था कि ब्रिटिश सरकार किसानों को असहयोग आन्दोलन से दूर रखना चाहती थी, न कि किसानों की समस्याओं का निराकरण करना चाहती थी। फलतः किसानों पर पुनः नयी लागतें लगा दी गई तथा पथिकजी को सवा तीन वर्ष के कारावास की सजा दी गई, जिससे पथिकजी के अभाव में यह आन्दोलन नेतृत्वहीन हो गया।

सन् 1923 में बिजोलिया के राव के विवाह के अवसर पर किसानों से बेगार लेने के प्रयास में किसानों पर पुनः दमनचक्र शुरू हो गया। सन् 1923-1926 तक मेवाड़ में बाढ़ व अकाल पड़े तथा ऐसे हालात में ठिकानेदारों द्वारा वसूला जाने वाले लगान व अन्य लागतों ने यहां के किसानों की स्थिति को ओर दयनीय बना दिया। ब्रिटिश सरकार ने ट्रेंच नामक अधिकारी को इस स्थिति से निपटने के लिए जनवरी 1927 ई. को बिजोलिया भेजा, जहां बैठक आयोजित कर बारानी[7] क्षेत्र (मालभूमि) के लिए लगान की मात्रा बढ़ा दी तथा पीपल (सिंचित) क्षेत्रों के लिए लगान की मात्रा अपेक्षाकृत कम कर दी। इस मसले पर विचार-विमर्श हेतु माणिक्यलाल वर्मा व रामनारायण चौधरी उपस्थित थे। इस सभा में बारानी क्षेत्र को छोड़कर अन्य

---

7. बारानी या मालभूमि : अलग-अलग प्रकार (किस्म) की भूमि जिनमें उपजाऊ, अनुपजाऊ भूमि के अलावा नदियों व तालाबों के किनारों वाली भूमि, शहर के पास वाली भूमि इत्यादि सम्मिलित थी। **मवेशीलाग** मवेशियों को चराने के उपलक्ष्य में लिया जाता था।

भूमि पर विचार-विमर्श जरूर हुआ, मगर अंतिम निर्णय पथिकजी पर छोड़ा गया। इन्हीं दिनों पथिकजी भी जेल से छूट गये, लेकिन निर्वासित किये जाने के कारण उनका मेवाड़ में प्रवेश करना वर्जित था इसी वजह से वे ग्वालियर के सिगोली इलाके के फुंसरिया गांव चले गये जो बिजोलिया की सीमा पर स्थित था तथा वहां रहकर वे किसान सत्याग्रहियों को दिग्दर्शन करते रहे।[8]

उल्लेखनीय है कि पथिकजी ने बारानी छोड़ने की जो सलाह किसानों को दी थी वह नाकाम रही। उल्टे मेवाड़ सरकार ने किसानों द्वारा समर्पित इन भूमियों पर नयी राजस्व दर कायम कर उन्हें दूसरे किसानों को बेच दिया। इस पर किसान हताश हुए तथा पथिकजी ने भी 'किसान पंचायत' की अध्यक्षता से इस्तीफा दे दिया। अब आन्दोलन का नेतृत्व माणिक्यलाल वर्मा ने हरिभाऊ उपाध्याय को सौंप दिया तथा पथिकजी व रामनारायण चौधरी को आन्दोलन से अलग कर दिया।

किसान अब भी अपनी बारानी भूमि वापस चाहते थे इसलिए वे हरिभाऊ उपाध्याय से मिले। उपाध्यायजी इस हेतु ट्रेंच से मिले, मगर इससे किसानों की भूमि वापस नहीं मिली। अतः किसानों ने माणिक्यलाल वर्मा के नेतृत्व में सत्याग्रह करने का निश्चय किया। पंचबोर्ड के माध्यम से अप्रैल 1913 ई. में समर्पित भूमि पर हल चलाकर किसानों ने सत्याग्रह शुरू किया। इस पर आक्रोशित होकर राज्य सरकार, ठिकानेदारों के कर्मचारी, सेना, पुलिस, भूमि के नये स्वामी सभी किसानों पर टूट पड़े, उन्हें निर्ममता से पीटा,[9] चौतरफ सेनाएं तैनात की तथा अनेकों को कैद कर लिया, इस प्रकार यह मामला राष्ट्रीय स्तर पर तूल पकड़ने लगा। गांधीजी की सलाह पर मदनमोहन मालवीय ने मेवाड़ के दीवान सुखदेव प्रसाद[10] को पत्र लिखकर स्थिति की गंभीरता से जांच करने का निवेदन किया, मगर सुखदेव प्रसाद शुरू से ही इस आन्दोलन का विरोधी था, इस वजह से उसने कोई प्रयास नहीं किये, उल्टे वर्माजी को जेल भेज दिया। अतः यह आन्दोलन नेतृत्वविहीन होकर सन् 1939 तक लडखड़ाता रहा।

---

8. रामनारायण चौधरी : *20वीं सदी का राजस्थान*, पृ. 103
9. आर.पी. व्यास : *राजस्थान का वृहत इतिहास*, भाग 2 पृ. 242
10. दीवान सुखदेव प्रसाद : इन्हें आधुनिक राजस्थान का 'चाणक्य' कहा जाता है। कभी उन्हें जयनाराण व्यास के आन्दोलन के परिणामस्वरूप जोधपुर से निर्वासित होकर अजमेर रहना पडा था। उनकी बीकानेर के महाराणा गंगासिंह से प्रतिस्पध र्ा थी। मेवाड़ में वे पथिकजी के किसान आन्दोलन के विरोधी रहे हैं।

इस आन्दोलन का पटाक्षेप सन् 1941 में हुआ। इस भय से कि कहीं किसान आन्दोलन गांधीजी के भारत छोड़ो आन्दोलन तथा मेवाड़ प्रजामण्डल के साथ न हो जाये। इसलिए ब्रिटिश सरकार ने सहानुभूति का रूख अपनाया तथा किसानों से बातचीत करने हेतु मेवाड़ के तत्कालीन दीवान टी० राघवाचार्य ने डॉ. मोहनसिंह मेहता को बिजोलिया भेजा, जहां किसानों की समस्याओं का समाधन हुआ। परिणामस्वरूप किसानों को उनकी जमीन वापस मिल गई।

बिजोलिया किसान आन्दोलन की समीक्षा[11]

(1) इस आन्दोलन में किसानों ने अधिक धैर्य एवं साहस का परिचय दिया यद्यपि उन्हें अनेक मानसिक एवं शारीरिक यातनाएं झेलनी पड़ी तथा अपूर्व बलिदान देने पड़े।

(2) इस आन्दोलन से न केवल मेवाड़, बल्कि पूरे राजपूताने की अन्य रियासतों के किसानों तथा जनता में एक नयी चेतना व जागृत्ति पैदा कर दी। इसके चलते सन् 1938 में मेवाड़, शाहपुरा, बूंदी इत्यादि में प्रजामण डलों की स्थापना हुई जिसकी आधारशिला इन्हीं किसान आन्दोलनों ने रखी थी।

(3) इस आन्दोलन के चलते राजस्थान को माणिक्यलाल वर्मा, हरिभाऊ उपाध्याय, रामनारायण चौधरी जैसे नेता मिले जो आगे चलकर राजस्थान की राजनीति के मुख्य कर्णाधर रहे।

(4) बिजोलिया का किसान आन्दोलन देश का पहला संगठित किसान आन्दोलन था, जो आगे चलकर भारत का प्रमुख आन्दोलन बन गया जिसमें महात्मा गांधी, पंडित मदनमोहन मालवीय जैसे नेताओं ने हस्तक्षेप किया इसलिए इस आन्दोलन का राजस्थान के इतिहास में ही नहीं बल्कि भारत के इतिहास में भी विशिष्ट स्थान है।

(5) इस आन्दोलन के चलते किसानों ने बेंगू में सन् 1921-27 तक, बूंदी के बरड़ में 1922-1925 तक, मेवात के मेवों ने 1932-33, सीकर तथा शेखावटी के क्षेत्रों में 1922-1932 ई. तक आन्दोलन चलाये जिनमें किसानों को सफलता मिली।

---

11. Ram Pande: *Agrarian Movement in Rajasthan: The Appraisal of Land Reforms of Rajasthan.*

उपरोक्त आन्दोलनों की प्रमुख सफलता में कई कारण आत्मसात रहे ये थे सन् 1857 का विप्लव, स्वामी दयानंद सरस्वती का राजस्थान में आगमन तथा आर्य समाज के सिद्धांतों के प्रचार हेतु इलाहाबाद से वैदिक यंत्रालय का अजमेर में स्थानान्तरण, 1883 ई में राजस्थान के उदयपुर में 'परोपकारिणी सभा' की स्थापना (जो एक सामाजिक संस्था थी), अंग्रेजी शिक्षा का राजस्थान में प्रसार, समाचार पत्रों का प्रकाशन यथा 'देश हितैषी', 'राजस्थान केसरी', 'परोपकार', 'जगहित कारक', 'राजस्थान समाचार', 'राजस्थान टाइम्स', 'राजस्थान गजट', जयनारायण व्यास द्वारा प्रकाशित 'राजस्थान हेराल्ड'। इसके अलावा प्रथम विश्व युद्ध में देशवासियों का बलिदान व अंग्रेजों द्वारा उनसे भेदभाव, विभिन्न क्रांतिकारियों, हरिभाऊ उपाध्याय, अर्जुनलाल सेठी, केसरीसिंह बारहठ, सेठ जमनालाल बजाज इत्यादि का अपूर्व सहयोग आदि रहा है।

17

सहकारी आन्दोलन : दशा और दिशा

डॉ० धर्मचन्द्र विद्यालंकार

सहकारिता 'सह' तथा 'कारिता' दो पदों से मिलकर बना है, जिसका तात्पर्य यह है कि बहुत सारे लोगों का एक साथ मिलकर किसी भी क्षेत्र में काम करना ही सहकारिता है। यद्यपि आजकल यह शब्द केवल आर्थिक उत्पादन-सम्बन्धों तक ही सीमित होकर रह गया है। वरना हमें अपने प्राचीन इतिहास-ग्रन्थों से यह ज्ञात होता है कि पहले महाजनपदकाल या वैदिककाल से लेकर मौर्यकाल तक चार प्रकार के शब्द सहकारिता के क्षेत्र में प्रचलित थे-श्रेणी, व्रात, पूग और संघ। श्रेणी यदि श्रमिकों या मजदूरों की जमातों का नाम था, तो व्रात किसानों का संगठन था। क्योंकि संस्कृत में कृषि को ही वार्ता कहते हैं। उसी को करने वाले शूद्र-किसानों को ही ब्राह्मण शास्त्रकारों ने व्रात्य और वृषण तक कहा है। व्रात नामक सहकारी संगठन ऐसे ही कृषि कर्मी लोगों का था। इस प्रकार धार्मिक और राजनीतिक समवाय ही संघ कहे जाते थे। जैसे कि गण संघ और और धर्म संघादि। दो या दो से अधिक गणों का परस्पर में सहकार भाव ही गण-संघ कहलाता था। यथाकि त्रिगर्त या त्रिजर्त या तीन जाटों के संगठन कुल्लू और कांगड़ा की घाटी में अवस्थित थे जोकि बाद में मिलकर छः बन गये थे। पाणिनी की अष्टाध्यायी और पतञ्जलि का महाभाष्य इस बात की गवाही देते हैं।[1]

इसी प्रकार के और भी गण-संघ कठ, मालव और शिवि संघों का भी तो था, सिकन्दर के आक्रमण-काल में तो हिसार से लेकर होशियारपुर तक अग्र, श्रेणि-अग्रवाल और सैनियों या मालियों का भी गठबन्धन था, जिसको लोग पौराणिक प्रभाव से एक शासक व्यक्तिविशेष : अग्रसैन भी मान लेते हैं। यह

1. डॉ० वासुदेवशरण अग्रवाल : *पाणिनी कालीन भारत*

संगठन सहकारिता में अग्रणी था, क्योंकि अग्रोहा का आवासन करते समय नवागन्तुक को एक ईंट और एक रुपये का सहयोग गण-संघ के सदस्यों की ओर से किया जाता था। यूनानी इतिहासकारों ने इस गण-संघ को अगस्सेनी ही लिखा है। योधेयों और त्रिगर्तों का पारस्परिक सहकार भाव भी प्रंशसनीय था। सिकन्दर से कठ और मालव मिलकर ही लड़े थे।[2] तभी उसे भारत भूमि से पराजित होकर बैरंग ही लौटना पड़ा था।

स्वतन्त्रता पूर्व काल : यहाँ पर हमारा ध्येय विशेषकर आर्थिक क्षेत्र में ही सहकारिता के महत्त्व को दर्शाना है। पुराकाल में व्यापारियों के पूग और निगम (Corporation) ऐसे ही सहकारी संगठन थे, जो परस्पर मिलकर वस्तुओं का आदान-प्रदान करते थे। बड़े-बड़े व्यापार-संघों और सार्थवाहों (कौरवों) का उल्लेख बौद्ध-साहित्य से लेकर मौर्य-काल तक के साहित्य में मिलता है।[3] लेकिन यहाँ पर हमारा सम्बन्ध ऐतिहासिक पृष्ठभूमि में न जाकर वर्तमान काल में सहकारिता के आन्दोलन का अवलोकन और मूल्यांकन करना ही है।

ब्रिटिश काल में 1904 ईस्वी में भारतवर्ष में सर्वप्रथम सहकारिता सम्बन्ध कानून बना था, जिसमें 1912 ई० में और भी कुछ संशोधन और परिवर्धन किया गया था। इन कानूनों का प्रभावी कार्यपालन संयुक्त पंजाब की यूनियनिस्ट या जमींदारा-लीगी सरकार ने किया था। जिसका 1923 ई० में ही वायसराय की कौंसिल या विधान-परिषद में बहुमत था और जिसके नायक सर फजले हुसैन और चौधरी छोटूराम जी थे। 1937-38 में पूर्णत: विधानमण डल का गठन होने पर जमींदारा-लीगी सरकार ने संयुक्त पंजाब के गाँव-गाँव में सहकारी ऋण-समितियों का जाल बिछा दिया था। उसी के कारण पंजाब का किसान सूदखोर-साहूकारों के मंहगे चक्रवृद्धि ब्याज से बच सका था। पंजाब विधान-सभा में पारित 'ऋण-विमुक्ति' कानून (Undebtation Act 1938) और पंजाब एकाउण्ट रेगुलेशन 1933 जैसे क्रान्तिकारी कानूनों के क्रियान्वयन से ही वहाँ के किसानों का कायाकल्प हुआ था। खोटे बाटों का मानकीकरण किया गया था और साहूकारों की घरेलू और निजी बहियों की मान्यता रद्द करके बैंकरों या मनीलैंडर्स का पंजीकरण (Registration) अनिवार्य किया गया था। पंजाब विधान-सभा में जमींदारा लीगी सरकार द्वारा पारित इन्हीं सुनहरे कानूनों के प्रभावी कार्यपालन के कारण ही पश्चिमोत्तर

2. *यथोपरि*
3. प्रभुदयाल अग्निहोत्री : *पतञ्जलि कालीन भारत*

भारत का ऋण के जुए में सदियों से जुतकर कराहता हुआ किसान देश का अग्रणी और कुछ समृद्ध व ऋणमुक्त नागरिक बन गया था।[4]

स्वातन्त्र्योत्तर काल : संयुक्त पंजाब में सहकारी ऋण समितियों के क्रान्तिकारी प्रभावों को परिलक्षित करके ही अखिल भारतीय राष्ट्रीय कांग्रेस के करांची अधिवेशन (1941 ई०) में किसानों की ऋण-मुक्ति का राष्ट्रीय स्तर पर संकल्प पारित किया गया था जिसका क्रियान्वयन स्वतन्त्रता-प्राप्ति के पश्चात ही हो सका। भारत के प्रथम प्रधानमंत्री श्री जवाहर लाल नेहरू भी रूस की समाजवादी और यूरोप की औद्योगिक क्रान्ति और उन्नति से अत्यन्त प्रेरित और प्रभावित थे। विशेषकर रूस की सामूहिक खेती से वे बहुत ही प्रभावित थे। इसीलिए उन्होंने 1956 ई० में अखिल भारतीय राष्ट्रीय कांग्रेस के अधिवेशन में कृषि के सरकारीकरण का प्रस्ताव प्रस्तुत किया था। लेकिन तब तक भारतीय किसानों के पास काफी हद तक पर्याप्त जोतें उपलब्ध थीं, फिर उनके अन्दर तब तक साथ-साथ मिलकर काम करने का सहकारी भाव भी नहीं पनपा था। संभवत: इसीलिए उत्तर प्रदेश में जमींदारी उन्मूलन कानून बनवाने वाले चौ० चरणसिंह जैसे कृषक-नायक ने उस समय की प्रतिकूल परिस्थितियों में सहकारी कृषि के प्रस्ताव का समर्थन नहीं किया अपितु विरोध किया। लेकिन बाद में उत्तर-प्रदेश में कृषि और राजस्व मंत्री रहते हुए उन्होंने ही भू-परिसीमन (Ceiling) जैसा परिवर्तनकारी प्रस्ताव भी पारित कराया था।[5]

आज किसानों के पास छोटी-छोटी कृषि भूमियाँ हैं जिन पर वे मंहगे खाद-बीज और कृषि-यन्त्रों का उपयोग नहीं कर पाते हैं। हर सीमान्त किसान के घर में ट्रैक्टर, पम्पसैट या ईंजिन और कार्बनहार्रवेस्टर संभव नहीं हैं क्योंकि ये बहूमूल्य उपकरण हैं। यदि प्रत्येक मध्यम दर्जे का या सीमान्त किसान भी इनको खरीदेगा, तो वह दस से बीस वर्षों तक उद्योगपतियों या पूंजीपतियों के लिए ही कमायेगा। जब एक ट्रैक्टर से बीस से पच्चीस एकड़ तक की जुताई-बिजाई हो सकती है तो फिर हर घर में उसका होना किसानों का ऋण-भार ही बढ़ाता है। ऐसी स्थिति में छोटी या सीमान्त जोतों को मिलाकर आज उनके बड़े-बड़े फार्म बनाकर उन पर सहकारी खेती से ही किसानों का उद्धार संभव है।

---

4. रघुवीर सिंह शास्त्री : *चौ० छोटूराम का जीवन चरित*, दिल्ली
5. डॉ० शिवकुमार गोयल: *चौ० चरण सिंह की जीवनी*

अन्यान्य क्षेत्रों में रोजगार के अवसर : सहकारी आन्दोलन आज केवल कृषि-उत्पादन या उपकरणों अथवा बीजों और उर्वरकों तक ही सीमित नहीं है। यद्यपि यह भी वस्तुसत्य है कि सहकारी संस्थाओं और निगमों के सुप्रयासों अथवा उपक्रमों से ही किसानों को आज सस्ते बीज-खाद और उर्वरक तथा कीटनाशक औषधियाँ मिल रहे हैं। इस क्षेत्र में हैपफेड, नाबार्ड और इफको का विशेष योगदान है। इफको तो आज उर्वरक उत्पादन के क्षेत्र में बहुराष्ट्रीय कम्पनी जैसी बन गई है। तो हडको बैंक और कॉपरेटिव सोसाइटियों ने कृषि-कार्यों के लिए ऋण-वितरण में उल्लेखनीय कार्य किया है। फिर भी अब सहकारिता का यह अग्रणी आन्दोलन यहीं तक सीमित नहीं है। अब तो उत्पादन से लेकर वितरण-भंडारण और प्रसंस्करण तक भी इसका विस्तार हो रहा है। आज 5 लाख सहकारी संस्थाओं के लगभग 23 करोड़ सदस्य हैं।[6]

कृषि के साथ ही साथ, हमारे छोटी जोतों वाले किसान और ग्रामीण मजदूर सहकारी आधार पर डेयरी-उद्योग चला सकते हैं-दुग्ध क्रान्ति या श्वेत-क्रान्ति सहकारिता का ही प्रतिफल है। गुजरात का 'आनन्द सहकारी दुग्ध उद्योग' और अमूल के दुग्ध-उत्पाद आज देश के लिए अनुकरणीय उदाहरण हैं। तो हरियाणा के करनाल सहकारी डेयरी संघ या वीटा घी भी अब अपनी चमक दिखा रहे हैं। छोटे-छोटे किसान और मजदूर सहकारी आधार पर मधुमक्खी पालन और मत्स्य-पालन जैसे काम कर सकते हैं। मजदूर महिलाएँ घर ही चाक-मिट्टी और प्लास्टर ऑफ पैरिस से चाक और खिलौने बना सकती है। वे मोमबत्तियाँ भी बना सकती हैं। मिलकर वे हथकरघा पर चद्दरें और गलीचे, दरी, तौलिये आदि भी बना सकती हैं। सौंदर्य प्रसाधन, साबुन, तेल, चूड़ियाँ और बिन्दी-पाउडर भी वे अपने ही घरों में सहकारी आधार पर बना सकती हैं। सहकारी प्रयासों से पूंजी-संचय भी संभव है। बंगला देश के ग्रामीण बैंक इस बात का उत्तम उदाहरण हैं। महिलाएँ 'स्वयं सहायता समूह' बनाकर भी सहकारी आधार पर कुटीर उद्योग लगा सकती हैं। तो सीमान्त या मध्यम दर्जे के किसान फलों के जूस और खाद्य पदार्थों के प्रसंस्करण के कुटीर-उद्योग मिलकर लगा सकते हैं। इस प्रकार से बेरोजगारी कम होगी।

---

6. *इंडिया टुडे* पत्रिका : दिल्ली, सितम्बर अंक

सहकारिता का महत्त्व :

सहकारिता मनुष्यों का, मिलजुलकर सामूहिक रूप से काम करने का एक स्वभाव है। किसी के पास यदि धन की बहुलता है तो वह इस क्षेत्र में अपना पूँजी निवेश करके लाभांश कमा सकता है। यदि किसी के पास शारीरिक श्रम करने की क्षमता है तो वह सहकारी संस्थाओं या उपक्रमों में सेवा पाकर अपनी आजीविका का प्रबन्ध कर सकता है। यदि किसी साधन-सम्पन्न व्यक्ति पर समय की अधिकता या बहुलता है तो वह सहकारी संस्थाओं के प्रबन्धन में अपना अमूल्य अवदान दे सकता है। सहकारी चीनी मिलों के निदेशक या डायरेक्टर से शुरु करके कितने ही जननायकों ने देश और प्रदेशों की राजनीति में अपनी अमिट छाप छोड़ी है। महाराष्ट्र का सहकारी चीनी मिल-उद्योग-संघ इस बात का जीता-जागता प्रमाण है।

सहकारिता, समता-स्वतन्त्रता या स्वैच्छिकता और बंधुता या भाईचारे के सिद्धान्तों पर आधारित आन्दोलन है। सहकारी क्षेत्र में एक व्यक्ति का चाहे कितना भी बढ़कर पूँजी-निवेश क्यों न हो, एक व्यक्ति के चाहे जितने शेयर या अंश सहकारी उपक्रम में क्यों न लगे हों, लेकिन चुनावों के समय ऐसा व्यक्ति केवल एक मत का ही अधिकारी होता है। इस प्रकार से सहकारी आन्दोलन स्वयं में एक जनतांत्रिक जनान्दोलन भी है। जबकि कम्पनियों में ऐसा नहीं होता। वहाँ पर जिस पूँजीशाह के जितने अधिक अंश या शेयर किसी कम्पनी में लगे होंगे, वह उतने ही भाग का स्वामी बन बैठता है। इस सबसे पूँजीवादी एकाधिकार को ही प्रोत्साहन मिलता है। लेकिन सहकारी संस्थाएँ समता या बराबरी के नियम पर काम करती हैं। सहकारी उपक्रम स्वैच्छिक होते हैं, आरोपित नहीं। अतएव उनमें व्यक्तिगत स्वतन्त्रता भी सुरक्षित बनी रहती है। एक व्यक्ति जब चाहे अपना अंश निकाल सकता है। या फिर वह स्वेच्छा से उसका आजीवन और सक्रिय सदस्य भी बना रह सकता है। वहाँ पर बन्धुता या भाईचारा भी बना रहता है क्योंकि उनके मध्य में स्वामी और सेवक या शासक और शासित अथवा शोषक और शोषित सम्बन्ध नहीं होते। सहकारी संस्थाएँ आपसी सहयोग और सद्भाव तथा भ्रातृभाव से ही काम करके आगे बढ़ती हैं।[7]

---

7. Dr. Subhash Yadav: *Rural Development & Cooperative Movement*

वर्तमान में मूल्यांकन : सहकारी संस्थाओं में राजनीतिक हस्तक्षेप के कारण भाई भतीजावाद और जातिवाद तथा क्षेत्रवाद बढ़ रहा है। सहकारी उद्योग और उपक्रम अब सरकारी उपक्रमों की भाँति अधोगति की ओर अग्रसर हैं।[8] यदि इन संस्थाओं में लोग मिलजुलकर ईमानदारी और लग्न के साथ काम नहीं करेंगे तो या तो ये संस्थाएँ राजनीतिक राजनेताओं की जागीरें बनकर रह जायेंगी, या फिर नौकरशाहों के हितकारी फरमानों में ही दबकर दम तोड़ देंगी। सरकारीकरण में केवल नौकरशाही ही सक्रिय होती है। उसमें जनसहभागिता नहीं होती। इसलिये सहकारी उपक्रमों में सरकारी हस्तक्षेप कम से कम होना चाहिए और जनता की भागीदारी अधिक से अधिक होनी चाहिए तभी उनका लोकतांत्रिक स्वरूप बचा रह सकता है। सरकारीकरण में व्यक्ति का प्रोत्साहन या अभिप्रेरणा समाप्त हो जाते हैं। अतएव वह वहाँ पर केवल वेतन पाने के लिये या केवल खाना-पूर्ति करने भर के लिए ही काम करता है। जबकि सहकारिता एक स्वैच्छिक और स्वयं में स्वायत्त संगठन है। इनमें सरकार का केवल नियमन (Regulation) ही होना चाहिए। वह केवल इन संस्थाओं के नियम-उपनियम ही बनाये, उनका नियन्त्रण या नेतृत्व जन प्रतिनिधियों पर ही रहने दे जिससे कि लोगों की स्वामित्व की भावना और अभिप्रेरणा बनी रहे। महात्मा गांधी स्वामित्व के अपहरण को भी हिंसा ही मानते थे। आजकल का उदारीकरण भी उसी भावना का विकास है। लेकिन सहकारी संस्थाओं का निजीकरण जैसा आजकल सहकारी चीनी मिलों के साथ हो रहा है, उनकी मौत ही है।

---

8. चौ० चरण सिंह : *भारत की अर्थनीति*, किसान ट्रस्ट, दिल्ली

List of Contributors

Dr. Ishrat Alam

Member Secretary, Indian Council of Historical Research, New Delhi

Sompal

Former Minister of Agriculture, L-502, Ambience Ist-Land, National Highway 8, Gurgaon, Haryana-122017

कप्तान सिंह

चेयरमैन, एकेडेमिक कमेटी, सूरजमल स्मारक शिक्षा संस्था, सी-4, जनकपुरी, नई दिल्ली-110058

Dr. S.S. Rana

Former Dean of Colleges, University of Delhi; B-13, IDC Aptts., Plot 8C, Sector 11, Dwarka, New Delhi-110001

Zakir Husain

Archivist (Rtd.), National Archives of India, Janpath, New Delhi-110001

N.S. Alam

Archivist (Rtd.), National Archives of India, Janpath, New Delhi-110001

Dr. Parwez Nazir

Assistant Professor, Department of History, Aligarh Muslim University, Aligarh

Ramesh Kumar

Research Fellow, University of Hyderabad, Hyderabad

Nasreen Naqvi

Associate Professor, Satyawati College, Ashok Vihar, Phase III, New Delhi-110052

Shirin Akhter

Assistant Professor, Zakir Husain Delhi College, Jawaharlal Nehru Marg, New Delhi-110002

डॉ॰ राम पाण्डे

सम्पादक एवम् सचिव, शोधक, बी-424, मालवीय नगर, जयपुर-302017 (राजस्थान)

Dr. K.S. Saxena

Former Director, U.G.C. (Rtd.), B-16, Chomu House, C-Scheme, Jaipur-302001 (Rajasthan)

S. Chandni Bi

Assistant Professor, Department of History, Aligarh Muslim University, Aligarh

Dr. Mohammad Idris

Assistant Professor, Department of History, Punjabi University, Patiala (Punjab)

Dr. Haroon Nayam Khan

Assistant Professor, Department of Social Sciences, Punjab Police Academy, Phillaur, Punjab

डा॰ मंजू पंघाल

असिस्टेंट प्रोफेसर, इतिहास विभाग, जीवन चानन महिला महाविद्यालय, असंध, करनाल (हरियाणा)

सुमेस्ता

शोधार्थी, के-104, कश्यप फार्म, गणेश नगर, शकरपुर, नई दिल्ली-110092

जोगाराम सारण

अध्यक्ष, श्री गंगाराम सारण मैमोरियल जाट समाज पुस्तकालय, गरल, बाड़मेर (राजस्थान)

मोनिका

रिसर्च ऐसोशिएट, महाराजा सूरजमल अनुसंधान एवम् प्रकाशन केन्द्र, सूरजमल स्मारक शिक्षा संस्था, सी-4, जनकपुरी, नई दिल्ली-110058

डॉ॰ मलिका बोहरा

व्याख्याता, इतिहास विभाग, महाराणा प्रताप राजकीय स्नातकोत्तर महाविद्यालय, प्रतापनगर, चितौड़गढ़, राजस्थान

डॉ॰ धर्मचन्द विद्यालंकार

ऐसोशिएट प्रोफेसर, जी॰जी॰डी॰एस॰डी॰ कॉलेज, पलवल, हरियाणा